# POLISH ORPHANS
# OF TENGERU

# POLISH ORPHANS OF TENGERU

## The Dramatic Story of Their
## Long Journey to Canada 1941–49

Lynne Taylor

DUNDURN PRESS
TORONTO

Copy Editor: Cheryl Hawley
Designer: Jennifer Scott
Printer: Marquis

Library and Archives Canada Cataloguing in Publication

Taylor, Lynne, 1958-
    Polish orphans of Tengeru : the dramatic story of their long journey to Canada, 1941-49 / by Lynne Taylor.

ISBN 978-1-55488-004-1

    1. Orphans--Poland--History. 2. Refugee children-- Poland--History. 3. Refugee children--Tanzania--History. 4. World War, 1939-1945--Children--Poland. 5. World War, 1939-1945--Refugees--Poland. 6. Orphans--Canada-- History. 7. Refugee children--Canada--History. 8. Canada-- Emigration and immigration--History. I. Title.

D810.C4T39 2009        940.53'161        C2009-900303-1

1    2    3    4    5        13    12    11    10    09

| Conseil des Arts du Canada | Canada Council for the Arts | Canadä | ONTARIO ARTS COUNCIL CONSEIL DES ARTS DE L'ONTARIO |
|---|---|---|---|

We acknowledge the support of the **Canada Council for the Arts** and the **Ontario Arts Council** for our publishing program. We also acknowledge the financial support of the **Government of Canada** through the **Book Publishing Industry Development Program** and **The Association for the Export of Canadian Books**, and the **Government of Ontario** through the **Ontario Book Publishers Tax Credit program**, and the **Ontario Media Development Corporation**.

Care has been taken to trace the ownership of copyright material used in this book. The author and the publisher welcome any information enabling them to rectify any references or credits in subsequent editions.

*J. Kirk Howard, President*

Printed and bound in Canada.
www.dundurn.com

Dundurn Press
3 Church Street, Suite 500
Toronto, Ontario, Canada
M5E 1M2

Gazelle Book Services Limited
White Cross Mills
High Town, Lancaster, England
LA1 4XS

Dundurn Press
2250 Military Road
Tonawanda, NY
U.S.A. 14150

# Table of Contents

# Acknowledgements

This has been an unusual book to write, very different from the traditional academic monograph. While anchored in the archives (all five of them), it is the interviews with some of the surviving "children," now in their seventies and eighties, that truly make the story. They invited me into their homes to share food, drink, and memories in equal measure. I deeply appreciate their willingness to broach what are still very painful recollections of a particularly dark part of their lives. To be able to put a face to the names in the dusty records, to talk to those being written about in the reports of those governments and agencies managing them, is a rare treat for a historian. For that I will be always thankful. I also wish to thank Basia Milligan, for generously allowing me to use photographs of Tengeru from a photo album compiled by the children in the orphanage of Tengeru, and dedicated to "our dear friend Mr. (Herbert Charles) Story" — her father. Finally, I wish to thank Liz Taylor (the red-haired, blue-eyed one) for her painstaking and invaluable work as both copy editor and cheerleader.

# Introduction

In September 1949, a group of 123 Polish Catholic child refugees arrived in Halifax, Nova Scotia, on the USAT *Heintzelman*. A few weeks later they were followed by another, smaller group. All of the children were coming from a refugee camp of several thousand Poles in Tanganyika (now Tanzania), called Tengeru, located just outside the northern city of Arusha. They had been sponsored by the Archbishop of Montreal who had heard about their plight, stranded in East Africa.

What should have been a straightforward movement of immigrants to Canada had become an international incident by the time they reached its shores. As they were moved through Europe on their way to Canada, the Communist Government of Poland vociferously and publicly attacked the International Refugee Organization (the IRO), Canada, the United States, and Great Britain for kidnapping these children to be used, in its words, as slave labour on Canadian farms and in Canadian factories, tearing them from their families in Poland in the process. The Polish Government pursued the children as they left Africa, across Italy and Germany, and even into the backwoods of Quebec, where the children were hidden upon their arrival in Canada. For all of Warsaw's protests, the Canadian Government refused to turn over the children. After a few final diplomatic sallies, Warsaw gave up and the children turned their attention to building lives in Canada.

Their journey from Poland to Canada, via Africa, was a complicated one, that began in February 1940, with four waves of mass deportations of Poles from Soviet-occupied eastern Poland deep into the interior of the U.S.S.R. (Poland had been divided between Germany and the U.S.S.R. in 1939, under the terms of the Ribbentrop-Molotov, or Nazi-Soviet, Pact.) By the spring of 1942, as part of the creation of a Polish Army from among the deported Poles and Polish prisoners of war, these children and what was left of their families were among tens of thousands who moved into Uzbekistan and Kazakhstan, and then on to Iran (then Persia). The mortality rate over the preceding two years had been horrifically high and by the time the Poles arrived in Iran there were many orphans and "unaccompanied children," children separated from their parents. The Polish forces were soon moved out to Palestine and other places, to fight alongside the British troops; just as quickly the Polish civilians that had been left behind in Iran fanned out across the British Commonwealth and beyond, to refugee camps. With them went the orphans. By 1948, a number of them had collected in Tengeru, which had a large orphanage. In 1949, those children were moved to Canada. It was an amazing journey, even when it is laid out so baldly. But the true power of their story and of their survival is in the details.

That experience created a bond between the children of Tengeru, that still ties them tightly together to this day, a bond that stretches across the breadth of Canada, a result of their shared experiences. Bereft of parents, taught by harsh experience at an early age to distrust all authority, these children turned to each other for support. When asked how it was that they did survive, the answer is very matter-of-fact. "You did what you had to do. What else could you do?" Whether it was God's will, luck, skill, or sheer bloody-minded determination, none can say with certainty. But survive they did, in spite of all odds.

# 1 | Deportation to the East

The night of February 10, 1940, was bitterly cold in Poland. In the small, dark hours of that morning, all along the Soviet side of the frontier that had divided Poland into two occupation zones — German and Soviet — teams from the NKVD (the People's Commissariat for Internal Affairs, an early Soviet police force) pounded on the doors of tens of thousands of homes, forcing their way in. Men, women, and children, still groggy from sleep, were dragged from their beds at gunpoint and stood against the walls of their kitchen, while the Soviet security personnel searched their homes, ostensibly looking for weapons. The inhabitants were told brusquely that they had anywhere from fifteen minutes to two hours, depending on the whim of the officer in charge, to pack up their belongings and get ready to leave.[1]

Only a few months before, the Soviet Union and Germany had divided the nation of Poland between them. On September 1, 1939, the German forces, one million strong, had poured over the German-Polish border, pushing back the desperately under-equipped and ill-prepared Polish forces. It was a hopeless battle. Poland was doomed when its two erstwhile allies, Britain and France, proved unable and unwilling to engage militarily with Nazi Germany, even after declaring war on September 3. When the Soviet Union invaded from the east on September 17, 1939, the Poles, both civilians and government, were nonplussed. No one knew why they were invading. Initially, many believed that they were coming to Poland's aid. The reason offered to the Polish ambassador in Moscow was that the Polish Government had disintegrated, and the U.S.S.R. needed to move in order to protect the life and property of the peoples of Western Ukraine and Western Belorussia.[2] The real reason was that the Soviet Union was moving to seize eastern Poland as its own.

At this point, no one knew of the now-infamous secret protocol of the Nazi-Soviet (Ribbentrop-Molotov) Pact signed between the U.S.S.R. and Germany. The pact itself was a non-aggression pact, in which each signatory had agreed to remain neutral if either became involved in a war with another nation. That much was made public. However, in a secret clause the two countries had also agreed to divide Poland between themselves. This, plus a part of Romania and Lithuania, was the price that Germany was willing to pay to the Soviet Union for non-interference in Germany's pending invasion of Poland. Thus, no one anticipated the Soviet invasion and the Polish forces were completely unprepared for a war on that front. On September 17, the Soviets were able to roll forward almost unimpeded.[3] In the face of the two invasions, the Polish Government decided it had no choice but to flee the country and on September 18, the president of Poland and other senior government officials fled to Romania, en route to Paris, where the government would reconstitute itself.

In the Soviet occupation zone the Soviet forces moved quickly to establish control over the territory. Soviet military occupation administrations were put in place, but soon replaced by the NKVD. Elections were held on October 22, to form new People's Assemblies for Western Ukraine and Western Belorussia. These new assemblies were just puppets that immediately petitioned the U.S.S.R. to be incorporated into the Ukrainian and Belorussian Soviet Socialist Republics. On November 1 and 2, respectively, the Supreme Soviet of the U.S.S.R. agreed, effectively absorbing them into the U.S.S.R. Soviet administration, and political structures were implemented; Soviet laws became the law of the land. On November 29, a decree was passed granting Soviet citizenship to all permanent residents of these provinces. It came with an obligation for all young men of a certain age in the region to serve in the Red Army.[4] The Soviets' objective in their occupation was the immediate sovietization of the newly acquired territories, which meant the nationalization of industry, the socialization of trade, and the collectivization of farms.[5]

Soviet occupation policy was also about pacifying the territories and eliminating all anti-Soviet elements. The first targets of the Soviets were the Polish prisoners of war captured by the Red Army in the military campaign of September 1939. The number captured is the subject of some debate, but ranged from 180,000 to 240,000.[6] Many of the younger troops were released and allowed to go home, not being considered dangerous. However, the officer corps was imprisoned and there were some one hundred prisoner of war camps established in both the former Polish and the Soviet Ukraine. There, the prisoners were used for heavy physical labour — construction, quarrying, logging. When the Germans attacked the Soviet Union in June 1941, these prisoners were quickly moved deeper into the U.S.S.R., under harsh and brutal conditions, where they were used again for heavy physical labour.[7]

As early as the fall of 1939, there were also massive waves of arrests of political, economic, and social leaders.[8] The purpose was to decapitate any possible resistance to Soviet rule by arresting its potential leadership. By the second half of October 1939, what had begun as individual arrests had swollen into massive roundups of all who were deemed a threat. Army officers who had evaded capture, landowners, businessmen, employers, policemen, members of the judiciary and court officials, local government officials, and anyone who resisted Soviet rule were considered dangerous. Anyone who had been a member of the political, trade union, or military elites was also a target.[9] However, these arrests were mere harbingers of more organized deportations that came in 1940 and 1941.

An estimated 320,000 to 980,000 Polish civilians were transported from their homes in four waves of deportations, between February 1940 and June 1941 (the exact number is a subject of considerable debate among historians).[10] These four deportations were carefully orchestrated exercises. The first, directed primarily against the *osadniks*, military settlers, and the Forestry Service, but also including civil servants, local government officials, court officials, and policemen, happened during the night of February 10.[11] The *osadniks* were Poles from western

Poland who had served in the Polish army during the Polish-Soviet war of 1920–21. In return for their service, they had been granted free plots of land in the eastern part of the state. Their presence was as much about Polonizing and policing that part of the country as it was about working the land. The *osadniks* soon filled the ranks of the local administration. For these reasons, they were deeply resented by the Ukrainian and Belorussian populations already living there. From the beginning of the Soviet occupation, these people had been the target of a heated propaganda campaign, labelling them as "enemies of the Soviet system."[12]

In the weeks leading up to February 10, the NKVD carefully compiled lists of who was to be deported, and constructed detailed plans for implementing the operations, including the complex logistical challenges of transporting at least 140,000 into the interior of the U.S.S.R. The *osadniks* were to be deported simultaneously, on a single day selected by the NKVD. It was not to be just the settlers, but also their families, for according to the Stalinist understanding of criminality, the individual was the product of his environment (i.e., his family). Thus, to weed out the "criminal" element, it was necessary to remove the entire family in which that criminality had flourished. Parents, wives, children, brothers, and sisters were all culpable in an individual's guilt, and the closer they lived in proximity to one another, the more invidious the threat to Soviet rule.[13] In the bitter cold of the early morning on February 10, 1940, the *osadniks* were rounded up and shipped into the deep interior of the U.S.S.R. — as far north as Arkhangelsk in the Arctic Circle, and Vologda, Irkutsk, and Novosibirsk in the east — a voyage that would take weeks. Some POWs and prisoners were sent as far as the Kolyma region in the far eastern reaches of the U.S.S.R.[14]

The second deportation's target was the families of those previously arrested or who had been taken as prisoners of war, as well as any anti-Soviet elements missed in the first deportation. These people were taken during the night of April 13, 1940, and mostly shipped to Kazakhstan, deep in the heart of Central Asia. At least 61,000 people, mostly women and children, were shipped out by cattle car. The third and fourth deportations were a smaller scale. On June 29, the third deportation numbered at least 61,000 more, and focused primarily on refugees in the former eastern Poland who had fled from western Poland in the face of the German invasion, including a large number of Jews. The final deportation, in June 1941, drew largely from the freshly annexed Baltic Republics and involved a minimum of forty thousand people. This transport was probably smaller than the others because it was interrupted by the German invasion of the U.S.S.R. that began on June 22, 1941. In the cases of the third and fourth deportations the transports scattered their cargo across the interior of Russia.[15]

The orders for the first deportation were issued by Lavrenti Beria, head of the NKVD, on December 29, 1939, just a few weeks before it would happen. The instructions for the handling of the deportees were thorough. They were to be allowed to take with them "clothes, linen, footwear, bedclothes, tablewear, tea and kitchen utensils, food provisions, household and domestic tools, an unlimited amount of money, domestic valuables," all to be packed into a trunk that could, in the final count, weigh up to five hundred kilograms.[16] The reality was starkly different and much less generous.

Sophia Wakulczyk was ten years old on February 10, when the NKVD burst into her home. She recalls that it was very early in the morning, perhaps around 3:00 a.m. Her father had worked as a policeman when he was younger, then as mayor of their small village, and finally for the Forestry Service. He was clearly someone who would be considered a threat by the Soviets. She remembers that the NKVD put her father in one corner of the room and her mother in the other, both at gunpoint. The soldiers told them that the whole family was leaving, and that they could not take anything with them except what they could carry. They were ordered to dress and get ready to go to the train station. Sophia, her parents, and her two younger brothers were put on a sleigh and delivered to the train station in Pinsk, about seven kilometres away. Her mother was six months pregnant at the time. There they were loaded onto cattle cars and shipped to Arkhangelsk, a voyage of several weeks.[17]

Helena Koscielniak was only three, but even she remembers that night — the terror and the bitter cold. Helena's father was a farmer, prosperous for the area. Helena's older sister Stella recalls that they had two beautiful horses, three cows, chickens, and a dog — the family pet. Helena's sisters told her that three soldiers walked into their house the night of February 10, and told the whole family to line up against the wall and not move. They then told the girls' father, Konstantyn, to get the sleigh and horse ready, and told their mother to collect whatever the family would need — warm clothes and a bit of food, but not too much, just whatever they could carry. Within a half hour, Stella remembers, the family was loaded in the sleigh, the dog howling. At the last minute, Konstantyn returned to the house and grabbed a half sack of flour and a feather quilt, which he put over his three daughters and wife who were already in the sleigh. Stella was quite distressed at having to leave her dog behind, with no one to look after it. The Soviets moved them to a nearby train station where, like Sophia's family, they were packed onto cattle cars.[18]

Kazimiera Mazur was nine on February 10, 1940, when, at six o'clock in the morning, the Russians came through their door. "Get up, dress yourself! You are going!" They were only allowed to take whatever they could carry — a little bit of food, clothes. The rest had to be left behind. Kazimiera, her father, her mother (who was two or three months pregnant), and five siblings were taken by sleigh and crammed into cattle cars at the nearest rail station.[19]

Janina Kusa, born in 1927, was the fifth of ten children. Her father, Jan, was disturbed enough by the increased activity in the area to have taken two of her younger sisters, Cecylia and Stanislawa, to their grandmother in Lvov on February 9. Fortunately, the oldest, Maria, had already finished school and had started teaching in a small village near the German-Polish border in September 1939. That meant one less child for him to worry about. Jan had only just returned from Lvov on the evening of February 9, and Janina recalls him telling her mother that he was very worried about the increased traffic he saw at the train station. There were too many soldiers around, and they were armed to the teeth, he said. He'd seen a whole train packed with Soviet military personnel. It didn't look good. If war did come, moving his remaining family of seven children westward was going to be a challenge. He had finally lain down to get some sleep at about midnight, but within hours the NKVD was pounding on the door. The immediate assumption was that they were coming for him because of his trip to Lvov, but the NKVD soon made it clear that the whole family was under arrest.

Janina's older brother, Ludwik, managed to escape. While the family was packing, he went to the outhouse behind the barn and just kept on walking. In the confusion of the remaining six children, he wasn't missed by the Soviets, nor by his parents immediately. When his father finally noticed, he kept quiet. Ludwik managed to get to the next village where the family had Ukrainian friends. They provided him with clothes, because he had escaped in only his pyjamas, and a bit of money. He eventually made it to his grandmother's home in Lvov, where he joined the Polish resistance.

Meanwhile, Janina's parents got the remaining children dressed and grabbed some food, and a few other things. Interestingly, among the things that Janina's mother packed were her wedding dress, some small rugs, and a small brass icon of the Virgin Mary. Her father put on his fur coat. In a couple of hours, the Kusa family was gone. Janina would never see her home again.[20]

Al Kunicki was very young when the NKVD came; four years old and the youngest of six (four sisters, one brother, and himself). However, he knows the family's story. By February 10, the Kunicki children were already parentless. His mother, Anastazja, had died in 1938. In 1940, some time before the deportation, his father, Filip, had been arrested. Filip had been in the Austrian army during the First World War, and in the Polish Army during the 1920s. He had been granted land in eastern Poland for his service in the Polish forces, and had become a farmer there. He was also a policeman. The combination made him an obvious target for the suspicious Soviets. Filip's arrest had left Al's two older sisters, Aleksandra and Antonina, aged nineteen and eighteen, in charge of the family.

Al's memories of that night are vague and based on family lore, but when the Russians arrived it was just him and his sisters at home. As the Russians surrounded the house, one sister, Jozefa, slipped out a window and ran to the orchard, tripping over a pile of mud in the process. She managed to escape to one of the neighbouring villages, where one of her mother's sisters hid her. The aunt had married a Ukrainian, so her family escaped the raids that night. Al's brother, Jan, later tried to find them in the Soviet Union, but to no avail. Al and his three remaining sisters, Aleksandra, Antonina, and Stanislawa, were sent to Siberia.[21]

Stan Studzinski was the same age as Al Kunicki at the time, and his recollections are thin, but he does know that when the Russians arrived on February 10, his father had already fled. He had also been granted land for serving in the Polish Army in the 1920s, which marked him as a potential threat to the Soviet occupiers. When the NKVD gathered up Stan's family and took them to the train station that night, it was just him, his mother, and the rest of his brothers and sisters. Stan's father remained in Poland.[22]

Michal Bortkiewicz was born in 1934, so he was six years old when the Russians rounded up his family and sent them into the Russian interior. His father, Bronislaw, was a prosperous farmer, having been granted land in eastern Poland. He had been an officer in the Russian Army at the time of the Russian Revolution, and had also been in the White Russian forces and blown up some Bolshevik officers. He was granted the land as one of the *osadnicy*.

The family lore holds that when Michal's father arrived in eastern Poland all he had was an axe and a rooster. Within a decade he had built himself a very prosperous farm. It was a combination of fields, a woodlot, and an orchard with twenty cherry and two apple trees, as well as livestock. Michal's life was idyllic for a young boy. There was a sauna in the back where men from the neighbourhood would gather and "booze it up" with his father, to use his words; his father took him trapping rabbits in the forest; they had beautiful horses. Working the land was deeply satisfying for Michal, even at a young age.

But all of that came to a crashing end on February 10, when the Russians arrived in the middle of the night. Initially, everyone in the family believed that they were there to arrest their father. This was not the first time the Soviets had come in search of him — they had tried several times before. Every other time he had slipped over the border into Lithuania. This time, however, he was at home.

The house had a front vestibule, which was unlit of course, since there was no electricity. When Michal's father opened the front door, the NKVD charged past him into the house proper, not seeing him in the dark. Believing that he was the only target for arrest that night, his father took advantage of the confusion of the moment to slip out the door and flee to Lithuania, not realizing that his whole family was about to be arrested and deported. The NKVD didn't realize they had missed Michal's father. They ordered his mother, Kazimiera, to dress the children and pack up. When she asked where they were being taken, the NKVD were vague. So she packed some clothes, some food, and other bits and pieces, and the family was put on the sleigh and taken to the train station.

In the midst of the chaos, Michal's older brother, Stanislaw, stepped outside. One Russian soldier had been left to guard the door, but when he saw the brother put on skis and disappear, he ignored it. An NKVD officer noticed something was amiss, but when he asked the guard what was going on, the guard replied, "Nothing." Michal suspects that he didn't want to shoot the boy. Stanislaw fled to the neighbours, but left when they challenged him. He found friends in the village who hid him, despite the Soviet threats to burn down the village if he wasn't turned over. He remained there for the duration of the war, working for some farmers. After the war, he rejoined his father, who had returned to Poland. Meanwhile, Michal and Stanislaw's mother, with four children ranging in age from four to twelve, was loaded on a train for Siberia.[23]

The operation was carefully planned in such a way as to minimize panic and resistance. That was the reason for the home invasions in the middle of the night and the very limited amount of time to dress and pack before being taken away. The element of surprise, combined with the bleariness of being jolted awake and the terror of being held at gun-point, induced both terror and passivity in the victims.[24] The scale of the operation, although not immediately apparent, was also intended to destroy any seeds of resistance in the remaining population, as well as deny leadership to any potential resistance.

No one had any idea where they were being sent or for how long. The NKVD teams, when asked, were either vague or lied outright, often saying that they were being moved to Germany (i.e., the parts of the former Polish Republic now controlled by Germany) or neighbouring districts.[25] People were told to pack only enough food for a few days. As Krzysztofa Michniak recalls, when her family was deported on April 13, 1940, the

NKVD continually edited what her mother was packing in the brief time she was given.

> They said, "You don't need this, you don't need that. Because in Russia you will have everything." And they said, "You should know how the other people are living. Because you have too much of everything here. You're not supposed to [have so much]." And always you heard this "bourgeois, bourgeois, bourgeois"!

Although she was ten years old, Krzysztofa was not able to help her mother because the terror of the moment had reduced her to tears. So much so that she was not even able to dress herself.[26]

The pressure of having to pack literally with only a moment's notice, at gunpoint, not knowing where you were going or for how long, made it almost impossible to decide what to take with any kind of logic. Dealing with terrified, crying children at the same time, with your husband unable to help — as he was pinned to the wall or in the corner — must have made the situation even more hellish for the women of the family, who had to bear the brunt of the organizing and packing, of spontaneously reducing their lives to whatever they could carry. To be torn from their homes, with no warning and no time, and then dragged out and onto sleighs in the dark hours of the early morning, not knowing where they were being taken or for how long, was traumatizing.

Yet this was only the beginning of the nightmarish journey. The trains onto which they were put were not passenger trains, but baggage or cattle cars, fitted out with crude plank bunk beds along the wall, sometimes with a small pot-bellied stove in the middle, and a hole cut in the floor in a corner that would serve as toilet. Sometimes there was something to burn in the stove, sometimes there was not. What few windows there were were boarded up, or had bars over them. Once the passengers were on board, the doors were locked from the outside and no one was allowed off the train or near it, at least not until it had crossed into Soviet territory. The transports could number some sixty cars, with up to fifty or sixty people jammed into each one. In many instances the trains sat in the rail stations for a couple of days before departing. Relatives and friends who had not been arrested and imprisoned tried to take their loved ones food and supplies while the cars sat on the sidings, but to no avail. The Soviet guards refused to allow them to approach.[27]

The voyages east lasted two to four weeks, and the deportees were scattered across the Russian interior. The travelling conditions were inhumane. For those transported in the winter months the piercing cold generated its own mortality rate among the very young and very old, who all too easily and inevitably froze to death. Many others died of starvation en route, because the rations provided by the Soviets were few and far between, and grossly inadequate when they were available, nor was there enough water. Helena Koscielniak's sister, Stella, explained to her what had happened to her family. Maybe once a day the guards on the train would throw a handful of old bread in, but you had to be close to the door or window when that happened, because there was never enough to go around. Helena recalls begging her father for bread, because she was hungry. Her father ultimately died on that trip, probably from starvation. He had been ill before, with lung problems, but on the train he always gave his portion of bread to his children. Without food or water, he died within a week or two. When it was discovered that he had died, Stella reported, "The train didn't even stop. They just opened the door and threw out the body. And there were a lot of bodies being thrown off that train."[28]

Krzysztofa Michniak's trip in April 1940 was no easier. A month long, the journey was a struggle to survive in horrific conditions. What shines through in Krzysztofa's recollections, and in the others', is how deeply degrading those conditions were. The lack of even the most elemental privacy — with a hole in the floor of the car serving as toilet; the way in which families were crammed together, literally on top of each other, twenty-four hours a day; the lack of any opportunity to practise even the most basic hygiene — all sapped the deportees both physically and emotionally. At the month's end, she recalled, the transport stopped in Novosibirsk and there, finally, they had a bath.

It was a beautiful building! Everything, because [it was likely built] when the Tsar was alive, probably it was for the army or something, because there was lots of marble, lots of showers, and hot water. But all the clothes you had, you were supposed to leave there, because they had to put a special disinfectant [i.e., treat them for bugs and lice]. Because the whole month you didn't have a bath! Not much water to wash, you know. And in that huge hall, people were naked. Everybody! Nobody mentioned this, but [that was] the way it was. Grown-ups and children together. Imagine that! All the women, they were holding children like that [in front of them, protecting them]. Because I remember my mother. It was shocking for us. She didn't know what to say, what to do. And she was holding herself. It was terrible. And after the bath, we went back to our car, to the train.[29]

Some had had enough foresight to grab some food when they had packed that fateful night. Janina Kusa remembers the only thing that kept her family of eight alive was the little bit of flour they had brought with them, because the guards on her train only gave them bread periodically, and hot water.[30] Water shortages were a serious problem on the transports. Krzysztofa Michniak shuddered to think of the pail of water that was sometimes given to the car. Half of it would be filled with mud. Her family of five would get one cup of water to share, and everyone would get just one sip from the cup.[31] Michal Bortkiewicz recalls trying to break ice from the door of the train car in an attempt to get something to drink.[32]

Once the Polish-Soviet border was crossed, the tight controls over the Polish deportees eased a bit. On occasion, the trains stopped and allowed the deportees to disembark in order to stretch and, most importantly, search for food. This could have dire consequences for families, however, as the train could and did start moving again without warning, leaving people behind.[33] This is what happened to Helena Koscielniak and her two sisters. Her mother and her older brother, Albin, had disembarked at a Russian rail station where they had stopped briefly, in search of food.

Before they returned, the train pulled out of the station with the three sisters on board. They never saw either their mother or brother again. The oldest sister, Katie, was ten years old.[34] In this way, with a chance decision, families were irrevocably broken apart and in an instant children were forced to assume adult responsibilities.

The first wave of deportations was sent deep into the Russian interior, to the north and to the east — Arkhangelsk, Irkutsk, Sverdlovsk, Novosibirsk, Komi. The second deportation was, for the most part, sent into northern Kazakhstan, although Krzysztofa Michniak's April 1940 transport ended up near Novosibirsk. However, it was not long before she was moved to Semipalatinsk.[35] The children who would end up in Tengeru followed these routes. What faced them at the end of their journey was daunting. Sophia Wakulczyk's family ended up in Arkhangelsk, where they were put into a small barrack, perhaps twenty feet by twenty feet, which they shared with three other families. The only furnishings were four plank platforms that served as beds, one for each family. Her parents were put to work as forced labour in brickworks, manufacturing bricks by hand, and the children were put in school. Sophia's younger brothers were put in kindergarten and Sophia herself was put in grade one, because she didn't know any Russian. There, they were taught Russian and indoctrinated in Communism. In Sophia's words,

> … [T]he schools were not too bad, but they tried to get us to tell whatever your parents were saying. So I said to my Mom and Dad, "I'm supposed to tell at school what you are talking about." And my father was just livid! He said, "Don't ever say anything!" Because they could imprison or separate us. So that was that for two and a half years.[36]

Kazimiera Mazur and her family were taken deep into the forests of Siberia. Although she doesn't know exactly where they were, she describes it as hopelessly remote and isolated. When the Mazur family arrived at their destination, it was basically a clearing in the forest, with a large barrack in the middle that looked very much like those in the

Nazi concentration camps. Twenty-three families were crammed into the open hall, with one little stove for cooking and heat. That spring the men in the barrack organized themselves and constructed walls in order to give each family its own room, small but private. Her father and her oldest brother were put to work in the forest, logging with hand tools — hard and dangerous work. Because there were six children her mother stayed in the barrack to tend them. There was no medical care provided and one of Kazimiera's sisters died of polio. They lived there for nearly two years.[37]

Janina Kusa and her family were sent to Novosibirsk, in Central Asia. After weeks on the train the deportees were unloaded, put on sleds, and taken through the woods and deep snow to a spot far into the forest, where they were housed in barracks similar to the one in which the Mazurs lived. Some families continued on to a village, but the Kusas stayed at the barracks. Within a day or two of their arrival, the Russian commandants of the camp came and ordered her father and two oldest brothers, along with the rest of the "able-bodied" adults, including pregnant women, to go work in the forest, cutting trees. After a few months, her father was shifted to caring for the horses, although her brothers continued to work as woodcutters. Like Kazimiera's mother, Janina's mother stayed in the barracks in order to mind the remaining children.[38]

It was a hard life. Families were crammed into roughly constructed, ill-heated barracks, with just a few square metres for each. The barracks were infested with cockroaches that crawled thick on the walls. Michal Bortkiewicz remembers that every year, the Soviet authorities came into the barracks and sprayed a poison to kill the cockroaches. As he described it,

> The cockroaches just fell down and they shovelled them away. They ate you alive at night! It was so bad in those barracks. I don't know how many times they came to put down this poison and picked up the dead cockroaches.[39]

Rations were determined brutally and were very limited, perhaps two or three hundred grams of bread twice a day, and watery soup. It was a fundamental Bolshevik principle that everyone worked and those who did not, didn't eat. The rule was made clear to the Poles upon their arrival in the camps. Those who worked got bread. Those who did not work didn't. The same principle applied to the Soviet labour force, which had, by this time, become quite militarized in its management. By 1930, Stalin's drive to modernize and industrialize the U.S.S.R. had resulted in a drastic labor shortage, which had necessitated the enactment of severely restrictive and militaristic measures to ensure the nation's productivity, including longer workweeks, restrictions imposed on workers' ability to move between jobs, and severe punishments for breaches of discipline, including tardiness and absenteeism. The Polish deportees were a much-needed source of labour for the Soviet industrial machine. The increasingly brutal labour management practices were merely carried over to, and exaggerated in, the forced labour camps, prisons, and work battalions formed with the Polish deportees.[40]

The work was hard, physical labour. All persons aged sixteen or older were expected to work, both men and women. In fact, that age limit was often lowered to fifteen, fourteen, and even twelve. In some instances children as young as ten were assigned compulsory labour. In the forests the labour was logging. In Kazakhstan, it was agriculture. The deportees were put to work planting and harvesting potatoes, picking vegetables, grains, and cotton, clearing and weeding fields, and herding and tending livestock. They were also used in major construction development projects, as well as heavy industries, such as brickmaking, quarrying, mining, factory work, and on farms or digging ditches. Payment generally took the form of food rations, although some deportees were occasionally paid a few rubles a month. The size of the food ration was determined by the worker's quota, but the quotas were set impossibly high. Failure to meet quota meant reduced rations and often additional punishment. To compound the situation, few deportees remained in one spot for long. They were moved between camps based on the seasons, the requirements of the central economic plan, or the whims of the local authorities. A few women chose not to work, but remained in the barracks to look after their children. If they could do this, it was because their husbands and older sons made it possible, if just barely. These were usually mothers of large families, like Kazimiera Mazur's mother, with six children, and Janina Kusa's mother. It was an enormous sacrifice and risk to take, trading their labor, and the food ration the mother could earn, for the preservation of the traditional family model that was the ideal in pre-war Poland. On the other hand, there was the very real and vexing problem of who would look after the children if both parents worked. If there wasn't a child old enough to take charge there didn't seem to be an option. More commonly, everyone in the family who could, worked. For those women who did not have their husbands with them, there was no choice. They had to work in order to feed their children.[41]

In this system it was impossible to survive on the rations received, even if one did work. For those who didn't, such as children and those mothers able to remain in the barracks to look after their children, the situation was much more grave, for they could expect no support from the state.[42] Resourcefulness and determination were needed to survive in those circumstances. Everyone had to contribute. One of the primary tasks of those too young, or unable, to work was to scavenge, beg, and steal extra food wherever and whenever possible. The younger children were sent into the forest to pick berries and mushrooms when in season.[43] If the family had anything it could trade for food, there was the possibility of bartering with the local Russians, although they had little enough of their own. Janina Kusa's mother, who had brought her wedding gown with her from Poland, trekked into the nearest village and traded it for a bit of food. Some planted small gardens in the midst of the forest, wherever a clear patch of ground could be cultivated. The Kusa family did that, in a clearing about one mile from the barracks. Unfortunately, it was a contest with the animals of the forest as to who would get the vegetables first. However, they did manage to harvest six small bags of potatoes, grown by carefully cultivating the eyes from potatoes they had been eating and planting them as seeds.[44]

Michal Bortkiewicz climbed trees to raid crows' nests for new hatchlings that his mother made into crow soup.[45] Those who still had family back in Poland sometimes received parcels from their relatives.

Janina's grandmother in Lvov sent a parcel of flour, which helped enormously.[46] Others received parcels of goods, especially clothing, that could be bartered.[47]

To a person, each of the individuals interviewed testified that the Russians were good people and that it was the Soviet system that was so horrible. Sophia Wakulczyk remembers that her youngest brother, Adam, was born in Siberia and quickly starved to death, as there was no food for the baby and her mother could not breastfeed him. A Russian woman with a goat, at great risk to herself, sneaked milk to Sophia's mother in a vain attempt to save Adam. While the baby soon died, Sophia still remembers the Russian woman's generosity.[48] There was never enough, and hunger was an unrelenting enemy. Stanley Paluch remembers that his eternal prayer while in Siberia was that God would allow him to eat his fill. After that, he would be content to die.[49]

In the winter, the shortage of fuel was as serious a problem as the shortage of food, for the temperatures habitually plunged down to between -30 and -40°C. In the forests, fuel was less of a concern because of the abundance of wood. For those sent to the Siberian steppes, where there were no trees, finding fuel for both heating and cooking was a constant challenge. All that was available to burn was scrub brush and manure. Collecting fuel was a task that often fell to the children. Krzysztofa Michniak and her older sister scoured the steppes for manure, which they would bring back to their hut, mix with straw, and dry into cakes of fuel.[50]

Yet, in the midst of these unremittingly harsh conditions, the children did find occasional moments to play. When asked about Siberia, Michal Bortkiewicz, who as a boy knew no fear and lived for the moment, recalls one winter's day when he and a bunch of the other boys in the camp took one of the huge sleds used to move wood and pulled it to the top of a hill. They all piled onto it and launched themselves on the enormous makeshift toboggan. "And then we were flying and everybody was jumping off! And I didn't jump! And I ended up on some roof! They had to dig me out of the snow!" However, this was an exceptional moment in a life that was almost unremittingly cruel. Michal reports that he spent most of the time in the hospital, unable to walk, unable to crawl, with bloody diarrhea, likely the result of either dysentery or typhoid fever.[51]

As a result of these terribly harsh conditions, the mortality rate in the camps, as well as the incidence of disease and malnutrition, was high. The very young and the very old were the most vulnerable. Janina Kusa's youngest sister died within months of arriving in Siberia.[52] Marian Kacpura's father had died on the trip to Siberia, and his mother died very soon after.[53] Sophie Matusiewicz, who had been shipped with her family to Irkutsk in February 1940, lost her youngest sister, born just months before the deportation. The infant girl died within a couple of weeks of reaching Irkutsk, for lack of milk. Her father died soon after, leaving her mother to look after five children — Sophie, her two sisters, and her two brothers.[54] Kazimiera Mazur lost one of her sisters to polio in Siberia.[55] Sophia Wakulczyk's mother gave birth to her brother Adam in Russia, who soon starved to death.[56] Helena Koscielniak lost her infant sister, Emilia.[57]

For the women in the forced labour camps, especially those who were single or who found themselves without their husbands — either because they escaped deportation, died on the way, or were somehow separated in the confusion of the transport — there were other risks as well. These forced labour camps were run by the NKVD and the inhabitants had no rights; they were prisoners. Women, especially (but not exclusively) those without men to protect them, were vulnerable to sexual predators. Krzysztofa Michniak explained that it was in the camps that she learned *gwalt*, the Polish word for rape.

> And there is one Russian man who is watching them, how they work. Work faster, do this and do this and…. But when we were, in the evening, all in bed, he used to come to [our] room! And I had a bad feeling about him. From the beginning, I saw, from the moment I saw him. Each time [he] approached, I had my eyes open and I'd lift my head and he couldn't stand this. And I don't know how many times he came there. How many nights. And he couldn't stand it. So he hired a young man to kill me. Yes. And my mother was … she sent us for a letter or something and we needed special

permission, and we [got] special permission. [But that meant] he knew I would be going there with my sister, my older sister! And we were walking and I said to my sister ... that man was maybe a quarter-mile from us, so he couldn't hear me when I was talking to my sister. I didn't talk loud. And I said, "I'm afraid of that man. He's going to do something to me."

And she said, "Oh no, just relax and talk and smile, and nothing is going to happen."

And I said, "You will see. He will do something." And when he was closer to us, and suddenly he was walking, was facing me. And when he was maybe that far, he took the knife. Then I screamed ... and I ran back to the camp. I don't know how. I am a very, very bad runner. I don't know how this happened. I always said, "God is always helping me." And I ran back to the camp and I was screaming like crazy.

My mother was standing in line to buy bread. When she saw me, she came to me. She asked me, "What happened?" My older sister, she was a very good runner, [yet] she was behind me! And he didn't even run after her. He didn't want to kill her, only ... me! And I wasn't able to talk probably for two days you see, and my sister said what happened.

Okay, so, during [another] night it was so hot that we weren't able to sleep in the barracks, so everybody was sleeping outside. When we were sleeping outside, that young man came again. He tried to kill me during the night. I was beside my mother. My mother caught the knife just in time. It was so close. So twice I [almost] had, that close, a knife through the heart ... because, I knew that my mother was raped, because when that man from work called her to his office ... I was, the first time, [pounding on] his door and screaming, "Let Mother out!"

Mother said, "It's nothing." Later, when she came out, she said, "Everything's fine, nothing happened."

I didn't know what means "rape", but that word was with me always. We call it in Polish, *gwalt*. So I heard a woman say "*Gwalt*" and my mother said, "Quiet."[58]

And then in 1941, came the amnesty.

While the Soviet Union was occupied establishing control in eastern Poland, after seizing the territory in September 1939, the Polish Government had fled westward, first to France. By September 30, it had reconstituted itself there, carefully ensuring that in the process it remained constitutional, and thus the legitimate government of Poland in the eyes of the Poles and, perhaps as important, in the eyes of the world. Wladyslaw Raczkiewicz was appointed president of Poland and, soon after, General Wladyslaw Sikorski was made prime minister and commander of the Polish Army in France. One of the first tasks the exiled government set itself was to construct an army, beginning with one division, headed by a Polish general. They would fight under the French High Command. The message was put out that any Polish soldiers or officers who could manage, should attempt to get to France. However, the government's haven in France was short-lived; France fell devastatingly quickly to the Germans in June 1940. By June 14, Paris had been taken and the chief concern of the Polish Government was its own evacuation, as well as the evacuation of its armed forces.[59] By June 21, 1940, the Polish Government had re-established itself in London, England, the guest of the British Government and financially dependent upon British loans to operate.[60]

The situation there was a bit precarious for the fledgling government. While it had been recognized as the legitimate government of Poland, the fall of France and the mad scramble to get to England had undermined the fragile peace that had been constructed between the various Polish political factions within the new Government-in-Exile. Furthermore, although it was acknowledged as the true government of Poland, that didn't garner it much in the way of influence with the major powers shaping events on the continent. The Polish Government was in quite a weak bargaining position and unable to exert much pressure on its allies, upon whom it was completely dependent.[61] For the next year Sikorski devoted his efforts to cultivating Poland's relationship with Britain, establishing Poland's diplomatic presence internationally, and rebuilding the Polish forces on British soil.[62]

Circumstances changed dramatically on June 22, 1941, when Germany invaded the U.S.S.R., sending over three million men pouring over a front line some three thousand kilometres long, stretching from the Baltic Sea to the Black Sea. Stalin had refused to believe his own military intelligence, which had warned him that the Germans were preparing for an attack. The borders of the Soviet Union were quickly overrun and the Soviets forced into retreat. By mid-July, the German forces had taken the Baltic Republics, Smolensk, and Kiev, and were only 320 kilometres from Moscow. On the day of the invasion, Winston Churchill, the prime minister of Great Britain, had gone on the radio and pledged unconditional support to the Soviet Union. The next day, perhaps even more controversially — at least within Polish exile circles — Sikorski also took to the airwaves to speak to the Polish nation about the new situation and to send a message to Moscow. It was surprisingly conciliatory. In the speech, he argued that the invasion negated the Molotov-Ribbentrop Pact of August 1939, which logically meant that both Poland and the U.S.S.R. had returned to their pre-war positions and to the 1921 border. He also suggested that this might be the time for Moscow to release the thousands of Polish prisoners currently in Soviet prisons. It was an invitation to a rapprochement between the two states. The British Government was mightily pleased with the overtures; they were keen to have Poland reconcile with their newfound ally. Many members of the Polish Government were less enthusiastic, being justifiably suspicious of the U.S.S.R. Within a few days the Soviet Union responded with cautious interest.[63]

The next five weeks were a whirlwind of diplomatic activity, with Britain acting as broker between the Polish and Soviet Governments. Several issues were serious sticking points, one being the Polish-Russian border. Sikorski wanted formal recognition from the U.S.S.R. that the boundary between the two countries was the one determined in the Treaty of Riga. The U.S.S.R. refused to acknowledge that and instead suggested that an independent national Polish State should be established, with borders corresponding to ethnographic Poland. This, Sikorski would not accept. However, rather than let the issue of frontiers sink the negotiations, and well aware that not only was the British Government very keen to see some kind of Polish-Soviet agreement, but also that there were thousands upon thousands of Poles in Soviet prisons and labour camps whose futures hung in the balance, he proposed that the question of frontiers be put aside for the moment. It was a proposal that did not sit well with many in the Polish Government, but it is one that was amenable to Moscow and the British. On July 30, 1940, the Polish-Soviet Agreement was concluded, over the protests and resignations of three Polish cabinet ministers, and in spite of the Polish president's refusal to sign. Instead, Prime Minister Sikorski signed on behalf of the Polish Government. The Agreement stated that the 1939 Pact between the U.S.S.R. and Germany, relative to the territorial changes in Poland, had lost their validity, and that diplomatic relations between Poland and the U.S.S.R. would be restored immediately. Both governments agreed to "render one another aid and support of all kinds in the present war against Hitlerite Germany" and, significantly, the U.S.S.R. agreed to allow the formation on its territory of a Polish Army, under a commander appointed by the Government of the Republic of Poland. It would, however, be subordinated in operational matters to the Supreme Command of the U.S.S.R. Further details as to its command structure, organization, and employment were to be worked out in a subsequent agreement. Importantly, in a protocol attached to the Agreement, it was declared that:

> As soon as diplomatic relations are re-established the Government of the Union of the Soviet Socialist Republics will grant amnesty to all Polish citizens who are at present deprived of their freedom on the territory of the USSR either as prisoners of war or on other adequate grounds.[64]

While the language stung, for it implied that the Soviet Union had both the right and justification for the internments, the end result, the liberation of Polish citizens, made swallowing one's pride worthwhile, or so argued Sikorski.[65] As well, to have refused might easily have incurred the loss of British support, as the British were keen to see the two countries reconciled.[66] The pledge to resurrect the Polish Army, combined with the amnesty granted in the protocol (which the Soviets finally issued on August 12, 1941[67]), would have a profound impact on the Polish soldiers and civilians who had been deported earlier that year and buried deep in the interior of the U.S.S.R..

Diplomatic channels were quickly established between the two nations. Sikorski appointed Professor Stanislaw Kot as Ambassador to the U.S.S.R. and selected General Wladyslaw Anders to lead the new Polish Army. Anders was, at that point, in the Lubyanka prison in Moscow. On August 6, General Zygmunt Bohusz-Szyszko, as head of the Polish military mission to the U.S.S.R., arrived in Moscow to begin the negotiations for the Polish-Soviet military agreement which would govern the shape of the new Polish Army. By this time, the U.S.S.R. was under considerable pressure from the Nazi invasion and wished to see the Polish forces mobilized as quickly as possible. Negotiations proceeded quickly and the accord was signed on August 14. General Anders, newly released from prison, was informed of his newfound office and, on September 10, was moved to his new headquarters in Buzuluk, in the western foothills of the Ural Mountains, north of the Kazakhstan border. His task was to bring together the Poles scattered across Russia and create an army.

This army was to be organized as quickly as possible. Although it would fall under the Soviet High Command, it would constitute a part of the military forces of the sovereign Polish Republic, its troops would be subject to Polish military law and regulations, and at the war's end, it would return to Poland, at least according to the accord. Once the troops were properly trained and equipped, it would be used against Germany, in conjunction with the Soviet forces and those of other allies. The U.S.S.R. pledged in the first instance to provide it with the necessary equipment, uniforms, armaments and supplies, including foodstuffs, to the extent possible, and then the Polish Government was obliged to make up the shortfall. Moscow agreed to provide rations for thirty thousand men, roughly the equivalent of two divisions and one reserve regiment.[68] Nothing smaller than a division was to be fielded at any time and only under direct Polish command. To facilitate communications, a Polish military liaison mission was attached to the Supreme Command of the Red Army and a similar Soviet mission was sent to the Polish High Command based in London. The Soviets' expectation (laughable in hindsight) was that the army would be in the field by October 1, 1941.[69]

The Soviet authorities finally issued the amnesty and called for volunteers for the army in late August, but the recruitment took much more time than originally anticipated. In many corners of the U.S.S.R., the Poles didn't hear about it for several weeks or even longer, as it was the NKVD who had to pass on the information. Sometimes they did, sometimes they did not. Some volunteers had begun gathering in Moscow, but by mid-September, Buzuluk became both the Polish military headquarters and a collection point, with the newly forming 5th Infantry Division located in Tatishchevo and the newly forming 6th Infantry Division and the reserve regiment in Totskoye. It was an inhospitable and forbidding location. Buzuluk and Totskoye, forty kilometres apart, were located at the point where the Central Asian steppes met the East European plain. The climate is continental in that part of the world and, in the winter, temperatures dip to -50°C and lower. Tatishchevo is located almost five hundred kilometres from Buzuluk, a trip that took up to eleven days then, given the deplorable transportation system and roads in the region, and the climate is no more hospitable than the roads were.[70] Buzuluk, as Anders described it in his memoirs, was a small, impoverished village in the middle of nowhere. None of the other sites were any better — there were no accommodations for the troops, let alone food, equipment, communication links, or even adequate transportation. In Totskoye, the troops lived in canvas tents in the forest. While the troops' morale was high, their physical condition after a year or more in Soviet prisons and forced labour camps was alarmingly poor. Most were emaciated from semi-starvation and in rags, without shirts or boots, in spite of the harsh winter. Lice- and disease-ridden, these were not men who could be considered in any way ready to be put in the field in just a matter of weeks. It was not an auspicious beginning, nor did it bode well in terms of Soviet support for the army.[71]

In fairness, this came at the nadir for the Soviet Union in the war against Germany. In the German advance during the spring of 1941, the Soviet army had been smashed. The air force had been largely destroyed. By the end of August, the Germans had captured 1.5 million Soviet prisoners of war. On June 22, martial law had been declared throughout the U.S.S.R.. A labour conscription law was issued requiring all men aged eighteen to forty-five, and all women aged eighteen to forty to work eight hours a day constructing defences. By June 26, the working day had been extended three hours and all leave and holidays were suspended. Stalin also ruthlessly purged the officer corps of those deemed responsible for the collapse on the front. On July 3, Stalin called on the population as a whole to mobilize against the invader. At the same time, a mammoth effort was made to move, literally, the entire Soviet industrial economy east. Within two days of the German attack, a Committee of Evacuation was established, responsible for orchestrating the dismantling of whole factories and shipping them to Siberia, the Urals or Kazakhstan, wholesale. Whenever possible, the train carrying the factory also carried its labour force. In the second half of 1941, some twenty-five hundred enterprises were moved. When a train arrived at their destination, the workers would boil off the train and instantly begin reassembling their factory. They were often set up in barren fields, with no amenities, little or no housing, nothing but what they brought with them. Some twenty-five million workers followed these factories into the interior, with families in tow. It was a herculean task, especially at a time of war, and one that threatened to overwhelm the transport and support systems of the country. There were drastic shortages of everything — food, clothing, transportation, fuel, weapons — even for the Soviet troops and civilians. The Soviet Union had also suffered the loss of its breadbasket (the Ukraine) and a significant part of its labour force. And in spite of the troops' tenacity and the mobilization of the citizenry, they were not yet able to stem the German flood. By July 21, Moscow was being bombed. By September 26, Leningrad was under siege, almost surrounded by German forces. By October 30, the Germans were within fifty kilometres of Moscow. The German advance would not lose steam until December 1941, and the U.S.S.R. did not begin to turn the tide until the spring of 1942. It was a brutal war and one which, at that point, the Soviet Union was losing.[72] Needless to say, during the winter of 1941–42 there was little extra to spare for the Poles.

Meanwhile, word gradually reached the Poles that the Polish Army was forming. Information was sparse, but everyone knew that the army was gathering somewhere to the south. By December 1941, between thirty-seven thousand and forty thousand Polish troops[73] (the exact number is a matter of debate) had enrolled in the army, far in excess of the thirty thousand men that the U.S.S.R. had agreed to supply. By this time it was clear the Soviet Union was unable and/or unwilling to adequately supply even thirty thousand Polish troops. Nor did it appear that the amnesty was being applied as it was supposed to be. Thousands of Polish citizens were not being allowed to leave the camps. Rumours suggested it was the strongest and most capable who were being kept. Many local Soviet authorities were apparently reluctant to lose their labour force, and either failed to tell their camp inmates of the amnesty or made it exceedingly difficult to leave.[74] Many Poles, especially army officers, had simply gone missing. On November 6, Anders was informed by the Soviet High Command that the total size of his army would be limited to the original August number of thirty thousand. Any troops in excess of that would have to be supplied by the Polish Government.[75] Meanwhile, tensions were mounting between the Poles, who were frustrated with the lack of support and with the obstacles put in the way of Polish recruitment by the Soviets, and the Soviets, who were increasingly frustrated by the Poles' failure to mobilize. Anders refused to let his men go into battle until they were properly trained and physically fit. He also refused to allow his men to be dispersed among the Soviet forces, insisting that the Polish Army, when it mobilized, would do so as a unit.[76]

Anders grew increasingly alarmed as the winter set in. His men remained in canvas tents, in temperatures dropping as low as -50°C, and in the midst of howling blizzards. To make matters even more complicated, at the same time as the troops were emerging from the prison and camp system, so too were thousands of civilians — women, children, the elderly — determined to seize what was seen as perhaps their one chance to escape Russia and the threat of another brutally harsh winter at the tender mercies of the NKVD. In desperation, Anders appealed to Sikorski and Stalin for aid. In December 1941, Sikorski flew to Russia and met with Stalin. The result of that meeting was a reaffirmation of the Poles' commitment to fight alongside the Soviet Union, but also an agreement from Stalin that the Polish Army could expand to a total of six divisions, or ninety-six thousand men (although he committed to supplying only one additional division); that it would move further south into Uzbekistan and Kazakhstan; and that the U.S.S.R. would loan the Polish Government one million rubles with which it could assist the Polish civilians who were on the move.[77] As soon as the weather permitted, Anders began moving his men southward.

The new headquarters for the Polish forces was Jangijul in Uzbekistan, near Tashkent and on the border with Kazakhstan. In the end, the transfer was a disaster. By all accounts, conditions were even worse in Central Asia. The climate in the winter was almost as bitter as where they had come from. In the summer it was impossibly hot and humid. The area was swampy and a breeding ground for mosquitoes, adding malaria to the list of illnesses plaguing the troops. Food supplies, housing, equipment, and clothing were all in extremely short supply. The troops lived in tents and mud huts; their rations were at a starvation level. The forces were ravaged with typhoid, malaria, dysentery, and typhus, along with other diseases resulting from malnutrition and an inhospitable environment. Thousands fell ill. Estimates were that by February 1942, almost 40 percent of the Polish forces were ill, with some units reaching 73.5 percent. To make matters worse, the troops were scattered over a huge area, some nine hundred kilometres wide, with only one single-track railway traversing it, making communications between units impossible. By this time, General Anders came to see his mission as being more about saving lives than constructing an army.[78] The notion of evacuating the troops to British-controlled Persia, now Iran, was tentatively floated.

To compound an already dire situation, the Soviet Union was working on the assumption that, with the amnesty, the Poles now had their own government to look after them, so the U.S.S.R. no longer had to do so. Abruptly, the Poles, both troops and civilians, found themselves "free" or, more accurately, left to their own devices. Some coming out of the prisons and labour camps were given a miniscule travel allowance to tide them over on their journey to Anders' army, based on an estimate of how long it would take them to get to their destination. Many were simply informed that if they wished to leave the camps, they were free to do so (with the notable constraint that they were not allowed to leave Russia). However, they had to finance and arrange their own way to the recruitment centres. This meant selling their remaining possessions in order to purchase train tickets south, or begging for the money from the Polish Embassy — provided they could make contact.[79]

The voyage southwards was one of chaos. There was no overall plan for the movement of the Poles and no one had expected the mass exodus, so no one was prepared for the sheer numbers. The trip was an arduous one, in the dead of the winter. In some ways it was even harder than the original deportation, because of the weakened state of the people. The Poles were simply released from the camps with travel documents and left to find their own way south. In many cases, fathers and brothers left their families behind while they sought out the army.

L.P.'s father was one such man. His logic was brutally simple. As he explained to his wife and his son, if they all remained in the camp they were all going to die. The Soviets were giving each of them two hundred grams of bread a day and very little else. They could not live on that. However, if he could sneak out of the camp no one would know that he was gone, so his two hundred grams daily could be divided among his wife and children — with luck, keeping them alive. So he and another man stole away one night and joined the army. L.P.'s mother took that bread and, each day, dried the ration and put it carefully aside against the day when the family would really need it. Ultimately, that bread and the blueberries the family picked during the summer of 1942, as well as whatever they could steal, would get the children to Uzbekistan, although not their mother, who died of starvation on the trek south. In one notable instance, L.P.'s sister was caught stealing sugar from a railcar. She saw someone helping themselves to something out of a railcar, standing on a siding, and went to investigate. When she discovered it was sugar they were stealing, she used her headscarf to take some for her family. As she was walking away, the makeshift rucksack flung over her shoulder, an NKVD officer saw her and arrested her. When he took her to the police station, she thought she was doomed. The NKVD chief screamed at her for stealing and told his officer to take the sack in the back room to see what was in it. When the officer and his chief returned to the room where she was waiting, they handed her the sack, now only half full of sugar, and brusquely told her to get back to the train.[80]

Families found themselves breaking apart under the dire need to keep moving south. Stan Studzinski was only five years old in 1942, travelling southward with his mother, uncle, three sisters, and two brothers. It was a desperate trip, with no food and no chance at finding any. Somewhere on that journey, Stan's uncle died. As he recalled, still shaken after all these years, the train didn't even slow down. They merely opened the door of the car and threw his uncle's body out into the snowbanks along the railway tracks. Somewhere along the way his other two brothers also died, something he only vaguely remembers. Stan himself was desperately sick, dying of starvation. At one stop, his mother got off the train with him and put him in a hospital. She told him to remember that he was five years old and then left; he wouldn't see his mother again until he visited Poland in the 1970s.[81] Stan Paluch also lost his oldest brother on the journey south.[82]

In many cases, the Polish civilians moving southwards were directed to *kolkhozes* (collective farms), rather than to the army recruitment centres, although they had been brought into the large catchment area for the Polish forces. The situation was dire. Now that the Soviet authorities had washed their hands of them they had no means to support themselves, and the Polish Army was even less able to provide them with the basic necessities of life. Many found, to their dismay, that moving south was perhaps the worst decision they could have made. Because they were "free," they were given nothing. There was no work, no housing, no food, and this part of Russia seemed even more impoverished than the north. Those who arrived first were sometimes lucky enough to get rudimentary housing — shacks made of mud, without windows or stoves. Others were less fortunate. Michal Bortkiewicz laughs wryly when he describes his family as living in a manger, because they lived with the farmer's livestock. His mother threw a pile of hay in the corner of the stable and that was where they slept.[83] Sophia Wakulczyk's family didn't even have that. When they arrived in Uzbekistan, her father dug a hole in the ground, made a roof, and that was where they lived.[84] A large number ended up working on *kolkhozes* picking cotton, onions, vegetables, harvesting grain or hay, weeding fields, or herding sheep or cattle. They were paid in food, and not much of that. This time, the whole family worked, even the very young.[85] What little they had left that was worth selling was sold for food. Michal Bortkiewicz' mother finally parted with the sheepskin jackets that she had carried from Poland, sending her two sons to the market to sell them and buy some sugar, flour, and salt.[86] Janina Kusa's mother traded her small brass icon of the Virgin Mary for a small bucket of green potatoes.[87] Theft was not uncommon. If something useful or edible could be taken, it would be.[88] It was still not enough, and to use the words of many interviewed, in Central Asia, "people were dying like flies."

As a result of the already compromised state of the Poles' health, combined with the abysmal conditions in Central Asia, the mortality rate climbed. Not only were people dying of starvation but, like the troops, they were also dying of malaria, dysentery, diphtheria, typhoid fever, and typhus. Orphaned children were becoming increasingly numerous, a problem that the Polish forces were keenly aware of. One of the tasks that the army took upon itself was to gather and care for the growing number of orphans. The armed forces had always been watching out for abandoned and orphaned children, but in Central Asia, in centres such as Tashkent and Semipalatinsk, and in smaller places, they organized army-sponsored orphanages. Life for children without guardians was particularly brutal, one in which they soon learned to fend for themselves or they didn't survive.

Stanley Paluch's story is a haunting one and all too common. When his family was deported from Siberia, it was his parents and six children, including him — three sisters and three brothers. By the time they arrived in Siberia, his oldest brother had already died. Two of his sisters died soon after the family moved to Uzbekistan, where his father left the family to join the army, arguing that it would be easier to get them out of Russia if he was in the army. Then his younger brother fell ill and went into the hospital, leaving Stan, his youngest sister, and his mother.

One day his mother went to visit his brother in the hospital. When she left, she told Stan, ten years old and now the oldest child in the family, that if she didn't return in two days, he was to take his three-year-old sister, Bronislawa, and go to the orphanage in Tashkent, forty kilometres away. They waited two days in the hut, but his mother never came back. After two days, Stan, now the adult of the family and caregiver for his sole remaining sister, set out with her to find the orphanage. Today he doesn't remember much of the trip, except stopping at a rudimentary soup kitchen to get something to eat; a place where, if you waited, you might get a scrap. When no one was looking, he tried to steal something for Bronislawa. Some man caught him and threw him out the window. He had no idea where he was going, but by asking directions he eventually found the orphanage.[89]

After losing one sister, Jadwaga, in Siberia, Michal Bortkiewicz and his older brother, Piotr, lost their remaining sister and then their mother in Uzbekistan. He and his brother buried them in the local Uzbek cemetery, where they decorated their mother's grave with a little stone heart and arrow, and the Polish eagle. How they survived without their mother is impossible to say. Michal remembers walking beside the river behind the local bazaar one day, where they threw the garbage. He saw a little chunk of bread floating in the water and, without thinking, jumped in the river to get it. His brother pulled him out as the bread disintegrated in his hands. Soon after that, they were put in a small orphanage.[90]

Sophia Wakulczyk's mother died of starvation in Uzbekistan, and her father was arrested, for what reason she still doesn't know. So at age twelve, Sophia was left in charge of her two younger brothers. They were soon brought to the orphanage in Tashkent.[91]

Sophie Matusiewicz's route to the orphanage in Bukhara was more circuitous, and reflects the important role played by chance in the way in which these children's lives unfolded. Her family, reduced from her parents and six children to just her mother and five children by the time they got to Uzbekistan, was soon further decimated. Upon getting to the south, Sophie's oldest brother left to join the army. Then her mother and both her sisters contracted typhoid fever and were taken to the hospital, leaving Sophie, aged nine, to care for her younger brother. She soon also got sick and had to go into the hospital, leaving her younger brother to fend for himself. She never found out what happened to him. When Sophie got to the hospital she actually saw her mother, but it was only a matter of days before a woman there told her that her mother had died. When the staff at the hospital asked her where her family was, she told them truthfully that she had no idea. They didn't know what to do with her, so they made up a mattress in the corridor of the hospital for her and there she stayed. She lived in the hospital for a while, until one day she heard two men speaking Polish. She started talking to them and one of the men asked her what she was doing there. When she explained her situation, he asked her if she would like to go to a Polish orphanage. She said yes, not having anywhere else to go. The next day he came and collected her, and took her to the orphanage.

Later, at the orphanage, a girl approached Sophie and said, "You know, you look like my sister." They started to talk and compare notes — things like their father's name and other family details — and concluded that they must be sisters. (What is dismaying is how quickly the children forgot what their siblings looked like.) The girl then told Sophie of her other sister, who was also in the orphanage. The reunion was not to last long, however. After a short while, both of the sisters became ill and they were taken back to the hospital. Sophie never saw them again. But at least now that she was in the orphanage she was getting something to eat.[92]

Other children, like Helena Koscielniak and her sisters, were found in Russian orphanages, having been put there after being separated from their parents or, as was Helena's case, because of their parents' death. That was also the case for Krzysztofa Michniak. At the end of 1940, she was still in the care of her mother and grandmother, but the living conditions and starvation rations they were receiving gradually wore them down. In January 1941, her mother died, likely of starvation, leaving only her grandmother to care for the three sisters. They were occasionally receiving parcels from Poland, which was, as Krzysztofa put it, "the way they existed." But they were literally starving to death, especially she and her grandmother. One day in March or April, in the most tragically banal way, her grandmother died, walking to the washroom. Krzysztofa ran screaming for her sister and then fainted in shock. By the time she came to, her grandmother's body had been laid out on the bed, dressed for interment. In May, she and her sisters were finally taken to a Russian orphanage in Semipalatinsk. There, Krzysztofa and her older sister, Felicia, were separated from their younger sister. She remembers that day clearly. It was just after the midday meal, when all the children were sent upstairs for a rest. Someone called her youngest sister downstairs. Krzysztofa had a bad feeling, and said to Felicia, "Maybe she's not coming back." Felicia dismissed her concerns, but Krzysztofa, restless, watched through the window. Suddenly she saw her youngest sister being taken to a car and she screamed out, "No! They are taking her away!" The two sisters raced downstairs and outside, screaming, in time to catch her at the gate to the yard. They had just enough time to say goodbye.

The two sisters remained in the orphanage, where they were put into a Communist youth organization and into a Russian school. There, the teachers tried to instill Communist values in them, albeit not very successfully. Krzysztofa found the whole experience bizarre. In the communist youth summer camp to which they were sent they were required to learn Communist songs, and practise marching and gymnastics, while in reality they were consumed with thoughts of food, because they were starving. At least, she said, this kept them busy and kept them from thinking about their hunger. It did not, however, make either her or her sister into a Communist. In school, the one bright spot was learning arithmetic, something her mother had always insisted she should do because she was going to need it. At least she could do that for her mother. Krzysztofa and Felicia remained in that orphanage until January 1942, when the director, an Uzbek, sought them out. He told them that he had Polish soldiers in his office, and they were going to pick them both up the next day and take them to a Polish orphanage. At that point, Krzysztofa broke down in tears. When he asked her why she was crying, she said, "Because our younger sister is in the other orphanage in Semipalatinsk." He said that she shouldn't worry, because she was already in the Polish orphanage, waiting for them.[93]

It did not take long for the Polish military authorities to realize that Central Asia was a death sentence for the tens of thousands of Polish troops and civilians gathered in the catchment area. Although the troops were sharing their paltry rations with the civilians, they were all doomed to starvation under the existing circumstances. The situation became exceedingly desperate on March 10, 1942, when General Kroulov, the Soviet general responsible for provisioning, informed Anders that as of March 20, 1942, the U.S.S.R. would only provide him with rations for 26,000 troops. By that point Anders had some seventy thousand troops in his camp who were not only feeding themselves with their rations, but also their families and dependants. In his mind, he was facing mass starvation. His response was to petition Stalin for relief, but Stalin's response was distinctly unhelpful. He informed Anders that he had been counting on a shipment of one million tons of wheat from the United States, but had only received one hundred thousand tons, due to the war between Japan and the U.S., which was compromising shipping on the Pacific Ocean. At best, he argued, he could offer thirty thousand rations, but they would be reduced in size.[94] At this point, evacuation of the Poles seemed the only solution.

Evacuation was an idea that had been bandied about for several months by the time Anders and Stalin met in mid-March. The resulting agreement was that Stalin would provide reduced rations for 44,000 Polish troops, men who would remain in Russia to fight beside the U.S.S.R. However, recruitment would continue, and any troops above that number would be evacuated to Iran and integrated into the British forces. Stalin himself sketched the evacuation route on the map during the meeting. The Poles would leave through Krasnovodsk, a port on the Caspian Sea, with an alternate route through Ashkhabad and Mashhad pencilled in. On March 19, Anders met with General Zhukov, who had been put in charge of the evacuation, to work out the details. Zhukov announced that the evacuation would be done in two weeks. That day, Anders issued the evacuation order and the first ship left Krasnovodsk on March 24. The British were aware of the decision and, in fact, had supported it. They hoped that these troops could bolster their beleaguered forces in the Middle East. However, while the British were expecting the evacuation, they were not prepared for either the numbers or the speed of the evacuation, nor were they expecting civilians. Instead of getting an army, as Keith Sword has so neatly put it, they were getting a welfare problem.[95]

The Poles were evacuated in two movements. The first was done quickly, largely between March 25 and April 5, moving a total of 43,858 people mostly to Pahlavi, across the Caspian Sea.[96] The second evacuation came in August, after a Polish-Soviet protocol was signed, allowing the remaining Polish troops and their families to leave. The British and the Polish Governments in London pressed Anders to stem the flood of Polish civilians in both instances, but to no avail. Anders fought hard to include civilians in the evacuations, believing that to leave them in Russia would be to condemn them to certain death.[97] On August 9, the second trek had begun. Over 69,000 were evacuated in those twenty-two days, including over twenty-five thousand civilians.[98] Once they crossed the border they became the formal responsibility of the Polish Delegation, with the considerable assistance of the British Government.

When word of the evacuations reached the Polish civilians there was a flood of people racing to get to Krasnovodsk. The train stations were inundated with people, camping out on platforms and around the stations, waiting for trains. Krasnovodsk itself was swamped with people desperately trying to get on the ships. Not everyone was going to be able to get out, but there didn't seem much rhyme or reason to who did get on board, other than the orphanages were given priority. Krzysztofa Michniak was in one of the first movements brought out. Her orphanage came through Ashkhabad in Turkmenistan, rather than through Krasnovodsk, and then on to Iran. Because they were among the first out, the orphanage was moved very quickly through the transit camps in Iran, and on to Pakistan, to avoid clogging the camps. They ended up spending some time on a British army base in Quetta, India (now Pakistan), where they had to wait for the monsoon season to end before they could move on. Their ultimate destination was a British refugee camp in northern India, outside a city called Jamnagar.[99] Kazimiera Mazur and her younger sister and brother, and Marian Kacpura and his siblings all followed the same route as Krzysztofa.[100] Helena Koscielniak and her sisters were brought out through Krasnovodsk to Pahlavi, in Iran — this was the more usual route. Stan Studzinski who had, by that time, been attached to a Polish orphanage, was also on the move southward. So were Sophia Wakulczyk and her brothers, Basel and Konstany; Michal and Piotr Bortkiewicz; Al Kunicki and his sister, Stanislawa; Sophie Matusiewicz; Stan Paluch and his sister, Bronislawa. — all orphans, all part of the mass exodus across the Caspian Sea. Some arrived relatively late to Central Asia and found themselves being moved through to Krasnovodsk very quickly. Such was the case for Stan Paluch, who said that almost as soon as he arrived at the orphanage in Tashkent, he and Bronislawa were on their way to Iran.[101]

Out of desperation, some parents turned their children over to the Polish orphanages when it appeared clear that they were not going to be able to leave as a family. Such was the case of Janina, Genowefa, and Bronislawa Kusa. When news of the evacuation reached the Kusas, Janina's father was very ill and in hospital. How he ended up there was revealing: He had tried to enlist in the Polish army, but had been rejected because his arm had been badly wounded in the First World War and hadn't healed properly. When he returned from the recruitment centre to the *kolkhoz* where his family was working, he was in despair. He was one of the few men left there and felt the burden of looking after all of the women and children. In a desperate attempt to get some relief, he walked to the Polish Embassy in Tashkent, some one hundred miles away, as Janina remembers it, to beg for food or money. When he got there, he was given some sugar and flour, but within blocks of the embassy, he was robbed. So he returned to the embassy and got some more supplies, although a smaller amount than before. With that he returned to the kolkhoz, where he carefully divided the sugar among the families, after having set aside a portion for the manager of the kolkhoz. With that bit of sugar, the families could barter for potatoes and other food.

Unfortunately, on that trip, he drank some contaminated water and soon after his return, developed dysentery. He was admitted to the make-shift hospital in the area, even though there were no medicines available. At that point he heard about the evacuation and that the orphanages were being shipped out. He was certain that this was going to be their last chance to get out of Russia, but he knew he was not going to be able to get to Tashkent, let alone to Krasnovodsk. So he told his fifteen-year-old son, Wladyslaw, to take his three sisters to the Polish embassy in Tashkent. And he gave him a note in which he explained that he had a son in the army and that he wanted the three girls put in the orphanage and to leave Russia. He told his daughters not to despair, but that as long as he was able to walk, he would follow and find them, so they should go. With that, he sent them to Tashkent with their brother. Bronislawa's first memory is of saying goodbye to her father through the window of the hospital. Her mother took Janina aside, just before they left, gave her a small, red, feather pillow and told her that it was for the youngest one, Bronislawa. She said, "Take care of her. Take care of the youngest one." Janina was thirteen and the eldest of the three; Bronislawa was four. The girls were admitted to the orphanage where they were given "new" clothes to replace their rags. Each child in the orphanage wore a blue Polish army shirt. It was long enough to be a dress on Janina and her sisters, which pleased them. They were also given berets to wear and were told to never take them off. It served as a uniform for the children and this way, the orphans could be easily identified in a crowd. Her brother returned to the *kolkhoz* to help his father and mother, who was sick with asthma. Two weeks later, Janina, Bronislawa, and Genowefa were on the boat for Pahlavi.[102]

Kazimiera Mazur's story is similar. Her parents were late in hearing about the amnesty and the formation of the Polish army to the south. As soon as they heard, in the summer of 1942, the family escaped the *kolkhoz* at night, trekking eighty kilometres to Tashkent. It was a nightmarish journey. Kazimiera's brother went with her father and they moved too quickly for her. Her legs were not long enough and she didn't have the strength, given that she was carrying her youngest sister, who was sick, on her back. At one point, when her father was ahead of her and her mother had fallen behind, they were passing a field where an Uzbek was working. He had a knife on his hip and he looked up at Kazimiera and her sister as they passed. Kazimiera panicked, thinking he was going to try to take her sister from her, so she started to run and her sister started to cry. After that, Kazimiera stayed close to her mother, because she couldn't keep pace with her father.

When they arrived in Tashkent, they didn't know what to do. They had nothing to eat and no way of getting help. It was three days before they got any food. And, even worse, by the time they got to the city, it was already too late for the family to get out. The border was about to close. However, there was one last transport happening and an orphanage was going with it. At the last moment, Kazimiera's father put her, her younger sister, aged three, and her brother into the orphanage so that at least they could get out. Their train left Jangijul on August 30. They left behind their parents, their oldest sister, who was sick with tuberculosis and couldn't travel, and an infant age one-and-a-half years — too young to be given to Kazimiera to look after. As her mother put them on the train, she told Kazimiera to never let the three of them get separated and that she was now responsible for her brother and sister.[103]

Stefan Koslowski was only seven when his mother put him and his younger brother, Henry, on the train bound for Bukhara. When his family was deported from Poland in February 1940, his father had been arrested and taken away, never to be seen again. Stefan, his mother, both his grandparents, and his brother and sister were taken to the interior of Russia. He doesn't remember much about Russia, but knows that by the time his family had moved to Uzbekistan, his grandfather, grandmother, and his little sister had died. When news of the evacuation came out his mother sent Stefan and Henry to the orphanage in Bukhara, knowing that it was the only way she could get her remaining children out of Russia. One of Stefan's first memories is of sitting on the train and, for a long, long while, looking back at where they had left, watching, waiting for his mother to join them.[104]

The trip across the Caspian Sea was hellish. Evacuees were packed into the ships like sardines in a can, with horrific sanitary conditions as a result. While the first evacuation had some semblance of organization and planning, the second evacuation, done in the heat of the summer, was pandemonium. By then the war in the Soviet Union was threatening the Soviet Caucasus in the north and transport was at a premium. Evacuees' luggage allowances were severely curtailed, there were fewer trains and ships available for moving them, and fewer provisions were made to help them along their journey. The Soviet authorities seemed determined to move out as many Poles as possible, as quickly as possible, with little thought to the conditions under which they were being moved. Janina Kusa recalls the deep heat and the chaos. Krasnovodsk was packed with people and there was little by way of aid offered to them. One of her biggest challenges was getting some water to drink for herself and her sister, Bronislawa. In Krasnovodsk, it was impossible, in spite of the fact that she had fifty rubles with her. When they finally got on the boat, Janina went in search of water. It was a frightening experience for a thirteen-year-old. Carrying a small can for water, she sneaked past a Russian soldier and disappeared into the dark interior of the ship. It was a maze of bridges and catwalks because it was a cargo ship, with water slapping around in the bilge and a huge wheel churning, a bizarre and frightening world. Deep in the hold, she saw the water tap, crept over, and filled the can. The Russian ignored her as she crept past again and made her way back to Bronislawa. As she was crossing the deck, a Polish soldier who was skinny — "like a ghost" — demanded that she give him the water. Janina was torn, but gave him the can. Before he could drink it all, however, another soldier tapped him on the neck and told him to stop. The soldier returned the can, so Bronislawa could have a drink too.

She recalls that many people on the boat were sick with dysentery, and the side of the boat, where a rudimentary toilet was constructed by affixing a plank to the rail, was soon red with their bloody stool. She remembers seeing a mother lying with her daughter, dying in her arms, under the steps for a bit of shade and fanning her daughter's face. There were deaths on the trip, Bronislawa recalls, with the bodies being slid over the side of the boat, into the water. Bronislawa's little red pillow was also a casualty of the trip. It got soiled, an inevitable thing. Janina decided it couldn't be salvaged and so tossed it overboard, much to the consternation of the adults onboard who thought someone was drowning.

It was almost as chaotic on the British side of the sea. Janina Kusa remembers that when they arrived in Pahlavi (and remember that she and her sisters were part of the second evacuation), there didn't seem to be anyone there to take charge of the orphans. The first night, they were put under rudimentary sunshades and left to sleep in the sand, without blankets, without shelter from the cold. The next day someone came to take them to the camp, where the delousing and medical examinations began.[105]

Most of the children remember little of Pahlavi. It was an enormous hastily-constructed tent city, right on the beaches of the Caspian Sea. It was intended to be a transit camp, where the evacuees would be isolated, deloused, treated for medical conditions, and restored to sufficiently good health so that they could be moved on to more permanent camps. The most crucial need, it soon became apparent, was for medical care. The evacuees arrived in miserable condition — half-starved, racked with a variety of seriously debilitating and life-threatening diseases. Many of the children had contracted trachoma, a dangerous and easily transmitted disease of the eye that, if untreated, leads to blindness. By all reports, it was rampant among the children, and the treatment was scraping the crust from the interior of the eyelids daily, followed by drops that burned. The treatment took months, if not a couple of years.[106] Delousing was also a crucial operation, as the refugees arrived infested with lice. This was typically followed by a medical examination. Marian Kacpura, aged four or five at the time, recalls being told to strip off all his clothes and stand in line, so that the doctor could examine him. His clothes were taken away to be burned and his head had been shaved. Most embarrassing, and the reason he remembers the moment, is that it was a female doctor doing the examination.[107]

Although most of the children remember little about Pahlavi, several things did stand out. The heat and the sand are mentioned by all. They went swimming in the sea, when they figured out how to get across the hot sands in their bare feet. One group of orphans had one pair of shoes between them, so whoever wanted to go swimming would borrow the communal shoes.[108] Another group used a bucket of water, pouring a little bit on the sand just before putting down your foot. With careful rationing, you could make the water last to the sea's edge.[109] They all remember that, upon arrival, they were stripped of all their clothing, which were then thrown on a huge pyre and burned. Then their whole body was shorn. After that, they were scrubbed clean and issued new clothes. Janina Kusa remembers the flowered nightgown she was given as a dress. When she cut the nightgown shorter, it gave her enough fabric for a belt. She still smiles when she recalls it, saying that it looked really nice. For the first time in a long while, she was clean and she felt good about herself.[110]

And then there was the problem of food. This time, it was not a problem of not having enough food. Rather, it was a problem of having too much. When the children first arrived — and the adults too for that matter — their food intake had to be very carefully managed and monitored. After years of starvation, to be given too much food, especially rich and fatty foods as the British first mistakenly provided, was not only very hard on the evacuees' digestive systems, but also very dangerous. Eating too much too quickly literally killed. So part of the recovery regimen in Pahlavi was to get the evacuees' strength back gradually, by slowly building up their systems. The evacuees stayed in Pahlavi from a couple of weeks to a couple of months, depending upon the state of their health and their destination.

As soon as the troops' health was satisfactory, they were shipped out to join the British forces, mainly in Palestine and the Middle East. The civilian population was a more problematic issue. To begin, the British set up more permanent refugee camps for the Poles in Tehran, four of them in the suburbs, plus a large orphanage camp, and then turned their management over to the Polish Civil Delegation (the Polish Government's representative body in Iran responsible for the evacuees). Pahlavi always remained a tent city, a temporary way station for the evacuees. However, a sizeable civilian Polish population soon established itself in Tehran's suburbs and a comprehensive camp system emerged, with a full-blown infrastructure of laundries, kitchens, bakeries, hospitals, schools, carpenters' shops, boot-repair shops, and seamstresses. In this environment the evacuees soon regained their health.[111]

The orphans did not remain there for long. Unlike many of the adults and families who remained in Tehran for a year or more, the orphanages were quickly moved on, generally leaving Iran within a matter of weeks. They were sent around the globe, but for the most part they went to India and throughout Africa, where it was thought that they would be safer and better cared for. There were several threats in Tehran: By the summer of 1942, the German forces were driving southward along the

German-Soviet war front, in the direction of the Caucusus and thus in the direction of Iran. It was thought that the refugees, especially the children, should be moved out of potential harm's way. Soviet forces controlled northern Iran and they were hostile to the Polish evacuees. Better to put some distance between them. Finally, supplying the refugees in Tehran must have been difficult and expensive, and it would make more sense financially to move them to areas where they could be more easily supplied.[112] The children were sent to refugee camps scattered across the British Commonwealth, especially to India and Africa, with the siblings carefully kept together.

The trip was a blur for most of the children, and uneventful — a steady stream of army barracks, schools, and tents, as they made their way to their destination. However, there were a few for whom it was not such smooth sailing. Stan Paluch and his sister were heading for India, attached to an orphanage run by a woman named Eugenia Grosicka. She had been part of the administration of the orphanage in Tashkent, and Stan and his sister had come out of Russia with her. However, when the group reached Karachi and was about to ship out to Africa, his sister fell ill and had to be hospitalized. The whole group couldn't wait for her to get better, so Stan chose to stay behind with her. He felt he couldn't leave her alone in Karachi; she was only five or six years old. Stan stayed in the transit camp in Karachi, and watched three, four, five orphanages pass through on their way to New Zealand, Argentina, or some other far-flung corner of the globe. Because it was a transit camp, there was little in the way of permanent accommodations. Stan eventually ended up bunking in with the British military, eating at their mess, playing soccer with the soldiers, and generally hanging about the camp. The men were very good to him, took him under their wing, and kept an eye on him. One even offered to adopt him and take him back to England, but Stan refused. He could never give up his sister, he declared. When his sister was well enough to travel again, they were attached to a group that joined an orphanage in a refugee camp in Kolhapur, India.[113]

Kazimiera Mazur had a more traumatizing experience. Just as her group was about to move out to India, her sister, Margie, fell ill with dysentery. She was very sick, but Kazimiera would not let her out of her sight. Her mother had instructed her to never let herself be separated from her sister and brother, and Kazimiera took her responsibilities as the eldest very seriously. However, at some point Kazimiera had to leave her sister to do something, she doesn't remember what, and that was when the people looking after the orphans took Margie to the hospital. Those in authority promised Kazimiera that her sister would follow her to India when she was better, so she and her younger brother left with the group for India, arriving in Jamnagar on December 8, 1942, (she remembers the date because it was a holy day). Losing her sister was devastating for Kazimiera because she had been told to keep the remnants of the family together. As the oldest, she was responsible for her family. Her brother kept asking for his sister and she was distressed because she didn't know how to answer him. After four or five months, a truckload of children arrived in Jamnagar from Iran. Kazimiera went to check for her sister, although she didn't expect her to be on the transport; she had learned not to hope.

> But she came with the other group of children. She was standing in that truck ... She was looking at me. And I stretched my arms like this, because I knew it was her, I recognized her right away. She had black hair and she's like my mother, so I recognized her right away. And I took her and I put her down. And she was looking around and she said to me, in Russian, "Take me in your arms because I am tired." And that is the first moment she remembers ... She didn't remember anything about my mother, about the rest of the family, nothing! That was the first thing that she remembers.

Her sister was four-and-a-half years old.

Most of the memories are patchy, some of the memories are searing. For the children especially, to be ripped first from their homes, and then from their parents and siblings, and to watch them die one after another, was a life-shattering experience. For the eldest child to suddenly become responsible for their younger siblings, at a moment's notice and when they themselves were still a child, was an overwhelming responsibility; one that many took seriously, with a gravitas and maturity that went far beyond their years. Aged ten, eleven, fourteen, these children cared for the younger as best they could, somehow getting them to safety against all odds. None can explain how it happened or why it was possible. Luck, God's will, sheer determination and perseverence, ingenuity, cunning — all played a part, they explain, in their survival. Siblings clung to one another, for they were all each other had. With no one else to count on, these children forged a bond, between siblings and eventually between orphans, that would last a lifetime.

# 2 | The Route to Tengeru

When the children left Iran, they went in a number of directions. Of those who ultimately ended up in the group that came to Canada, some were sent straight to Africa. Others were first sent to India. The trip from Iran was rapid and only remembered vaguely. What the children do remember, however, was the harrowing trip through the mountains to Tehran, on narrow, winding roads with cliffs soaring up on one side, deep gorges on the other, and hairpin turns. They didn't know whether to be fascinated by the dramatic scenery flashing past, or terrified by the careening bus that seemed certain to plunge over the edge at the next turn, taking them all to their death. From Tehran, they were dispersed across the British Commonwealth. By 1948, they had all gathered in Tengeru. From the children's perspective, to use the words of many, they had stumbled into paradise.

For several of the children, the route to Tengeru was quite circuitous. Some were sent to India, first to an orphanage outside of Jamnagar, and then on to another camp in Valivade, before moving to Africa in 1947. Others were sent to a camp in Kolhapur in India, near Bombay (now Mumbai). Still others were sent directly to Africa, but even then not always to the same camp, and not necessarily straight to Tengeru. There was a network of twenty-two camps spread across the British colonial possessions in Africa where a number of orphanages were established: Uganda, Kenya, Tanganyika, South Africa, and Rhodesia (now Zambia and Zimbabwe).[1] For this particular group, the group sent directly to the African continent, the most common routes seemed to be twofold — either they were taken directly to Tengeru, a refugee camp located just outside of Arusha, a town in northern Tanganyika (now Tanzania), or they arrived in Tengeru later, in 1947 or 1948, having first spent time in the orphanages in the Masindi (Uganda), Rongai (Kenya), and Ifunda (Tanganyika) camps. The movement between camps, which was very disruptive for the children, was the result of decisions made at various times to consolidate the camps into larger, more economically feasible, and more viable operations.

In India, the decision to move the children and other Polish refugees out of the country and to Africa was also, in part, a response to the growing tensions in the country between the British colonial powers and the Indian independence movements. India was no longer considered a particularly safe place for the children, as the tensions seemed set to boil over. In Africa, consolidation was also the order of the day and over the period of 1943–1948, the African camps were gradually rolled together. This was driven by three key factors: One was the sheer difficulty in trying to administer these camps. The camps were typically located in remote regions, isolated from the towns and cities, as well as from each other. Communications and movement between camps was very difficult and laborious, making effective and efficient administration a serious challenge. Consolidating the camps into fewer, larger entities simplified their administration considerably. Second, some camps proved too difficult to maintain or were dangerously unhealthy, such as Masindi, which turned out to be malarial. Many of the camps were costly to maintain, partly because of their remoteness and partly because a smaller camp could not realize the economies of scale of a larger camp. Finally, over the course of the mid-1940s, the Polish refugee population in the camps was declining.

It was a case of natural attrition. Some found opportunity in Africa and India, and chose to leave the camps to establish new lives in their newfound homes, making a temporary refuge into a permanent future. Others found opportunity elsewhere. In the years after the war, numerous countries sent selection missions to the DP camps, primarily in Europe, but elsewhere as well, seeking potential immigrants. These resettlement schemes were almost always directed at employable adults. In this way a number of Poles in the camps found a chance to rebuild their lives in Canada, New Zealand, Australia, South America, and the United States. Still others moved to Great Britain. In May 1946, the British Government announced that it would allow any member of the Polish forces who had fought under British command and enlisted before June 1, 1945, to settle in Great Britain, through a newly created institution called the Polish Resettlement Corps.[2] This was soon followed by a scheme called Operation Pole Jump that brought in the families and relatives of those same troops, which was the most common means for Polish civilians to move to Britain, and then by a much smaller scale program called the European Voluntary Workers scheme, intended to recruit single adults to work in British industry and agriculture.[3]

In some cases it was also about tracking down and reuniting remnants of families spread over the camps. This was Stan Studzinski's story. He had been brought to Jamnagar from Iran, but wasn't destined to stay there long. He befriended a boy there, who was soon moved to Tengeru to join his mother and sister. It turned out that the boy's mother was one of the supervisors in the orphanage. There, he heard about two girls whose name was Studzinski. He asked them if they had a brother and they replied that they did and that his name was Stan. So he told his mother and she wrote to Jamnagar and arranged for Stan to be moved to Tengeru to join his sisters. Father Krolikowski, a young Catholic priest based in Tengeru and someone who would come to figure prominently in the children's lives, explains:

> The sisters went to the boys' quarters with their curious friends. Suddenly the girls stopped, fearing that they might be laughed at if the boy was not their brother. The boy brought in was looking around in fear and distrust, his ears burning. He shifted from one foot to the other, twisted his fingers and looked at the toes of his dirty shoes. Zosia [one of the sisters and his twin] sized the boy up, and in the tone of an investigator, asked, "Is your name Studzinski?"

"Yes," said the boy quietly in half-shy, half-exasper-
ated voice, "so they say."[4]

Stan did not recognize his sisters, not even his twin, nor did they
recognize him. It is astonishing how fleeting the children's memories
were. To this day, Stan insists that he did not know his own name and
that he still has no idea how anyone was able to keep track of it for him.
But the details all matched, so these had to be his sisters.[5] Lives were
profoundly altered by such random happenstance.

Too young to work and without families to claim them, they had little
by way of options for resettlement. They got shunted from camp to camp
as the consolidation process continued, uncertain as to their fate. Life in
the camp orphanages took on a common pattern. In some cases, such as
Rongai, the orphanage was the camp. In others, the orphanage was part
of a larger camp of Polish civilians, which included single adults as well
as families. The camps ranged in size from several hundred refugees to
several thousand, with Tengeru being one of the largest, with a population of some five thousand at its peak. In every instance the orphanages
operated as a separate, and often isolated, entity from the rest of the camp.

The exodus out of Russia had come as a surprise so accommodations, especially in Africa, were makeshift, and planning for the children's
care was done on the spot, with considerable improvisation and, at least
initially, minimal resources. Many camps were still under construction
when the children arrived, including Masindi in Uganda and Tengeru
in Tanganyika. Janina and Bronislawa Kusa remember Masindi vividly.
The actual camp was located outside of the city of Masindi, surrounded
by elephant grass and jungle. They arrived in November 1942, and the
British were still clearing jungle and building barracks when the children
got there. The camp consisted of two rows of barracks that ran down
either side of a dirt road. The first barracks, which housed twelve girls to
a room, were rather rough and ready, with dirt floors and only burlap to
cover the windows. The buildings were so newly built that when Janina
looked under her bed she discovered grass still growing there. It soon
became clear that the dirt floor was going to be a problem, because of
small insects known locally as "jiggers," a small black flea that lives in the

soil and lays eggs in human flesh, especially under toenails. Many of the children ran barefoot, so this became an ongoing concern. Eventually, they would have barracks constructed out of clay, with brick floors, but that was still months away. Meanwhile, they were moved back and forth between the camp in the jungle and a school in the city.[6]

Tengeru was much the same. Sophie Matusiewicz was one of the children sent directly to Tengeru from Iran. At that point, Tengeru was still a small camp. There were just a couple of blockhouses, or blocks, built for the children. Each had two wings that slept twelve apiece, with separate living quarters in the middle for the block's supervisor. Those children who didn't fit into the barracks were housed in small round houses with thatched roofs. The camp was surrounded by bushes and tall grass. But the plans for the orphanage and the camp were much more ambitious, and construction went ahead in leaps and bounds. Day and night, they were burning bush and grass to clear the land. The fire burned incessantly, or so it seemed to Sophie. They were constantly putting up new blocks for the orphans who were arriving, as well as more small houses for the families coming to the camp. They soon built a church and then a school.[7]

The pattern their lives would take from that point on was much the same, no matter which camp they were sent to. The children were divided into age cohorts and by gender, and housed in barracks, often supervised by Polish adults who had also escaped Russia, usually Polish nuns and priests. In this way, siblings were separated in their sleeping arrangements, but could, and did, still see each other daily. Life became very regimented and school became a central element of their lives, or so the supervisors hoped.

Stan Studzinski; Kazimiera Mazur, with her sister and brother; Al and Stanislawa Kunicki; Marian Kacpura and his two sisters; and Krzysztofa Michniak and her sister were among those who ended up in an orphanage located just outside Jamnagar, in northwest India, on the ocean. Somewhat removed from the city, the orphanage was sponsored by the maharajah of Nawanagar, His Highness Jam Saheb.[8] The maharajah had heard of the children's plight in Iran and had offered to take in one thousand of them. The reasons for his generosity were uncertain, even to the children, but two explanations are generally offered. One is that the maharajah, when he was a young man, was studying in London or Edinburgh (it varies between sources). He was arrested for some kind of political activity, likely participating in a demonstration demanding India's freedom or autonomy within the British Commonwealth (a very sensitive issue in Britain at the time). While in jail, he was befriended by a Polish student. The offer to help was, therefore, his way of expressing gratitude. An alternative version suggests that the maharajah's father had a chalet in Switzerland and his neighbour was the Polish Foreign Minister. The two had become friends and from that friendship came the offer to take in the Polish orphans.[9] Whatever the reason, hundreds of children were brought to Jamnagar in 1942 and 1943. There, the orphanage was run by a Polish Catholic priest, Father Franciszek Pluta.

The camp was specially built for the children and was removed from the main refugee camp in Jamnagar. Life in Jamnagar's orphanage was extremely regimented. As the children tell it, Father Pluta was a strict disciplinarian and ran the camp like the army. The day began with a bugle playing reveille, often before dawn, as Krzysztofa Michniak recalls. The children had to get up instantly and go outside to do calisthenics, march, and sing. Everything was rushed, she remembers. If you were too slow, you would immediately get behind! After morning exercises, the children raced back to the barracks, grabbed their towels and soap, and rushed to the showers. Depending on how much time they had, they washed up, showered, or bathed. Then they raced back to the barracks again and dressed in long pants. If they didn't wear long pants, they would be punished because they were needed for protection from the mosquitoes. Malaria was rampant in this part of India, so every child had to wear long sleeves and long pants at dawn and at dusk. After they were dressed, the children marched in columns to the chapel for a morning service. From the chapel, they marched to the courtyard to raise the flag. From there, they marched in columns to the dining hall for breakfast. After breakfast, they ran to the barracks to change their clothes to something lighter for the day — skirts and short-sleeved blouses for the girls, shorts and shirts for the boys. They grabbed their books and ran to school. Classes were held six days a week, with only Sunday off. At school the schedule varied, depending on which subjects they were taking that day. When school was finished for the day (classes were half days), the children returned to their barracks, washed up and lined up again to march to lunch. After lunch they dashed back to the barracks where they had a rest period of thirty to forty-five minutes, depending on how long lunch had taken. Then they returned to school to do homework. After school the children were given a snack, often an orange or banana, and then they would go to the playground, swimming in the ocean (the beach was about half a mile away), or they were given a project, such as knitting or sewing. Krzysztofa recalls one rather disastrous knitting project. Each girl was supposed to knit a sleeveless vest for one of the boys, but the gauge of the needles they used was so small that, in the end, the sweaters would only fit the very youngest boys, much to the girls' amusement. The girls were still keen to learn, and even before they received proper knitting needles had been experimenting with the spokes from a bicycle and with broom handles.[10] So went the routine, with the children in bed by 10:00 p.m. every day. On Sundays and holidays the children could read, play, sing, and use the recreation centre.[11] The pattern repeated itself throughout the orphanages both in India and in Africa.

There was considerable emphasis placed on education. Indeed, education was one of the central missions of the orphanages. Some of these children had received no education to date, having been taken from Poland at too young an age, and others had had their education abruptly interrupted by the deportations. Either way, they were seriously behind in their studies and the orphanage administrations were determined to correct that. Instruction sprang up spontaneously everywhere. Even in Pahlavi, using the sand and a stick to write, classes were organized, if on an ad hoc basis. In every camp, schools were established. An elementary school was established in Jamnagar, but Valivade became a true mecca for schooling, with three kindergartens, four primary schools, a grammar (middle) and secondary school, a trade school, a school of domestic management, and a teachers' school, with a total of 2,500 students, including children and adults.[12] It was not uncommon for young adults in their late teens and early twenties to attend class, having also had their education interrupted.[13] In each camp in Africa, schools were among the first institutions established, at the same time as church services and religious instruction.

Initially, the teaching was very haphazard and spontaneous. An individual would take a group of children in hand and begin to teach them to read and write, as well as perhaps basic arithmetic. Usually this person was not a trained teacher. There were very few of those around, especially those trained to teach at the upper levels of education. Often they were simply one of the older children, trying to teach the younger ones what they knew. Such was the case with Stanislawa Kunicki, who taught the younger children in her orphanage when she was a teenager. She recalls that it was a bit difficult to do, with her younger brother, Al, sitting in the back making faces at her, but she persevered.[14] There were no school buildings and classes happened in the open air, under a tree.[15] The students might be taught their letters by writing on a scrap of paper or by drawing them with a stick in the sand.[16] Eventually they received exercise books for writing, but they were precious and few. The teachers had no manuals so subjects were taught when there was someone who could teach them. Gradually the Polish Government in London brought some order to the chaos and attempted to impose a curriculum. Manuals and books started to make their way to the camps, largely through the efforts of the Polish Army in Palestine, as well as the teachers, who copied the manuals out on their summer vacations. Still, a chronic shortage of supplies and teachers continued to plague the camp schools, making it difficult for the children to get a comprehensive education. It was a situation that lasted until the camps were finally disbanded.[17]

Stan Paluch had finished high school in Tengeru in 1948, and had hoped to go on with some advanced training in commerce. Unfortunately, there was only one year of the program available, so he never completed it.[18] That was often the case with the technical schools and upper level programs, as they were highly dependent on having the appropriately skilled teaching staff, as well as the equipment and resources. This sometimes meant moving children from one camp to another in order to be able to continue their education. Such was the case in Jamnagar, where the older children were moved to Valivade once they had completed primary and middle school, as Valivade had a high school and Jamnagar did not. That was what happened to Krzysztofa Michniak and Stanislawa Kunicki.[19]

One way in which the teachers tried to compensate for the lack of resources was to do field trips. Excursions to Victoria Falls, an ostrich farm, Mount Kilimanjaro, and going on safaris were part and parcel of the educational experience. Scouts also figured prominently in the children's lives, for both the boys and the girls. It provided a focus for extracurricular activities, as well as a sense of community.[20]

*A field trip for the children.*

Another obstacle to the children's education was medical. While their health had improved decidedly with the transfer to India and Africa, and many had bounced back amazingly quickly, others remained fragile. While Jamnagar was a decided improvement over Russia, and even Pahlavi, the weather was still problematic because it was very wet and humid and malaria was very common.[21] Many of the children came down with it, including Kazimiera Mazur. Krzysztofa Michniak had already contracted malaria in Kazakhstan, but it recurred in India with alarming frequency and virulence.[22] The situation was similar in Masindi, where malaria was rampant. Kazimiera Mazur missed a considerable number of classes because she had several episodes when her temperature reached 105°F and she was unconscious. She would suffer relapses of malaria well into her twenties, even after she had arrived in Canada.[23] By the time Krzysztofa was moved to Africa in 1948, her overall health, especially her heart and her back, was bad enough that she was put on a course of injections for one and a half years, intended to strengthen her. All of that impacted her studies, as might be expected, and she had to struggle to get through high school. She fought malaria relapses, headaches, and a myriad of other complaints. To compound that, much later, when she miscarried her second child in Canada, a tropical abscess was discovered in her stomach.[24] With the improved diet, generally the children's health rebounded, but a number faced long-term health consequences as the result of being deprived of a healthy diet during their prime growing years. Yet there were others who survived their childhood in remarkable health, such as Michal Bortkiewicz, who took up running marathons in the 1980s.

A further obstacle to education was the constant transfers. Those sent to Jamnagar remained for two years before being moved to Valivade. There, they remained for another two years or so, and were moved to Tengeru in 1947. Those sent to Kolhapur, like Stanley Paluch, followed suit. Even those sent to Africa were shunted around as camps were consolidated. One common route was to be brought to Masindi in 1942, from Iran, where the children spent about two years. Then they were moved to Rongai, for another two or three years, followed by a stint in Ifunda. Only then did they get to Tengeru, usually around 1948. Four camps in six years meant less than two in each, on average. With each move, although they weren't exactly starting over, they were set back yet again. For some it was disheartening and frustrating. This was especially true, it seems, among the boys. The girls, although not all of them, seemed to embrace school, and the structure and discipline it provided. The boys rebelled. For them, the fascination lay with the world outside the camps.

Many of the children chafed at the constraints on their lives and the discipline that was meted out that, to them, seemed both without reason and excessively harsh. Each camp had a bit of a different tone to it, as the degree of regimentation varied with the inclinations of the

*The orphans gathered around a car in Tengeru.*

individual administrators and block supervisors. Nonetheless, regimentation was considered necessary, as these children were without parents and therefore missing essential parental guidance and supervision. The philosophy across the camps was that the children needed to be constantly kept in hand. Any breaches of discipline were punished immediately and harshly. Corporal punishment was not unusual.[25]

Krzysztofa Michniak was glad to move from Jamnagar to Valivade. She had moved there in order to begin high school, but with the move came freedom. As Kazimiera Mazur explained, Father Pluta would not let any of the children leave the camp, except on authorized and supervised trips, not even the older ones. Even swimming in the ocean had to be organized for them. By this time, both Kazimiera and Krzysztofa were in their mid-teens and the restrictions were frustrating. In Valivade, which was a bigger centre and a larger camp, there was more independence. There they received an allowance from the Polish Delegation responsible for the Polish refugee camps (funded by the Polish Government-in-Exile). It was not a large amount, but for children who did not have anything, it was a fortune. That pocket money represented freedom and dignity. As Krzysztofa explained,

... [P]ocket money, it gives you a better feeling. Not
because this is money. Because you can go to the movies.
Of course in Jamnagar they took us to the movies. But
[in Valivade] you [could go] on your own. And when
you didn't have ink, because you used to write with ink,
you didn't have to go and beg for it. And when you
need paper, you didn't have to ask anybody for paper or
a pencil. You went ahead and purchased it yourself.[26]

For the younger children, it was not so easy to escape the discipline. While Janina Kusa admits the discipline was extremely strict in Masindi, she accepted it as necessary, because the children needed the structure. Her younger sister, Bronislawa, has very different recollections. Seven years old and traumatized by her experiences in Siberia, she found herself in a block supervised by a very strict disciplinarian who believed in corporal punishment and seemed to have no mothering instinct. As Bronislawa remembers it, the children were constantly being punished for small, insignificant infractions. Once she recalls that all the girls were forced to hit one of their own, as punishment for some small mistake. She can't even remember now what it was this girl had done to deserve this punishment. If any of the girls didn't hit her hard enough, then they were hit as well. Another time, she and a friend, Aniela, were being chased by a large dog. They ran and Bronislawa fell, and the dog pounced on her back. Both girls were badly frightened, although not hurt by the dog. Aniela's supervisor cleaned her up and consoled her. Bronislawa was made to kneel in penance the whole night. A final example of the woman's unjust discipline was when the supervisor decided to teach them all some table manners. Apparently they had been pushing and shoving in the dining hall, especially when picking up their cups. So the supervisor brought a cup to the barrack, put it on the table and made them all line up and learn how to pick up the cup "properly." In the midst of the lesson in manners, a small earth tremor struck and the table shook, sending the cup to the floor, where it smashed. The supervisor declared that this was a sign from God and the whole barrack was punished for the smashed cup.[27]

Stefan Kozlowski remembers the priest who taught him religion in Tengeru. If he asked a boy a question and the boy didn't know the answer, he would strike the boy. If he was writing at the blackboard and someone in the class spoke, he would turn around and strike the nearest boy. If the boy protested that he wasn't the one who spoke, the priest would reply, "Well, thank your friend!"[28]

This was not necessarily the norm, however. It differed between camps and between supervisors. By most accounts, Rongai was a paradise. Not only was it a very healthy camp, with none of the malaria that plagued Masindi and Jamnagar (and to a lesser extent, Tengeru), it was located in a beautiful corner of Africa. Rongai was also just an orphanage, so all its resources were channeled towards the children's needs. Mimosa trees bloomed everywhere and the scent was heady in the spring. Eventually a swimming pool was built for the children. Sophia Wakulczyk has fond memories of the nuns who ran the camp, who she says were very kind to them. The food was also very good. It was in Rongai that she, Janina, and Bronislawa Kusa (the three first met in Rongai), had chocolate for the first time since leaving Poland — chocolate and whipped cream! To this day, she can still almost taste it.[29] Janina Kusa recalls that there were lemon and orange orchards in the camp, with real grass growing between the barracks and flowerbeds around the buildings.

Stefan Kozlowski remembers Rongai differently, as the place where he spent two-and-a-half years and never had a full stomach. At that point, a growing boy, he was constantly hungry. Instead, for him, the best camp was probably Ifunda, because it was a very small orphanage and there he got to eat his fill. As well, there was some sort of abattoir near the orphanage, and when they slaughtered a cow they would give some of the meat to the orphans. In his words, "That was about the best. I was never hungry then. We had fruit, we had good meals, everything was fine, because there were so few of us." As well, the priest who ran the orphanage ran bingo games for the children and, as Stefan explains, everyone always won something.[30]

One of the drawbacks of institutional living was that the children got fed on a schedule and there was no cupboard to raid in the middle of the afternoon if you were hungry. This proved to be less of a concern for the girls than it did for the boys. Still, food was a preoccupation of all the children, and figures prominently in their recollections. Fruit was ample and the variety was amazing. As Al Kunicki put it,

> ... [In Africa] they had all kinds [of bananas]. They had big, large ones. And the very tiny ones, they are so sweet, they almost hurt your mouth, you know. And then there were some red ones. I mean, the variety was something else! We didn't get much in India, we had bananas. But India was more about mangoes. Fantastic tasting mangoes.[31]

Kazimiera remembers the bounty in Jamnagar. "Bananas, oranges, papayas. I loved that papaya. I always buy it now, even. We had pears, special pears. What else did we have? Oranges, mandarins, tangarines, you know. But every, like every lunch, we always had fruit. Suppertime, always fruit. It was good."[32] Sweet, succulent, bursting with flavour, the fruit was an important part of their diet, both in India and Africa.

Still, the boys complained that there was never enough to eat. And they particularly resented the discipline of the camps. For the younger ones it was difficult to avoid. For the older ones, now in their early and mid-teens, the world outside the camps was their escape. Their memories are full of the strange and amazing things they discovered in those parts of the world that they had never expected to see. And their curiosity drove them to explore. On the train ride down from Jamnagar to a camp outside of Bombay, as part of their eventual move to Africa, Al Kunicki remembers one day when a group of boys, including himself, got into serious trouble with the Hindu guards on the train. At one point in the voyage the train had stopped on a siding. One of the boys, who knew reasonably good Hindu, said something that greatly angered the guard. The boy took off with the guard in pursuit. At the same time, the other boys had noticed a dark cloud in the sky. It was not a normal cloud, but seemed to be a dense flock of birds. Curiosity bested them, and a number, including Al, left the train and went to check it out. They discovered it was a Parsi Tower of Silence, used for the disposal of corpses. When a member of the Parsi faith dies, his corpse is carefully prepared and then laid out on a special tower, exposed to the elements. It is left there while nature takes its course. Part of the purpose of putting it on the tower is to encourage carrion birds, especially the white-backed vulture, to feast on the corpse, as a means of disposal. This is what the cloud was, a thick flock of vultures. This is what the horrified boys saw, before the guard was able to catch up with them.[33]

Marian Kacpura remembers India well. He had been taken to Jamnagar and then Valivade. On one organized trip he visited some monks who lived in caves they had dug in the side of a mountain, where they slept and meditated. He was just a kid, he says, so he didn't think anything of asking one of the monks if he could look inside. The monk acquiesced and he took a peek. It was a comfortable square room, about six feet high, six feet wide, and eight feet deep. There was a rope bed and two oil lamps, and that was it, which Marian thought was strange. Vignettes of India at the time still stick out in his mind. On one occasion he had gone off exploring and was walking back to the camp. While he doesn't remember where he had gone, what he does remember is that as he was walking along the side of the road, an Indian man driving a cart being pulled by a bullock offered him a lift, a time-honoured version of hitching a ride. So Marian climbed up beside the driver on the cart and the two talked for the whole trip. Marian didn't speak much Hindu or Urdu, but enough that they could communicate.

> Yeah, it's amazing. In India, you go from one village to the next, it might be a different dialect. But when you are a kid you learn quick to differentiate and express yourself in their language. And here I go. This cow is pulling that cart and clop, clop, clop, clop. It was a brick-laid ... a cobblestone road. And that road was, on each side, [lined with] either walnut trees or mango trees. And we used to climb and get those mangoes. No, not walnut, it looked like a bean. It's fruit. But it was delicious. You eat the thing, but you only eat the pit itself. It had a pit inside, but it was fresh fruit only on

the inside. And all the mangoes! Lined all the way on the road there. So when the season came, we used to climb and get those things.[34]

During the sugar cane harvest, he again experienced the generosity of the Indians.

> You know, they had, in Valivade, they had fields and fields of sugar cane. And when the harvest came around, they would bring kettles and boilers, and squeeze the juice out of the canes and boil this liquid so it became like molasses. It was thick sugar. And once I had two pennies and I asked the Indian fellow there, that was working there, how much I would get for two pennies? He grabbed some of that sugar thing, slapped it on my hand, and closed the money in my other hand. And he said, "I don't want any money. Go!" So I had a handful of fresh sugar from the cane and still had two pennies in my pocket![35]

These were heady experiences for an eight-year-old boy from rural Poland.

By 1948, the last of this group had arrived in Tengeru. The camp was located in northern Tanganyika, near the town of Arusha. By that time it was one of the largest camps, numbering some five thousand inhabitants, including two orphanages. It was located near the equator, in the southern hemisphere, about eighty kilometres from Mount Kilimanjaro and almost at the foot of Mount Meru, which is 14,960 feet high. In the words of Father Krolikowski, who lived in Tengeru and worked with the orphanages, among his other responsibilities, the camp looked like a large park, with trees dotting the landscape, and "colonies of cacti and agave" hiding the small huts in which most lived. In the centre of the camp was the church. There were also recreation halls, schools, an outdoor theatre set into a natural amphitheatre, a shop, administrative offices, warehouses, and the residence of the British officer who ran the camp. Beyond that were coffee, papaya, and corn plantations, as well as a hospital and a farm operated by the camp's inhabitants. The camp was surrounded by jungle that soon gave way to the African savannah, which stretched to the horizon. Not far away was Lake Duluti, a spring-fed lake that had formed in an ancient volcanic crater. The two orphanages were housed in a number of barracks, one of them located beside a river that passed through the camp. Because of its location Tengeru had a pleasant climate, with a cool breeze blowing from Mount Kilimanjaro that kept it from getting too hot.[36]

*The orphanage's barracks, Tengeru.*

The structure of the children's daily life in Tengeru was the same as it had been all along. They lived communally in barracks, sorted by gender and age, and supervised by an adult who lived in private quarters between the two wings of the barracks. Mrs. Eugenia Grosicka was the director of the orphanages. School happened six days a week, half days, and was better organized by then, although still very short on supplies. The children were expected to do chores around the orphanage — wash dishes in the dining hall, peel potatoes, or set and clear the tables, for example.[37] On Sundays they attended mass. For the younger children, the discipline, structure, and restrictions continued. Stan Studzinski remembers life in Tengeru as very disciplined. He explains that you weren't allowed to leave the orphanage's grounds unsupervised, which was terrible for those who were still hungry after a meal. If he wanted to buy some bananas he had to sneak out. They were expected to do their chores, attend school, and abide by the routine. It was very difficult for the young ones to escape the regimentation.[38]

*Gymnastics class for the orphanage, Tengeru.*

On the other hand, the oldest children, now in their late teens, enjoyed considerable freedom. Unlike the younger children, they didn't live in barracks but in small round houses that could accommodate four. On top of receiving a small monthly allowance from the Polish Delegation, they had the opportunity to work for wages around the camp, as the camp was intended to be self-sufficient. They could work in the offices, on the farm, in the kitchen or laundry, or in a variety of other ways. For those who had finished high school, there was also the opportunity to work outside the camp. The local European population occasionally advertised for help from among the camp population. Although no one was required to work, everyone was encouraged to find something to occupy themselves. Those who chose not to work outside the camp were given work in the camp.

Two orphans who took advantage of this opportunity were Janina Kusa and Sophia Wakulczyk. Sophia, then eighteen years old, went to work as a nanny for a British family, the Ramsays. They had a farm near a village called Amani, near Arusha. Sophia lived with them for eight months. Her job was to look after the two Ramsay children, Celia and Colin. She didn't know how Mrs. Ramsey kept herself busy, as she had servants to do everything for her and Sophia minding the children. Sophia was given her own room and the Ramsays treated her like family. It took a bit of adjusting at first, as it had been years since she had lived in that kind of environment. In the orphanage, where you basically looked out for yourself, manners easily slipped. In the Ramsey household, Sophia had to brush up on them quickly. Although Sophia spoke no English when she arrived, she quickly started to learn some of the language. The two children helped her in that regard, with Colin reading stories to her out of his books. It was a wonderful opportunity for her. When they went on holidays, the family took Sophia with them, including to the sea. On top of her room and board, she was also paid a regular salary for her services. It was, she says, smiling at the memory, an absolutely lovely time.[39] Janina Kusa worked for one year as a nurse's aide, for a doctor who ran a private hospital in Moshi, a town beyond Arusha, at the foot of Mount Kilimanjaro. She had no medical training, but it was a chance to learn. She, too, was paid for her work and lived in Moshi for the year.[40]

Interestingly, unbeknownst to each other, the first thing they each bought for themselves from their wages, the first money they had ever earned for themselves, was a watch. For both of them, it was the first watch they had ever owned. To this day, although the watches stopped working long ago, they both still have them.[41]

However, living outside the camp didn't mean that they were free of the camp administration's control. They were still charges of the Polish Government. This meant that in 1949, when the opportunity came to go to Canada, they were asked whether they wished to go or to stay in Africa permanently, as they were considered old enough to make their own decisions. They could have chosen to stay in Africa, which would have meant moving out of the camp permanently and forging a future

*Another gymnastics class.*

for themselves in Tanganyika. Neither did, as they did not want to be separated from their brothers and sisters, for whom they still felt responsible. They reasoned that they would have a better future in Canada. The families had to stay together.[42]

The girls of all ages seemed to settle into the routine of camp life easily, adapting to the regimen quickly, blossoming with the supervision, structure, and schooling. The boys had a harder time adapting. However, for the boys in their mid-teens, Tengeru was heaven-sent, because by then they had figured out how to work around the restrictions of camp life. From their perspective, school was a waste of time. There seemed little point in learning Latin in the middle of the Africa. Life was to be lived by the day and it was about survival — a lesson learned the hard way in Russia, and seemingly reinforced by the ever-present jungle. School got in the way. The jungle and Lake Duluti beckoned, and the boys escaped there as often as they could. And that was frequently, as supervision was limited. As Michal Bortkiewicz explained, as long as you "performed" — did your homework (no matter how perfunctorily), did your chores, were there for the headcount at night, showed up for mass on Sunday — there was no one really keeping track of the children in between. This meant that once they had figured out when they had to put in an appearance, the rest of the time was theirs.[43] In the heat of the day, Lake Duluti was too inviting to resist, deep and clear, and both boys and girls skipped class to go for a swim. There were snakes and leeches, which terrified some, but only added to the sense of adventure that seemed to permeate most of the children's lives in Tengeru.

To add to that sense of adventure, the jungle grew up to the banks of the lake at certain points and it was possible to swing on lianas or vines, like Tarzan, out over the water, let go at its farthest reach, and drop into the inviting water. Every weekend, there was a movie night at the camp, and *Tarzan* had just been released. It was a movie that fired the imaginations of the boys, although it could have dire consequences. One friend of Al Kunicki's dropped from the vine too soon and broke both his arms.[44] Once, Marian Kacpura was trying to swing out over the water, but the vine jerked and he fell into the grass. It was a tall, hard, fruit-bearing grass that had been recently harvested, so the ends were quite sharp. One blade pierced his chin badly. It was a mile to the hospital from where they had been playing, a distance he had to walk, his chin bleeding, crying from the pain and shock. When he got to the hospital, the doctor patted him on the head consolingly, took a needle and thread and sewed up the gash, without the benefit of anesthetic or even local freezing, put a bandage on it, and sent him on his way.[45]

*Tree climbing, a favourite pastime.*

Michal Bortkiewicz was acknowledged as the best in the jungle, earning him the coveted nickname of Tarzan. He had the advantage of having lived in Tengeru since 1942, so he knew the camp and the surrounding jungle well. At thirteen or fourteen years old, Michal had mastered the liana, could climb trees like a monkey, and had a network of nests in the trees, where he would disappear for hours. He would collect wild bananas, papayas, and figs, settle into a nest and watch the snakes in the treetops — black, brown, green — as they slithered past. Michal lived for the jungle and for swimming. He wasn't especially successful in school, not having much patience for, or interest in it, although he did acceptably well in geography and mathematics, as well as singing. He much preferred to be outdoors and on the move. He took being Tarzan very seriously and when another boy wanted to hang out with him, Michal insisted that he had to learn to yell like Tarzan across the lake. Another time, several of them were swimming in the lake and saw some Africans chasing an antelope. The antelope leaped into the water to escape, which should have saved it, as the Africans couldn't swim. However, Michal and his friends swam after the antelope and drowned it. They dragged the carcass back to the Africans, who promptly butchered it and gave the boys the hide and the heart as a reward. That night, the boys built a fire back at the camp, roasted the heart and ate it, believing that eating the heart of the beast made them strong.[46]

The children's understanding of the world was very much shaped by their experiences in Russia and by the movies that they watched each week, which gave them a window onto the world beyond Tengeru and Africa. Movies like *Tarzan*, the cowboy films of the 1940s starring Roy Rogers, the Cisco Kid, and Hopalong Cassidy, and *The Jungle Book*, resonated with the boys who had been taught harsh lessons at an early age. The movies showed them a world in which life was "mostly stormy, adventuresome, filled with glory and easy living."

The values that were prized by these boys were, according to Father Krolikowski, "Physical strength, cleverness, and courage."[47] Life was simple, primitive, and lived for the moment. *The Jungle Book* inspired one of Michal's most daring plans, which was to run away into the jungle with some of the other boys, and carve out a life for themselves much like

Mowgli had done in the movie. Mowgli was a young boy who had been abandoned in the jungle as a baby and raised by the animals. The story appealed to some of the boys and, with Michal as ringleader, they plotted their escape. One early morning they were to gather by the river. It was five o'clock, still dark. Michal sat on a rock, waiting for the others. He had even made arrows and stolen some matches. He waited and waited, but the others had lost their nerve and never showed up, so Michal had to return to the camp.[48]

*The jungle's trees were the children's playground.*

Perhaps one of the most dangerous escapades that these boys got into was the result of idle hands being too clever in the technical school's machine shop. Unbeknownst to the teachers, two boys crafted handguns for themselves and decided to stage a shootout with them, just like in the cowboy films. The camp's administration only found out about this when one of the boys appeared at the hospital with a bullet wound in his chest, the bullet lodged near his heart. Ironically, the British experts in the region were "full of admiration for their excellent craftsmanship." The revolvers fired cleanly, the barrels were well-made, and the ivory handles carefully carved with scenes of jungle life, like that of a hunting lion. It turned out that the boys had not just made the two revolvers, but had also made a number of other handguns, knives, and primitive rifles, which they were selling.[49] Not to be outdone, Michal and a friend made a big hunting gun of their own and took it out on the savannah one morning. They saw giraffes and bison, but then Michal's buddy yelled, "Hey a black panther just jumped in that tree!" The two bolted for the river and clambered up on the rocks. After a couple of hours, discretion being the better part of valour, the two returned to the camp.[50]

Michal and some of the other boys were also, at heart, born entrepreneurs. In an environment where you are guaranteed food, shelter, and clothing, but not much more, other than two shillings a month for an allowance, there was an incentive to make money. The young men who were making firearms and other weaponry for sale were one example. Michal never engaged in entrepreneurial activities of that scale, but for a thirteen-year-old he proved very good at turning a shilling. Among a certain segment of the children in the camp, it was a measure of status to have one's own rooster for cockfights. Michal, of course, saw an opportunity to make some money. His logic was that, if his rooster won the fight, he won the pot. If his rooster lost the fight, he could always cook it and sell the meat. A true businessman, he bought the rooster for two shillings, and sold each leg and each wing for a shilling apiece — a tidy profit.

Another source of income came from acting as broker for those Poles leaving for England. Michal was a regular in the local bazaar and had learned some Swahili in the process. His Swahili was not sophisticated, but he could get by when dealing with the locals. And he was a born haggler. When people found out that they were going to England or elsewhere, they often wished to sell some of their clothes and other now unnecessary household items, which they either couldn't take or couldn't use in their new home. Michal would take their goods and hawk them on the side of the road outside of the camp in the market that had sprung up. As he explained the math,

> I'd say [to the Polish person selling the goods], "How much do you think you want for those [referring to the items]?" The woman would say, "Oh, ten shillings." And

I'd go and sell them for twenty shillings. I'd give her ten
shillings, and she'd give me two shillings' reward![51]

Theft was also common, especially of communal goods within the
camp. They didn't steal each other's personal items, but they would take
communal items such as bedsheets, blankets, clothing, underwear, and
footwear. These they traded for fruit or sold in the market.[52] The children saw no crime in what they did, and even openly bragged about it.
Michal and his brother, Piotr, often stole papayas from a local papaya
farm, although one day they had a near miss. The Masai guard with a
dog saw them and started chasing them. Every time the dog got too
close, Piotr hit it so they could get away. They just made it to the camp
and slid under the fence, the Masai in hot pursuit. As he came up to the
fence, yelling at the boys, the camp guard yelled back, telling him that
he couldn't enter the camp.[53]

Few were as rebellious as Michal, but they still took advantage of the
lax supervision, and proximity of the lake and jungle to indulge in some
wanderlust and impromptu "science lessons." Al Kunicki, then eleven or
twelve, readily admits to skipping school, taking his dog and going to
jump in the lake. One night he also decided to camp out at a cave above
the lake. All his buddies knew where he was, although the "authorities"
didn't. As he describes it, "The nighttime is kind of interesting. I lit a fire
and you could see those shiny eyes! The jungle noises! It is amazing what
goes on! It was a very long night." He didn't repeat the experience.[54]

Marian Kacpura was another boy who went into the jungle on a
regular basis. In part he went in search of wild fruit, to assuage his hunger. While the food provided in Tengeru was adequate, both in taste and
quantity — being generally Polish cuisine consisting of meat, potatoes,
and bread — growing boys were always hungry. The jungle's bounty was
one way to alleviate those hunger pangs. Marian and his friends would
also play with the red army ants, nasty things with a vicious bite. When
the ants moved, it was en masse. They would follow a trail, with guards
on either side, protecting the worker ants. The guards would wave their
pincers in the air, ready to snap at anything close by. The boys used to
prod them with sticks, teasing them. Still, they had to be careful. The

boys ran barefoot, leaving them rather vulnerable.[55] Al Kunicki remembers that one of the games they used to play was to see who could get a scorpion to walk across his hand without being stung.[56] On another occasion, Marian and a friend went to the savannah in search of turtles. Someone had told them that they could have fun playing with them, so they headed out one afternoon. They did, indeed, find turtles, but by that time it was dusk and night falls quickly in Africa. Within half an hour it was dark and they were about an hour's walk from the camp. As they were heading back, scared, they heard lions roaring on one side of them, and then lions roaring on the other side! Although they had the presence of mind to not run, as that would have attracted the lions' attention, they hurried back as fast as they could.[57]

Michal was also not the only child to mingle with Africans. The children have fond memories of the Africans who they said were, for the most part, very kind to them (unless given a reason not to be, like stealing their papayas). Marian Kacpura remembers walking in the jungle once and stepping on a prickly plant by accident. Of course, he was barefoot and got a huge thorn in his foot. As he was hopping home, crying from the pain, a Masai who was passing by stopped him and asked what was wrong. Marian showed him the thorn and the Masai pulled out a pair of tweezers he had hanging on his belt, as well as a small knife. He made a deft cut and neatly pulled the thorn from his foot. With that, he said, "Okay, boy, now you're all set."[58]

Most of the older children visited the local market regularly, often to buy fruit. Al Kunicki remembers how cheap the fruit was, and how delicious. He could get two dozen bananas for five pennies, which was as many bananas as an eleven-year-old could carry. The first time he did this, he ate them all during the midday break from school. Needless to say, the rest of the afternoon was a trial to get through and he regulated his consumption of bananas more carefully after that.[59] After the starvation diet of Russia, the children could never get enough food or fruit. It was a constant preoccupation.

Not all entertainment happened in the jungle. The camp also had many amusements available to the children. The boys played soccer, volleyball, basketball, and other games. They made toys, such as tops and

*St. John's Night Akademia, amateur theatrical production.*

wooden tractors, with which they fought one another to see whose trac-
tor was the strongest. The shortage of toys meant that the children had
to call on their imagination or copy from others more inventive than
themselves.[60] There were two recreation halls for the orphans, with "a
piano, table tennis, a record player with a good supply of records, games
of chess and checkers, a library, and a corner for reading. The youngest children had their own corner too — the kingdom of dolls, clowns,
teddy bears, toy soldiers, balls of all sizes, and rubber wheels."[61] The
theatre was used regularly for movies and special performances, both
by camp residents and visiting performers. It was an open-air theatre, a
natural amphitheatre carved into the side of the jungle and on the edge
of the lake. The site was idyllic and excellent for performances, with
impressive acoustics. It was Mrs. Grosicka, now running the orphanage,
who organized an ensemble of the best singers and dancers from among
the children. They performed regularly and soon developed a reputation
beyond the camp. They were invited to perform in Dar es Salaam, the
capital of Tanganyika, and even in Nairobi, the capital of Kenya. The
theatre was one of a number of ways, then, in which the children were
kept occupied and entertained.[62]

*Fairies in St. John's Night Akademia.*

The older siblings, especially the girls, tried to take care of their younger brothers and sisters, as much as the structure of the camp would allow. Katie Koscielniak collected her two younger sisters' monthly allowances for them, giving them a portion to spend in the camp store or the market, but setting aside the rest. At one point, she had saved enough to buy Helena a pair of white shoes to wear to mass on Sunday. Helena was inordinately proud of those shoes and guarded them jealously, as the children typically had very little by way of personal possessions — perhaps two or three changes of clothes, a few handmade toys, and a hat.[63]

A very few children had established connections with Polish soldiers serving in the Polish forces. Sophie Matusiewicz had stayed in touch with the Polish soldier who had found her in the hospital in Bukhara. Perhaps out of loneliness for his own family, this soldier corresponded with her regularly, sending her money and, on occasion, fabric for dresses. One Christmas, he sent her a doll. Sophie was thrilled, for it was the first doll she had owned since leaving Poland and no one else in the orphanage had a doll. It was a beautiful thing and, she reports, as a result, all the girls wanted to play with her. The soldier had talked of adopting her but nothing came of it, and eventually he stopped writing. Sophie never knew why.[64] According to Father Krolikowski, many of the orphans corresponded with soldiers who they had never met, but who had taken an interest in them. Generally, there was a genuine attachment that grew out of the correspondence, but some children took advantage of the soldiers' concern and generosity, exaggerating the inadequacies of camp life and playing on the soldiers' sympathies, and inveigling money and gifts from them.[65]

Father Krolikowski's observation was that the majority of the children were fine, but that there were a few boys who were a serious problem and he worried about them. They did not form gangs, nor did they engage in destructive practices, but he was concerned about their attitude nonetheless. He became increasingly alarmed at the growing barbarity of some of them, fuelled by the "lax conditions in Africa," as he put it. The lack of male teachers to act as role models, and the poor quality of the few male teachers they did have, were an important contributing factor.[66] Many of the men who were sent to the camps to act as policemen, and in other offices, and who might have been possible role models were, to use both Father Krolikowski's and Al Kunicki's words, rejects. Father Krolikowski described them as "psychopaths, hot-heads, moral degenerates," men dismissed from the army at a time when the

*Field trips were regular events in Tengeru.*

army needed soldiers — obviously of questionable character. While not all men would have fit this description, it took only a few to have a disturbing influence.[67]

As well, the camp was already a very unnatural society, unbalanced in a variety of ways. Although the size of a small town, it did not have the same web of economic, social, and political relationships that make up a functioning society. Even the families were incomplete, because most fathers were serving in the military. Husbandless mothers were in the majority and, although they tried to exert influence over their children, by the time the children were teenagers their mothers had usually lost any influence they might have had. For the orphans, there was not even that leavening agent. The female teachers had little authority over the teenagers, and there was no effective way of imposing sanctions on the children. No matter what the children did, they knew they were guaranteed food, shelter, and clothing. Even if they behaved, the camp had little more to offer them, so there was no tangible reward for good behaviour and no effective punishment for bad. To compound the situation, their experiences in Russia had taught them to distrust all authority and that the only people who would take care of them would be themselves or their siblings.[68]

There was also considerable sympathy for the orphans among the rest of the population in the camp. There was a general feeling that all the children had suffered enough, which worked against dealing with their poor behaviour too harshly. This sentiment was felt all the more strongly when confronted with the orphans' misbehaviour. These were children who had lost everything and so deserved leniency and sympathy, not harsh punishment. As Al Kunicki wryly pointed out, the supervisors could not get too aggressive when dealing with them, because there were other people in the camp to whom the orphans could turn who would tell the authorities to back off.[69] As a result, as Marian Kacpura put it, "You could go anywhere and nobody said anything."[70] That all of the children did not fall into delinquency, argued Father Krolikowski, was testimony to the positive effects of "conscientious teachers, devoted mothers, scouting programs and religious organizations, and the great majority of worthy youngsters who responded to these efforts themselves and helped save their weaker friends."[71]

What is striking when talking to the children, now adults, about their experiences so many years ago, is how none identified any adult in the camp who might have acted in any way as a surrogate parent. Few can remember the names of their block supervisors. None really knew Father Krolikowski until leaving Tengeru. Mrs. Grosicka, they knew, but she appears to have been a distant figure for most of the children. Instead, the family that emerged from these orphanages was a family of brothers and sisters, made up of the children. They developed a deep, special, lifelong bond with one another, a result of their shared experiences in both Russia and Africa. Although many of the children in Tengeru didn't arrive there until 1947, or even 1948, they were all quickly absorbed into this emerging tribe. They turned to each other when looking for support, consolation, friendship, help, and explanation, not to the figures of authority in the camp.

Unbeknownst to the children, tensions were brewing at the level of local government and in Britain over the fate of the camps. Almost from the beginning, questions were raised about the camps' administration, locations, and funding. While the camps were not luxurious by any stretch of the imagination, they were significantly better than what the Poles had left behind in either Iran or the Soviet Union, and

*Field trip to the savannah.*

generally better than the conditions of many living in Africa. Not only were the physical facilities quite satisfactory, but the Poles received generous allowances from the Polish Delegation in Nairobi, funded by the London Polish Government-in-Exile. No Pole was obliged to find paid work. The initial assumption was that it would have been impossible to find work for all the refugees (there were too many of them) and they were, in theory, only there for a short period of time, so finding a job was unnecessary. As well, private enterprise in the camp was forbidden, putting a brake on individual initiative. Instead, all businesses had to be sanctioned by, run by, and paid for by the Polish authorities.[72] Furthermore, the wages they were being paid for working in the camp were significantly higher than local wages.

This ultimately proved to be very disruptive for the local economy, upsetting the local population. Not only were the Poles earning considerably more than locals, as well as receiving supplementary allowances (even the children), but they could purchase clothing, furniture, trinkets and all manner of stuff from locals at higher prices than locals could, thus causing inflation with "serious and negative" repercussions for the native population. The end result was the camp's existence badly destabilized the local economy, much to the frustration of the native administration.[73] The East Africans, after having warmly welcomed the Poles, became increasingly hostile. There was "a feeling that the Poles were alienating sympathy by their ungrateful behaviour," by taking everything for granted and failing to recognize the need to conserve resources.[74] The concern among the British officials in East Africa about the mounting tensions between the Poles and Africans was enough to warrant Mr. Gurney, of the Conference of East African Governors in Nairobi, to write the Colonial Office to draw attention to the problem.[75]

There were also tensions between the Poles and the British over the administration of the camps, including Tengeru. In late 1942, and the first half of 1943, as the Polish refugees were being moved into the various refugee camps in East Africa, there was considerable discussion within the British Government about how to handle the Polish refugees. Although the refugees were located in British territories, they were the officially responsibility of the Polish Government-in-Exile, not the British Government. This created some tricky administrative questions that could not be ignored. While the refugees were only expected to be in East Africa for the duration of the war, that was also expected to mean a stay of approximately two years. Some structure and definition of responsibilities had to be imposed, if only to bring some order to the chaos.

In July 1943, a memorandum was finally signed regarding the respective responsibilities for the Polish refugees of the East African Governments and the Polish authorities in East Africa. In it, the East African Governments accepted responsibility from the British Government for the Polish refugees' general welfare "for whom they were providing a domicile during the war." The governments expressed a desire for advice and assistance from representatives of the Polish Government-in-Exile in London, but reserved for themselves executive authority, meaning that they would decide on all questions regarding the discharge of their responsibilities, subject to direction from London. However, the memorandum stated that they intended to make full use of all available Polish resources in the administration of social, religious, cultural, health and educational life, and services in the camps, and were willing to delegate authority on these issues to Polish leaders in the camps as much as possible. In the memorandum, the Polish Government also acknowledged its responsibility and duty to:

> ... [A]lleviate the burden of refugee life and to help the
> refugees both spiritually and mentally, to educate the chil-
> dren, to re-establish the other refugees morally so that they
> may form a useful community on their return to Poland,
> preserving as far as possible their religious sentiments.

Thus, the East African colonial governments assumed responsibility for the physical maintenance of the camp — housing, security, health, as well as the supply of food and clothing. The Polish authorities assumed responsibility for supplementary welfare services such as education, religion, cultural welfare, and sport, as well as for Polish security services internal to the camps, and the organization of work. The ultimate aim was to make the camps self-supporting and the East African governments expected to gradually reduce the supply of food and clothing it provided over time, as this goal was achieved.

The officers in charge of the camps would be appointees of the East African governments and responsible for security, discipline, sanitation, fire precautions, and the physical maintenance of the facilities and equipment, the employment of native labour in the camps, entrance and exit passes to the camp, and meeting the material needs of the refugees (food, clothing, et cetera). This camp commandant would work through a Polish camp leader, who would be responsible for the "loyal execution" of his orders. The camp leader would be appointed by the Polish delegate, who reported ultimately to the Polish Government in London, as would all Polish camp staff. Preference would be given to Poles for the performance of camp duties and the Polish authorities would be responsible for the internal organization of the camps.[76]

In reality, the British Government wanted little to do with either the administration or financing of these camps, including Tengeru. The Conference of Governors of the Territories of British East Africa (Tanganyika, Uganda, and North and South Rhodesia) had established the East African Refugee Administration, which acted as a clearinghouse for information on the refugees in those territories. It was, for all practical purposes, dependent on the territorial governments, and had to get those governments' consent before implementing any policy, so it played a largely advisory role. However, it also appointed the British camp commandants, who did carry considerable responsibility.[77] The financing of the camps was also a complicated affair. While the camps were built by the territorial governments, they did not maintain the refugees. The camps were officially funded by, and ultimately under the jurisdiction of, the Department of Social Welfare of the Polish Government-in-Exile.[78] But in practice, the funding came from the British Government in London, who loaned the money via the territorial governments to the Polish Government-in-Exile.

Within the camps the administrative structure was unclear. One of the chief purposes of the memorandum was to lighten the burden of the British authorities, who were feeling rather overwhelmed by the situation. They simply didn't have the resources to manage the sudden influx of some twenty thousand Poles. The purpose of this scheme was to establish a Polish organization that would minimize the work of the Territories. It would be responsible for organizing the cultural, national, and religious life of the camp, providing schooling for both children and adults, preparing them for the future, and helping the adults to overcome the demoralization of the preceding years. While the idea was to make the camps as self-sufficient as possible, both administratively and ultimately economically, through manufacturing and agriculture, the Territories' economies and native populations had to be protected as well, so the British territorial authorities were not willing to abandon all control over the refugees' activities. Thus, for example, the Director of Refugees, who represented the East African Refugee Administration, had to approve any economic enterprise, to prevent any possible disruption of the local economy (as seen, ultimately a vain hope).

In practice, at the camp level, the result of the memorandum was two parallel administrations, one British, responsible for the physical plant and general administration of a camp, as well as its interaction with the outside world, and one Polish, responsible for the service functions of the camp. In practice, the camps tended to be self-sustaining and self-administering, with little interference from either the territorial governments or the British Government. It very quickly came to be the Poles who ran the camps, with little British input or interference.

This did not mean the end to the tensions, which continued to grow, both among various factions of Poles over how to administer the camps, and between the Poles and the British authorities. The British authorities in East Africa had always favoured a decentralized structure and wanted the Polish administrative officers located in the individual camps, rather than in Nairobi, where they were then based. The Poles, on the other hand, seemed to be pushing towards an evermore centralized structure, based in Nairobi and rather removed from the camps, and one that neutralized or undermined British authority, especially at the camp level.[79] The British authorities were also increasingly upset at the cost of the camps, which were turning out to be much more expensive than originally expected.[80] The solution to Britain's dilemma came in the form of an international refugee organization, the United Nations Relief and Rehabilitation Administration (UNRRA).

# 3 | The Postwar Settlement

During the war there was a strong sense of a debt owed to the Polish by the British. However, by 1944, the British authorities were increasingly perturbed at the cost of the camps. They were turning out to be more expensive than originally expected, especially the maintenance costs (the costs of maintaining the Poles on a daily basis, including the allowances), for which the Poles seemed incapable or reluctant to account. By June 30, 1944, the cost of the refugees in the Tanganyika Territory alone was £108,000 over budget, with an additional deficit in the second half of 1944 expected to amount to another £100,000.[1] The British were also becoming concerned because it appeared increasingly unlikely that the Polish Government-in-Exile would ever be returning to Poland. That summer, a Soviet-supported Polish Communist regime had been established in Lublin, proclaiming itself the government of Poland. By September 1944, with the might of the U.S.S.R. behind it, the new Lublin Government was well-entrenched, though not very popular. The non-communist resistance in Poland fought its installation and seizure of power, and by that fall Poland was on the verge of quasi-civil war between the two factions. Nonetheless, the battle was decidedly one-sided, as the Lublin Committee had the strength of the Soviet Union behind it, as well as its immediate presence. By the end of 1944, the Lublin Committee was already fashioning itself as the Provisional Government.[2] If the Polish Government-in-Exile was not to return to Poland and the Lublin committee was to form the postwar Polish Government, it was extremely unlikely that the British Government would ever see a penny back from the loans made to the London Poles. The solution to Britain's dilemma seemed to come in the form of an international refugee organization, the United Nations Relief and Rehabilitation Administration (UNRRA).

UNRRA came into being on November 9, 1943, the creation of forty-four different nations. The agreement's signatories pledged to provide aid and relief to the population of any area liberated from Axis control. UNRRA's purpose was to:

> ... [P]lan, coordinate, administer or arrange for the administration of measures for the relief of victims of war in any area under the control of any of the United Nations through the provision of food, fuel, clothing, shelter and other basic necessities, medical and other essential services.

It was also to assist in the return home or repatriation of those who had been displaced by the events of war.[3] UNRRA was always intended to be a temporary organization, as it was expected that everyone would want to return home quickly. Thus its initial postwar lifespan was set in terms of months, rather than years.

As early as September 1944, rumours were flying that UNRRA would take over responsibility for the Polish refugees in East Africa and elsewhere, and the reaction among those loyal to the Polish Government-in-Exile was not favourable. On September 23, 1944, the British Delegation to the UNRRA Council, then meeting in Montreal, reported to the British Foreign Office that a delegation of Poles in Canada had complained to the Foreign Office about this possibility. The Polish diaspora, which was largely sympathetic to the anti-communist London Poles, was clearly mobilizing. The Canadian Poles' chief concern was that the current administration of the camps, which was staffed by, and responsible to, the Polish Government-in-Exile, not change. They also argued that Britain should have no fears about repayment, as the Polish Government was good for the debt. The British Delegation demurred, arguing that, in fact, having UNRRA take over would be an advantage to the Polish refugees, as it would give them the best possibility of "securing proper assistance." It further explained that the British Government much preferred to have UNRRA paying for the refugees' maintenance, not the British taxpayer, as UNRRA had been established and was funded internationally to do expressly that. Nor did it expect the camps' administrations to change significantly. Nonetheless, the British Delegation made it clear to the Foreign Office that it thought the possibility of UNRRA taking over the East African camps should be pursued as quickly as possible.[4]

The Foreign Office agreed wholeheartedly. While the Polish Government-in-Exile was officially funding the camps, the fact of the matter was the monies were being borrowed from the British Government and the bill was mounting. However, shaking free of this burden was not as straightforward as it seemed. It was uncertain whether these displaced persons fell within UNRRA's mandate, as they were in a territory that had never been occupied by the enemy. Second, the British were also uncertain as to who should approach UNRRA — the British Government or the Poles — as the camps were officially the Polish Government-in-Exile's responsibility. Finally, it was unclear whether UNRRA should be asked to assume responsibility not only for those Poles located in the African territories, but also for those located in other British colonies and refugee camps. The Dominion Offices, who were responsible for the camps' budgets, felt strongly that UNRRA should be asked to take over all of them, but there was a fear this might be an overwhelming project for UNRRA, who might reject the proposal because of its scope.[5]

The first concern, whether these displaced persons fell within UNRRA's mandate, was resolved when the UNRRA Council passed a resolution in its Second Session held in Montreal, allowing it to assist displaced persons located in territories never occupied by the enemy. The second concern, whether Britain had the authority to approach UNRRA, was also resolved. The Council decreed that the camps were the responsibility of the Polish Government-in-Exile, not Britain. Britain merely lent the operating funds to the Poles. Thus, it was not for Britain to ask UNRRA to take over the camps. Rather, the Polish Government-in-Exile had to be persuaded to do so and the British Government began to push the Poles.

In November 1944, the British Foreign Office wrote a formal request to the Polish Ambassador that his government approach UNRRA about assuming responsibility for the Polish displaced persons, not only in East Africa, but also in the Middle East, India, Southern and Northern Rhodesia, and New Zealand. The Foreign Office argued that this would be of enormous benefit to the Polish Government. Although London had always considered it "a privilege and duty to do what it could to alleviate the distress and hardship of the Polish displaced persons," their maintenance was a heavy burden to the Polish Government. While London had tried to alleviate that burden with credits and advances, having UNRRA assume this financial responsibility would help enormously by reducing the financial burden ultimately being carried by the Polish Government. The letter went on to recognize that the Polish Government might be reluctant to request such a change, because it did not want to see any changes in the camps' administration or welfare arrangements. The British Government itself also preferred "as little modification as possible." However, London firmly hoped that UNRRA could be persuaded to assume formal responsibility for the maintenance and eventual repatriation of the displaced persons, without requiring any change to the present camp administration or personnel. In reality the British Government believed that UNRRA had little choice in the matter. It suggested that the Polish Government remind UNRRA, if it proved reluctant, that the organization "cannot escape from the commitments laid down by its mandate, particularly as now affected by Resolution 46 of the Montreal Conference [one of the formative meetings of UNRRA]." The British Government concluded its note verbale by urging the Polish Government-in-Exile to approach UNRRA, and reassuring the Poles that they had the full support of the British Government in doing so.[6]

The Polish Government-in-Exile clearly did not think this was an attractive proposition, and apparently did not pursue it, as nothing changed in the status of the camps until 1946, when the question reared its head again. By this time, the international situation, and Poland's position within it, had changed dramatically and, from the displaced Poles' perspective, for the worse.

Over the course of three major international conferences (Tehran in November to December 1943, Yalta in February 1945, Potsdam in August 1945), the major powers — Great Britain, the United States, and the Soviet Union — to a large extent determined the shape of the postwar settlement. One part of those discussions became known as the Polish Question. At its heart was a debate over the future of the Soviet-occupied territories in the former Polish Republic, and which government would rule in the resurrected Poland — the one based in London or the Soviet-sponsored Provisional Government already in Warsaw. The conversation began at Tehran (November 28 to December 1, 1943) in a meeting between Prime Minister Churchill, President Roosevelt, and Joseph Stalin. There the three signed a secret provisional agreement that the Soviet Union would keep the territory it had occupied in 1939, and the Curzon Line would be used as the new Soviet-Polish frontier. As compensation the Poles would receive lands from eastern Germany, up to the Oder River. It was implicitly acknowledged that Stalin had the right to act unilaterally in the territories liberated by his forces, and that Poland would be liberated by Soviet forces, not Anglo-American. This was the context in which the conversation about UNRRA assuming responsibility for the camps was occurring.

By the time the three met again, this time in Yalta on February 4–11, 1945, the Soviet Union had liberated Poland and the Lublin Committee was firmly established in Poland as the Provisional Government. The Soviet Union was riding a crest of victory into eastern Europe, pushing the German forces back before the Russian steamroller. Stalin was in a particularly strong bargaining position, and Churchill and Roosevelt knew it.[7] At Yalta, the realities were acknowledged formally. Churchill and Roosevelt agreed to the establishment of a Polish Provisional Government, but pushed for it to be reorganized "on a broader democratic basis with the inclusion of democratic leaders from Poland itself and from Poles abroad." The new government was called upon to hold "free and unfettered elections" as soon as possible and when such a government was properly formed, the three signatories — the U.S.S.R., the

U.S., and Great Britain — pledged to recognize it diplomatically. In addition, the Yalta agreement confirmed what was provisionally agreed to at Tehran: that the eastern border of Poland would follow the Curzon Line, with some minor adjustments, and that Poland would receive territorial compensation in the west (the exact extent of which was left undefined).[8]

When the terms of the Yalta Agreement were announced, the Polish Government and political parties in London, as well as the Polish military leaders and the majority of their troops, were terribly shocked. Some of the leaders of the pro-London political organizations and parties realized the sobering reality underlying the decisions at Yalta, and the necessity of working with the U.S.S.R. and the Polish Communists. Indeed, many returned to Poland to join the new government, including Stanislaw Mikolajczyk, then Prime Minister of the Polish Government-in-Exile, believing that perhaps they could ameliorate the Communist rule and negotiate with Moscow for an independent and democratic Poland. It was a false hope. While the new government was nominally a coalition of five parties — the Polish Workers' Party (the Communists' vehicle); the Polish Socialist Party; the Peasant Party (led by Mikolajczyk); the Democratic Party; and the Labour Party — in reality, the new government was decidedly dominated by the Communists. Although the opposition parties were given sixteen of the twenty-one ministries, the Communists retained control of the key ministries responsible for defence, public security, the Western Territories, industry, and foreign affairs. Through them the Communists controlled the army, the police, and a huge patronage system.[9] The Communists' control was unassailable.

Many Poles refused to return, in spite of strong urging from the British Government. The British logic was twofold: The London Poles and the Polish Armed Forces, in spite of having fought beside the British forces in the Middle East and in Italy, were now considered an embarrassment and a burden. Relations had to be normalized with the new Communist Poland and with Moscow, and the London Poles' presence, as well as the tens of thousands of Polish troops that were still mobilized, were a sore point with the erstwhile allies. As well, the Poles were expensive to maintain. There was also the hope that the presence of the strongly democratic Polish troops in Poland might favourably sway the pending elections. Thus, it was in the British Government's best interest that these Poles return home as quickly as possible.

The Poles' refusal to repatriate to Poland was just as logical. Many of them had been part of the brutal evacuation out of Siberia and knew first-hand what the Soviet occupation was like. They had no desire to return to a homeland under Soviet domination, justifiably fearing harsh persecution if they did. Indeed, General Anders had explained this to Winston Churchill quite bluntly, when Churchill informed him of the results of Yalta. Anders declared then that no Polish soldier would return to Poland.[10]

This was the context in which Churchill publicly made a pledge that would haunt the British Government in the future. When explaining the terms of the Yalta Agreement to the House of Commons on February 27, he suddenly stated:

> In any event, His Majesty's Government will never forget the debt they owe to the Polish troops who have served them so valiantly, and for all those who have fought under our command, I earnestly hope that it may be possible to offer the citizenship and freedom of the British Empire, if they so desire. I am not able to make a statement on that subject today because all the matters affecting citizenship require to be discussed between this country and the Dominions, and that takes time. But as far as we are concerned, we should think it an honour to have such faithful and valiant warriors dwelling among us as if they were men of our own blood.[11]

Thus, although the British hoped that most could be induced to return to Poland, none would be repatriated against their will. And in an effort to quell the panic that was spreading through the ranks of the Polish Armed Forces, as a matter of honour the British Government pledged to continue to provide pay, maintenance, and provisions for the Polish forces, even after the formal de-recognition of the Polish Government-in-Exile.[12]

Of course, this did little to improve British relations with the Warsaw Government, who strenuously objected to the continued existence of Polish formations that were openly hostile to it. Nor did things stabilize in Poland, where the hunt for the non-Communist resistance continued. At the end of March 1945, the Soviets caught sixteen leaders of the pro-London resistance, breaking the resistance loyal to the Polish Government-in-Exile and seriously compromising the anti-Communist resistance in Poland, at least temporarily.[13] On April 22, the U.S.S.R. signed a twenty-year Treaty of Friendship, Mutual Assistance and Cooperation with the Lublin Committee (who had no real authority to conclude such a treaty), which allowed Soviet troops to remain in Poland and lay the groundwork for future relations between the two countries.[14] And at the Potsdam Conference in July 1945, the Big Three decided that the moment had arrived to formally recognize the Polish Provisional Government of National Unity as the official government of Poland.

However, doing so meant withdrawing international recognition from the Polish Government-in-Exile. De-recognition also meant cessation of the Government-in-Exile's operations and the surrender of its assets to Warsaw. Britain's worst fears — that the extensive loans it had made to the Polish Government-in-Exile would never be repaid — were becoming reality. Bringing the London Polish Government's activities to an end served two purposes for the British Government: it would end the drain on the Treasury posed by those credits, and it would allow the British Government to begin negotiations to persuade the Warsaw Government to assume the debts incurred by the London Polish Government.

The process of de-recognizing the Polish Government-in-Exile was involved. London created the Interim Treasury Committee for Polish Affairs (the ITC) to supervise the orderly dismantling of the Polish machinery of state and the liquidation of its assets. For the period of liquidation the ITC managed the London Poles' foreign affairs, diplomatic activity, home affairs, information services, and social welfare programs for the Polish refugees scattered throughout the Dominion. The last could not be ended too abruptly without causing considerable hardship. Although initially consisting of only British civil servants drawn from the Treasury and Foreign Office, it was soon realized that the ITC needed Polish representation in its ranks. Count Raczynski, the Polish Ambassador to London for the now defunct Polish Government-in-Exile since 1933, was invited to join the ITC, as the head of a Polish delegation attached to it. These Poles were all former employees of the London Polish Government and were chosen for that reason. The logic was they were the most familiar with its operations and commitments, so they were the best equipped to facilitate the closure of operations. However, this had the unintended effect of granting these Poles a quasi-official role as salaried Treasury staff, which did not sit well with Warsaw, and which gave the London Poles a vehicle for continuing to influence policy and reach the Polish exile community, in spite of the gradual dismantling of the Government-in-Exile's administration.[15]

Another side effect of the creation of the ITC was to bring the approximately 178,000 Poles scattered around the globe in refugee camps from India to Mexico, Sweden to South Africa — the diaspora who had fled from Siberia and Central Asia, as well as from elsewhere — under its authority, and thus under direct British authority. Some host countries agreed to assume responsibility for the Poles in camps on their territory, such as France, but most did not. The British Government suddenly found itself directly responsible for the financial upkeep and administration of camps in India, Palestine, and Lebanon, and throughout Africa. It was not a minor expense. The monthly cost to the British Treasury for the maintenance of these refugees was £256,000.[16] Thus, London was increasingly keen to have UNRRA take over responsibility for the camps. On the other hand, recent history meant that the British also felt some obligation to the London Poles and they could not simply abandon them.

The London Poles, as well as the Poles in the camps, were extraordinarily suspicious of UNRRA. Although removed from the continent, they were not unaware of what was happening, and what they saw frightened them. With the war's end in Europe in the spring of 1945, the continent faced numerous challenges, including the problem of millions of people who had been displaced from their homes by the war. There were over twelve million displaced persons in the western part of Germany alone, who were liberated by the Western Allies. Millions returned to their homes voluntarily, in a mass movement of people across the face of the continent. However, many others, primarily Soviet citizens and prisoners of war, were forcibly repatriated to the U.S.S.R., in fulfillment of a clause in the Yalta Agreement requiring the Allies to facilitate the return of all Soviet citizens to the Soviet Union, whether they wished to return or not.

The forcible repatriation was a nasty piece of business, with hundreds of thousands being herded unceremoniously across the line demarking the Soviet occupation zone in Germany. Many fought repatriation, some choosing to take their own lives rather than return to the U.S.S.R. They rightly feared persecution or exile to the forced labour camps in Siberia or Central Asia at best; summary execution at worst. Stalin had little patience for those who had allowed themselves to be captured by the Germans. For him, they were traitors to the nation, who had now been infected with Western ways of thinking. They could not be trusted, although he made sure not to tell his erstwhile allies this. When queried, Stalin explained that if the repatriate could demonstrate his or her good faith and lack of corruption, he or she would be welcomed back into Soviet society. But he insisted that all had to be returned and held accountable.

Initially, the western Allied powers, and especially the American forces, who liberated the part of Germany that contained the largest number of displaced persons, cooperated in the forcible repatriation of the Soviets. However, the panicked reaction of the repatriates soon sickened the American troops, as well as others, and the forced repatriation fell to a trickle and then stopped. In January 1946, orders were issued to the American military forces to cease the forced repatriation of any Soviet citizens, with the exception of: those captured in German uniform; those who were members of the Soviet Armed Forces on and after June 22, 1941, (when Germany invaded the U.S.S.R.) and who had not been discharged from those forces; and those who were "charged by the Soviet Union with having voluntarily rendered aid and comfort to the enemy, provided the Soviet Union satisfie[d] the US Military authorities of the substantiality of the charge...."[17]

While none of the Poles in East Africa considered themselves Soviet citizens, nor were they, the Poles believed they had reason to fear forcible repatriation. First, they came from eastern Poland. In the postwar territorial settlements, the eastern Polish territory occupied by the Soviet Union in 1941 was now recognized internationally as a permanent part of the U.S.S.R. Poland had been compensated for this land with territory carved out of eastern Germany. For the vast majority of the Polish displaced persons in the camps around the world, this meant that their former homes now fell within the borders of the U.S.S.R. They feared that this might make them eligible for forcible repatriation in the first months after the war, although the frenzied repatriation drive of 1945 never reached outside the European continent, and they would have not been swept up in it even if they had been in Europe. Still, it created a great deal of consternation among the Polish displaced persons, and the Allied and UNRRA's 1946 assurances that no one would be repatriated against their will seemed thin comfort.

Matters were not helped any by the actions of UNRRA. The terms of UNRRA's mandate were simple: to provide aid and relief to displaced persons, and to facilitate their repatriation. UNRRA's constitution did not allow any resolution to the displaced persons' situation other than repatriation. UNRRA also faced considerable pressure to deal with the displaced persons problem promptly, as it had a very short lifespan. Initially, it was expected to finish operations (i.e., to have emptied the camps) by mid-1946. When, at the eleventh hour, it become clear that that was not going to happen, UNRRA's operations were extended for a further six months, with a clear mandate to settle the problem. UNRRA would fight for yet another reprieve at the end of 1946, but the situation made UNRRA aggressive in its promotion of repatriation. Resettlement in other countries was not yet a viable option; UNRRA could not pursue resettlement opportunities and possible receiving nations were reluctant to take in destitute immigrants at a time when they were absorbing the return of their own nationals, and trying to regain some normalcy after years of occupation and war. So UNRRA promoted repatriation with vigour. While forcible repatriation was not allowed anymore, to many displaced persons it seemed that UNRRA still strongly believed that they should return home, willingly or not. Many in UNRRA (including then Director General F. LaGuardia), had a difficult time understanding their deep-seated horror of returning home to a Communist-governed country, making them less than sympathetic.

Furthermore, it must be remembered that UNRRA was an international body, to which not only the U.S. and Britain belonged, but also the U.S.S.R. and Poland, to name a few. With the international recognition of the Warsaw Provisional Government and de-recognition of the London Polish Government, the Poland sitting on the General Council of UNRRA was Communist Poland. To the suspicious Poles in East Africa and elsewhere, it appeared that UNRRA was a puppet of the Soviet bloc. The reality was that UNRRA found itself torn in two, caught in the middle of the growing struggle between West and East. In many instances that resulted in paralysis at the upper levels of the organization, and ad hoc crisis management at the lower levels. The result was little consistency in policy. Because the upper echelons could not agree or provide any guidance to the field workers, individual staff members carried inordinate *de facto* authority, at least in the first year or more of operations. Those staff who were sympathetic to the eastern bloc had considerable freedom to strongly encourage repatriation, even though they did not have the power or the resources to forcibly repatriate anyone. Their zeal was often construed by the displaced persons and their advocates as undue pressure. For the Poles in East Africa, the notion of UNRRA assuming responsibility for their camps was an alarming one.

By late 1945, the British Government was quite keen to have UNRRA take over the camps. Being forced to assume direct financial responsibility for the camps when UNRRA had been established to deal expressly with the refugee problem, and was being partly funded by the British Government to do so, was particularly galling. And although London had pursued negotiations with Warsaw, hoping that the Provisional Government would assume responsibility for the Government-in-Exile's debts, they proved fruitless. To the British officials it made sense to have UNRRA assume control of the camps.

In part, the British also wanted some resolution of the refugees' fate. The camps were never meant to be permanent institutions. The

Territories had agreed to take in the Poles only for the duration of the war, and were beginning to complain about their continued presence. Now that the war had been over for a number of months, there was a growing belief that the Poles needed to decide what they wanted to do with the rest of their lives. There was also a growing fear in London that these Poles expected to simply be given British citizenship and moved to Britain, and were content to remain in the camps until that happened. Churchill's pledge of February 1942, the continued support of the Polish Armed Forces, and the steady admission of thousands of Polish soldiers and their dependants to Britain, all reinforced that expectation. However, in Whitehall, it was generally felt that Britain had already done enough, both during and after the war, in alleviating the distress of the refugees. Furthermore, bringing the remaining Poles under the wing of UNRRA would open up opportunities for a resolution of their situation that was not available if they remained in the care of the British Government. The sense of urgency was also driven by the fact that UNRRA was due to shut down operations in mid-1946. This would seem counter-intuitive, but there was already much discussion at the U.N. about replacing UNRRA with another international relief agency that would assume UNRRA's responsibilities, but with a slightly different mandate, including allowing it to pursue resettlement opportunities. Thus, if London could get UNRRA to take over the camps, then they would also be assumed by the new organization and London would be freed from the financial burden it had been carrying. Furthermore, the Polish refugees would be able to take advantage of the considerable resources of UNRRA and its successor organization.

The situation was made more critical when, in December 1945, the Warsaw Polish Government approached C.M. Drury, Chief of the UNRRA Mission to Poland, to discuss the possibility of it assuming responsibility for its refugees, including the camps in East Africa and elsewhere. The Polish estimated there were a total of 38,290 potential repatriates in Palestine, Egypt, Iraq, Iran, Syria, East Africa, India, New Zealand, and South Africa. The Warsaw Poles hoped that the repatriates could be moved by sea, by far the easiest way of moving them, but Poland would need UNRRA's help in arranging the transportation, as

the country did not have its own shipping. Drury allowed that, in principle, UNRRA assistance was possible, although it couldn't happen before
the spring of 1946. He also suggested that the Warsaw Government
would have to send representatives to the camps to advise the potential
repatriates on conditions in Poland. Drury made it clear that UNRRA
could not forcibly repatriate anyone, which the Warsaw Government
acknowledged. On the other hand, the Warsaw Poles reserved the right
to refuse admission to any Pole they considered undesirable. In fact,
Warsaw proposed sending a mission to Cairo to "tell the expatriates of
conditions in Poland and do something to counteract the influence of
those who were inimical to the regime." They were well aware of the
hostility of the pro-London Polish camp administration.

Drury's superiors at the European Regional Office (ERO) of
UNRRA were cautiously optimistic about this possibility. Although the
ERO could do nothing about the refugees in New Zealand or South
Africa, as they fell outside its territorial mandate, it might be able to assist
with the rest. However, there were several concerns: UNRRA's Middle
East Office (MEO) estimated that, at most, a mere 10 percent of the
displaced persons would actually be willing to repatriate. Many of the
displaced persons were physically fragile. Women, children, the elderly,
and the sick had special requirements that had to be met before being
moved. Even if these questions could be resolved, the ERO realized it
would still take some time, as there was an acute worldwide shortage of
shipping, even for short distances.[18] But none of those issues seemed
insurmountable and on December 26, 1945, the Polish Government
formally requested that UNRRA assume responsibility for the refugees'
repatriation, to begin on April 1, 1946.[19]

Still, nothing could proceed until the British Government had also
agreed to the proposal, as required by UNRRA's own policy. In a series of
meetings in early January 1946, Drury met with representatives from a
number of departments of the British Government — the Treasury, the
India Office, the Foreign Office, and the War Office. Their reaction was
one of alarm and they raised a number of objections. First, given that
the overwhelming majority of the population in the camps was hostile
to repatriation, and to the Communist regime in Warsaw, they predicted

that introducing administrative personnel appointed by Warsaw to the camps would be very problematic. Second, the representative of the War Office feared that introducing that kind of changeover, at that moment in time, would make it extremely difficult to sort out the remaining displaced persons who were eligible for Operation Pole Jump. Third, and perhaps most importantly, while the British were very interested in having UNRRA assume responsibility for the camps, they were not willing to consider it if it meant that UNRRA would be forcibly repatriating the Poles from the camps. While Drury reassured them that UNRRA did not repatriate anyone against their will, London remained uncomfortable with the situation.[20]

Meanwhile, UNRRA itself had begun to have its own reservations about the whole plan to take over the camps. While in principle UNRRA expressed a willingness to accept the responsibility, it could not justify or afford their present maintenance payments, as it paid less to other displaced persons. Thus, the Poles would necessarily see their standard of living drop if UNRRA took over, not something for which UNRRA wanted to be held responsible. UNRRA was also becoming increasingly nervous about the possibility of repatriating these Poles. UNRRA was bound by its own Resolution 71 to both work with the Polish Government as the national government representing these displaced persons and to encourage, but not compel, repatriation. With a camp population openly opposed to repatriation, this would put UNRRA in the awkward position of having to proselytize to the adamantly disinterested. Finally, the issue of the camps' administration would also continue to be a thorny one, and perhaps irresolvable for UNRRA, which, according to its mandate, would have to allow the Polish Government to shape it.[21] Drury was further put off by wrangling within the Foreign Office and between the Interim Treasury Committee and the Welfare Branches, and by the Foreign Office's insistence on keeping the Polish Government out of the camps. UNRRA and the Foreign Office had fundamentally disagreed over whether a Polish Government mission should be sent to Cairo to investigate the situation, and whether information liaison officers and priests should be sent from Poland to the various camps. UNRRA wanted them, the Foreign Office did not.[22] In the end, on behalf of UNRRA, Drury politely declined the invitation to take over the camps, suggesting that it made sense for the camps to remain a responsibility of Britain, given the problems that appeared to exist: the issue of the camp administration, which Warsaw would not be willing to leave as it was; and the potential resettlement of a number of these people in Britain as dependants of the Polish forces who had fought for Britain.[23]

The matter did not end there, and the debate continued to roil through the corridors of government in London. In mid-January the London Poles, without a government to speak for them, mobilized the Chief of the Polish General Staff of the Polish Forces to make their case to the War Office. Apparently, the rumours that UNRRA would be taking over the camps were still flying. In fact, in spite of the conclusion reached at the end of the early January meetings between Drury and the British Government, the British had not yet given up hope, so the rumours were not completely unfounded. The Chief of the Polish General Staff complained that UNRRA delegates in the Middle East and Africa appeared to be planning how to administer those refugee camps, should UNRRA take over responsibility for them. While the problem seemed to be a civilian one, and therefore not his concern, because of the reality that many of the refugees were dependants of his military personnel, he argued that it was actually very much a military affair. The rumours were very vague, simply that there might be "possible changes in the future circumstances and eventual fate of these people." That was enough to cause considerable anxiety and unrest among the Polish military personnel, who were rightly very concerned about the fate of their loved ones. The Chief of the Polish General Staff argued that this close connection with the Polish Forces under British Command meant that these refugees fell outside UNRRA's mandate, which was restricted to displaced persons and did not include the care of military personnel. He raised the now well-rehearsed concern that transferring the camps' administration to UNRRA would be putting it in the control of Warsaw, with predictably disastrous consequences. He also made the point that to turn the camps over to UNRRA would mean a serious deterioration in the standard of living in the camps. Surely, he concluded, if the reason for considering the transfer was financial, the British had already made reductions in personnel and administrative costs and they should continue to do so, as long as it didn't affect the status, rate of the allowances, or actual place of residence of those concerned.[24]

And the debate continued. The War Office, in spite of its sympathies for the London Poles, was very clear in its desire to be relieved of the responsibility for the Polish displaced persons in the Middle East, India, and Africa as soon as possible, and believed that UNRRA was the only body appropriate for the task.[25] The Foreign Office was torn between the War Office's position and the concerns of the Polish General Staff. On one hand, they wanted to be able to reassure the London Poles that nothing significant would change, but on the other, the Poles' position was fundamentally contrary to that of London. Ultimately, they had to acknowledge that the British Government could not speak for UNRRA.[26]

Those who supported the idea of UNRRA taking over argued that if UNRRA had pledged not to forcibly repatriate the Poles, that was good enough for them. Regarding the issue of replacing the administrative staff with Warsaw Poles, they argued that they could hardly ask UNRRA to take over the camps and then tell them what they could or could not do once they were in charge. One had to let them do as they saw fit. The heart of the opposition to UNRRA's takeover came from the Interim Treasury Committee, led by Mr. Eggers. The ITC had a close relationship with, and a strong loyalty to, the London Poles. Eggers was extremely reluctant to agree to UNRRA's assumption of the camps, because he didn't want to see the London Polish administration in the camps replaced by Warsaw Poles. He argued that since the majority of the Poles in the camps were "bitterly anti-Russian," and had refused to return to Poland, it would be unfair to hand them over to the Warsaw Poles "who would be certain to try to indoctrinate them and would probably annoy and victimize them a good deal."

It was a widespread concern. Mr. Hancock, of the Foreign Office, echoed a common sentiment when he maintained that there would be unrest and even violence in the camps if the Warsaw Poles were put in charge. This would have been a disaster for the British administrators in the colonial territories, especially in Tanganyika, where there were twice as many Poles as there were Europeans of other nationalities. The Treasury also argued that Britain had commitments to the Poles that it would be breaking if they agreed to UNRRA's terms. Then there was the very thorny problem that many of the Poles in these camps were not repatriable. UNRRA's mandate restricted its aid and relief efforts to candidates for repatriation. If a refugee was deemed non-repatriable for any reason that instantly put them outside of its mandate. Although UNRRA had made a commitment to support such former displaced persons for a reasonable time, the support was not unlimited. Eventually, the refugees would have to move out of the camp and fend for themselves. It was unclear what that would mean for those who would inevitably be evicted from the camps in East Africa. It was not a corner of the world easily capable of absorbing a sudden increase in its permanent European population.[27]

All the while, the Foreign Office continued talks with UNRRA. London's choices were, in reality, very limited — either to continue funding the camps itself and allow the camps to continue to exist for the foreseeable future, or to turn them over to UNRRA. On March 8, 1946, London finally formally requested that UNRRA assume responsibility for the maintenance of the Polish refugees in the Middle East, India, and the British territories in Africa, proposing that it take over the camps as of April 1, 1946. UNRRA was noncommittal at first, explaining that whatever their eventual decision, April 1 was an impossible date.[28]

UNRRA's reluctance to take on this particular group of refugees had grown as the conversation with London had continued. Its earlier concerns had not been allayed. There would be no way around giving Warsaw access to, and control over, the camps' administration; there was the problem of the excessive maintenance payments that would have to be reduced if UNRRA took over; and there was the real possibility that most of the refugees were non-repatriable, resulting in an indefinite commitment on UNRRA's part to maintain them, which would be unacceptable. And from past experience, UNRRA knew that these people were not easy to deal with. While the camps in East Africa had never been a priority for UNRRA, especially not the Poles, who seemed well taken care of by the Polish Ministry of Social Welfare in London, UNRRA had not completely ignored them. The Administration's impression of these particular displaced persons was not a favourable one.[29]

In 1944, H.H. Lehman, Director General of UNRRA at the time, had inquired about the feasibility of UNRRA assuming responsibility for the Polish camps in East Africa, Iran, India, and Palestine. It was in the early days of UNRRA, when the organization was still trying to define its role and establish its legitimacy, so the question made sense. C.M. Pierce, of UNRRA's Division on Displaced Persons, informed him that it would be a very difficult and problematic thing to do, as well as very expensive.[30] The logistics of administering the camps would be nightmarish. There were a total of twenty Polish camps in East Africa, scattered from northern Uganda, down through the heart of central Africa to the Dominion of South Africa. Administering those camps, given the distances involved and the physical challenges of transportation on that continent, would be tremendously difficult, but responsibility could not be left in the hands of the Polish Government-in-Exile, as UNRRA would have no control over the operations or their cost. Pierce suggested that if UNRRA was to take over the camps one massive new camp, or a network of camps, with a capacity of fifty thousand, should be established in the Middle East, near a seaport to which they would move all the Poles. This could then be a purely UNRRA operation, without assistance from either the Polish Delegation or the military. The result would be a much more viable and simpler operation.[31]

While these discussions were underway, UNRRA had decided to register the displaced persons in these camps, to get a sense of the size and nature of the problem. S.K. Jacobs, a Displaced Persons Specialist for UNRRA, was dispatched to East Africa to do the registration in late 1944, and early 1945. It was a disaster. The Poles proved extremely suspicious of being registered, and the Polish camp administration was not terribly co-operative. Before Jacobs set out for Tengeru, his first test site for the registration drive, he had met with the Polish Consul General and the Polish Delegation to inform them of his plans and ask them to notify the camp leaders of his purpose. When he arrived in Nairobi, en route to Tengeru, to his dismay he found out that no one had passed on the message to the camps. Instead, they assigned a Delegation representative, Dr. Kon, to introduce him at the camps, as well as to observe the registration process. When the two men arrived in the camp, Jacobs discovered that not only was the Camp Commandant, Colonel Minnery, not there (he had gone on a cattle-buying expedition and his car had broken down), but that the telegram he had sent to the camp five days earlier, announcing his pending arrival, had only arrived the same day he did. Thus, no one knew he was coming — not an auspicious beginning.

Jacobs immediately met with the camp's Polish leader, an interpreter, and Dr. Kon to discuss the registration process. In spite of the mix-ups Jacobs still felt optimistic. School was out and there were fifty teachers available who could help. That afternoon the teachers were gathered and the process was explained to them. Meanwhile, the camp as a whole was told that registration would begin the next morning at 9:30 a.m. At the teachers' meeting Dr. Kon spoke first, in Polish. Jacobs got the first inkling that something was amiss when he thought he heard Kon mention the Soviet Government, which he could not understand as the U.S.S.R. had no role in the registration exercise. It quickly became clear that something was very wrong. The teachers were getting quite upset, although he had no idea why. When Jacobs asked the interpreter what was going on, the interpreter explained that the camp population was very suspicious of the registration plan and "up in arms" about the whole thing. To Jacobs' dismay, Kon played on the crowd's fears, whipping it into a mild hysteria. In the midst of the increasingly raucous meeting, one woman collapsed with a heart attack and had to be carried away, apparently overwhelmed by memories of her cruel time in Russia. According to Jacobs' report, at that point there was no holding them back; in his words, "[t]he priest, who can always be relied on, got up and with a good deal of fist shaking made a violent denunciation of communism." When Jacobs finally got the floor, he desperately tried to defuse the situation. He explained, through the interpreter, that there was nothing binding about the registration and that no one would be forcibly repatriated anywhere. He tried to point out that this was a United Nations effort, supported by their own government, but it was to no avail, the audience was in no mood to listen.

The teachers finally agreed to assist in the registration, but only if they could enter "Poland" as their declared destination. Jacobs told them it wouldn't be very useful, but that he agreed to the compromise.

As most of these displaced persons had come from eastern Poland, the territory now absorbed into the U.S.S.R., this was a deliberately provocative demand, a thinly veiled declaration of their refusal to accept either the Soviet annexation of eastern Poland, or the new Communist Government of Poland. They then announced they would refuse to assist unless they could put on every card that they would only return to a Poland that was governed by the London Government (the Polish Government-in-Exile). Jacobs explained again that this wouldn't be very helpful, but if they wished, they could put it under "remarks" on the registration card. Then they dug in their heels, flatly refusing to do the registration at all. In the midst of this, some of the people hanging around outside burst into the room and disrupted the meeting. One individual in particular was especially obnoxious, waving his fist and threatening Jacobs. The camp leader refused to do anything to maintain order in the meeting, merely shrugging his shoulders when Jacobs appealed to him for help. Jacobs even appealed to the priest to restore some order to the meeting, but he said he had nothing to do with the registration and refused to help. Meanwhile, "There was a racket going on like feeding time at the zoo!" According to Jacobs this was, in part, because "one of the good ladies recognized me from Russia where I had been a member of the OGPU (the Russian secret police of the early 1930s)." Jacobs, as an American Jew, found this particularly amusing, commenting in his report that he really had to be more careful with his disguises. Giving up on the meeting as a lost cause, he retreated to his quarters.[32]

Jacobs was not the only one appalled by the course of events. Herbert Story, a member of the Friends Relief Service, a Quaker organization operating in the camp, was as shaken by the Poles' reaction. As he observed to his superiors in the United States,

> I wonder now how he managed to leave the meeting
> unscathed. Believe me this is no exaggeration.... People
> became hysterical, one person fainted, some swore they
> had seen Mr. Jacobs in Russia.... The same suspicion
> and hatred of Russia was behind all the questions [posed
> by the teachers], although never openly expressed....

[A]n inspector of schools, a man I know very well since
he has been my neighbour for close on a year, and whom
I always found had very sane ideas, stated quite frankly,
"I don't trust this fellow, he is a Jew. The Jews, our own
Jews, fired on us when we were fighting the Russians
between the Great War and this one."[33]

When Minnery returned to the camp, he and Jacobs held a conference with all the supervisors and a representation of five from the ranks
of the teachers (selected by the teachers themselves). At that meeting,
they were all quite contrite, at least according to Jacobs. By this time, Dr.
Kon had conveniently disappeared with the car. Minnery addressed the
meeting impressively, berating the people for their misbehaviour and
lack of courtesy, and assured them that Jacobs was an accredited representative of UNRRA. He also explained what UNRRA was, and that
it did not pose a threat to them. Then Jacobs spoke. He told them that
he had been genuinely surprised and taken aback by his reception, as
he was a representative of UNRRA, not Joseph Stalin, and that their
own government was contributing to his salary. He pointed out that
UNRRA was as much their organization as it was his. He explained that,
while UNRRA could facilitate anyone's repatriation to Poland, if they
wished to go, no one would be forced to repatriate against their wishes.
The registration was simply intended to get more complete information
about the camp population and did not commit the displaced persons to
anything. In the end, Jacobs reported that the people were very apolo-
getic but, given the furor and upset in the camp, there was no point in
attempting to register anyone at that time. Minnery, meanwhile, promised to hold a series of meetings to explain the registration and its purpose, as well as UNRRA. True to his word, Minnery did so.

In spite of the improved state of affairs by the time Jacobs left the
camp, he was of the opinion that registering these people would be a
waste of time. He didn't see the point in wasting a lot of resources on
people who, he believed, were going to "be the root of future troubles
in Poland." He didn't blame the refugees themselves, as he thought they
were largely ignorant and illiterate peasants with no way of knowing what

was in store for them, having been bombarded by anti-Soviet and anti-UNRRA propaganda, and isolated as they were from the outside world. As well, the camps themselves would be problematic to run. He was dismissively contemptuous of the refugees, with no comprehension of what these people had endured in the Soviet Union and no sympathy for their very real fears. In this way, he was a particularly bad choice to have sent into Africa. Unfortunately, his was not an uncommon opinion. In a private conversation with the Polish Consul in Nairobi, the Consul was quite frank, confirming Jacobs' opinion. He expressed little confidence in the Polish Delegation, and complained that the Polish administration was bloated, inefficient, and not particularly interested in working in the camps. The East African Refugee Administration, on the other hand, was very thinly staffed, and unable to control the Polish Delegation as a result. Officially, of course, both the Consul and the Delegation expressed surprise at the fracas, explaining it away as a momentary upset because of the present circumstances. Jacobs' final conclusion was that it would be a serious mistake for UNRRA to take on these refugees, unless it was possible to move the refugees into UNRRA-administered camps outside of East Africa.[34] This was the message that was communicated with the upper levels of UNRRA.

From the perspective of those who had to deal with the Poles after Jacobs left, he had done considerable damage in the short time he was in Africa. Herbert Story was amazed at the panic and vitriol he had roused in the camp, explaining that Jacobs, "Partly due to his very undiplomatic approach, and refusal to face facts, and partly as a result of the non-preparedness of the people to receive him brought this feeling to the surface and it appeared in a unified form such as we here have never before experienced."[35] The British administration in Tanganyika (the East African Refugee Administration or EARA), for its part, was furious. Jacobs' unannounced and abrupt arrival in the camps, and the manner in which he pursued registration, had been very disruptive and had caused considerable unrest and confusion in the camps. The Poles were now convinced that his objective was to register them for compulsory repatriation to Poland and, since most of them came from eastern Poland, they believed that meant compulsory repatriation to the Soviet Union.

The EARA's reassurances that no one would be forcibly repatriated fell on deaf ears. In communications with UNRRA, EARA insisted that it should have been informed of the pending registration before Jacobs was sent to the camps so they could have prepared the way for him. They also made it clear that Jacobs was "hardly the tactful choice for the job."[36] EARA sought to discourage UNRRA from the plan, arguing that, in its experience, these refugees were reluctant to register and any new registration would simply create more "apprehension," as had been witnessed in Tengeru. The distances involved, and the limited staff available at the settlements, would make registration very difficult anyway. Instead, it would be better to wait until it was certain that UNRRA was going to assume responsibility for the camps, and then do the registration after the refugees had been moved to a central camp.[37]

If the experience in Tengeru was not enough to convince UNRRA that these refugees spelled trouble, Jacobs ran into a similar problem in another camp in Uganda, the Masindi Camp. He arrived there in February 1945, to register its inhabitants. The opposition, violence, and vitriol was, if anything, even worse than what had erupted in Tengeru. Ultimately, Jacobs managed to get the camp registered, but only after the Polish Consul came to the camp and spoke several times to the people there, and after the priest spoke in favour of registration. He had had to agree to three modifications to the registration process as well: registrants had to be allowed to leave blank the space for "desired destination"; they were not required to sign the cards, as they were "deathly afraid of signing anything"; and they were allowed to put down their birthplaces as they stood that day or just before the war. Thus, as he put it, "If some old goat was actually born in Russian territory which later became Polish, he ... put down Poland." Without these concessions, registration wouldn't have happened. Even with them, it was an uphill battle that was not helped by letters from Polish soldiers in Italy, warning their relatives to watch for someone coming from Lublin to register them and not to sign anything under any condition.[38] Given Jacobs' reports it is no small wonder that UNRRA was reluctant to take on these displaced persons.

Jacobs' experiences were not the only disincentive for UNRRA. There was considerable concern about the ticklish political position in which

UNRRA could find itself, running camps of anti-Communist Poles with Communist Poland and the Soviet Union sitting on its Council. Many felt that the situation was "loaded with political dynamite." The potential embarrassment of having the U.S.S.R. and a Communist Polish Government as members, while supervising camps of Polish refugees, hostile to both, was tremendous. The fear was that these governments would argue that they had a right of access to these displaced persons (and so they did, according to UNRRA's policy), but "in view of the high emotional pitch of these refugees and the direct relationship to the Polish army with the Allies in Western Europe, such visits ... would create tremendous difficulties in the centers and perhaps in the army as well.... If such representatives were admitted ... troops would be required to maintain order in the camps." On the other hand, if Warsaw was denied access, it was not improbable that Warsaw would revoke the refugees' citizenship, rendering them stateless.[39] This would have the effect of rendering them permanently homeless and throwing them to the mercy of an already strained international relief community. This change in status would, by default, put a number of them in UNRRA's charge indefinitely.

Finally, there were the serious logistical obstacles to assuming responsibility. By late 1945, rumours of Pierce's proposal to move all the Polish refugees into one big camp, or network of camps, in the Middle East, were running rampant and the Middle East Office (MEO) of UNRRA was getting nervous. In a slightly panicked telegram to UNRRA headquarters in London, the MEO asked for some clarification as to the rumour's veracity, as the Egyptian authorities were beginning to ask questions which it could not answer. If the camp was going to happen, the MEO had no idea how it would manage it, as it had neither the staff nor the resources to manage such an enormous endeavour. It was rightly concerned about having this project dumped in its lap.[40] Headquarters quickly got back to the MEO with reassurances. By this time, the interest in Pierce's new camp had waned. Now the preference was for the British authorities to continue to care for the refugees through the local authorities, a much cheaper alternative.[41]

Meanwhile, Director General H.H. Lehman, who had initially been so keen to take on these refugees, had become increasingly pessimistic.

His concerns were, by now, familiar. He was dismayed by the evidence of corruption, mismanagement, and inefficiency in the camps' administration. He was worried about the generous monthly allowances enjoyed by these Poles, which exceeded those that UNRRA would or could provide. Reducing them to the level of UNRRA support would be difficult, as any efforts along those lines would "undoubtedly meet serious resistance on the part of the officials and refugees now benefitting from wasteful administration." He knew that both the general refugee population and the supervisory personnel were actively hostile to UNRRA, didn't want its assistance, and that this hostility was fostered by the leaders and members of the Polish Army. He also recognized the intractable problem posed by the fact that most of the Polish administrative personnel were appointees of the former Polish Government-in-Exile, to which Warsaw was certain to object. Nor would they be acceptable to UNRRA, for UNRRA's mandate obliged it and its staff to encourage repatriation whenever possible. Thus, those appointees who would fight against repatriation would have to go. Finally, recognizing Pierce's and Hoehler's concerns, Lehman acknowledged that UNRRA just didn't have the personnel, supplies, or equipment to effectively administer such a large number of camps spread out over such a broad expanse of territory. It would be a major task to correct all these ills, Lehman concluded, and one that UNRRA might want to avoid.[42]

Lehman's conclusions were buttressed by yet another UNRRA official's tour of the camps. W. Langrod visited the Middle East between October 26 and November 8, expressly to evaluate the state of affairs there. His observations echoed those of every other UNRRA official — that logistically the project was nigh impossible, and that these displaced persons would be a difficult challenge to deal with, as they were hostile to UNRRA and to the notion of repatriation.

> From a psychological point of view, the Polish displaced persons in the Middle East and Africa are very difficult to handle. Their previous sufferings and the years of more or less abnormal conditions of their refugee life have left deep traces in their characters and reactions.

They are excitable, suspicious and subject to mass suggestion. The religious attitude of women in East African Polish settlements often takes forms of fanaticism (*sic*) and bigotry. The DPs fear above all repatriation by compulsion. They mistrust UNRRA; an attempt to accomplish a preliminary registration in January 1945 in Africa was interrupted by an open, hysterical hostility against the Representative of UNRRA. There were analogous reactions against local Polish social workers. The refugees have, therefore, to be handled with skill and tact.

As regards the repatriability of Polish displaced persons, until now, a very small number of them have declared their willingness to go back to Poland under the present circumstances.... It has to be borne in mind that in a very large number of cases the decision of these people depends on the decision of their relatives serving in the Polish Army, and that as long as the latter refuse to go back, there is no possibility of obtaining a favourable decision from their wives and children.[43]

If UNRRA assumed responsibility for them, then these Poles would be UNRRA's for a considerable time.

However, it was not politic to reject the possibility out of hand, so Lehman crafted an alternative, one which was very similar to what was eventually proposed to the British Government. He suggested that UNRRA assume only financial responsibility for the camps, not administrative, and limit that financial responsibility to the per capita cost that was its present standard for the camps it already administered in the Middle East. The British Government would be free to augment the per capita allowance if it wished. While UNRRA reserved the right to monitor the camps' operations, maintenance of them would continue to be a British responsibility. If conditions were found to be substandard, or the administration inappropriate, UNRRA also reserved the right to station its staff in any camp or office, even to the point of taking over a camp's administration, and even to withdraw its financial support, if the situation warranted it. UNRRA would make every effort to encourage repatriation at the earliest moment, in co-operation with the Polish Government. The British Government would be expected to offer all possible assistance in this effort.[44]

Meanwhile the London Poles, by this time without formal representation but still having considerable influence, continued to press the British Government to cancel the plans with UNRRA and continue to maintain the Poles itself. If that was not possible, they pressed for restrictions on UNRRA's operations and control of the camps. It was Count Raczynski, Chief Polish Representative on the Interim Treasury Committee for Polish Affairs (ITC) and a leading figure in the London Polish community, who brought their demands forward. They were, by now, very familiar. The London Poles should be involved in the negotiations, or at least be given the chance to review the agreement before it was signed. No one should be forcibly repatriated and UNRRA must be made to explicitly guarantee that this would not happen. UNRRA should also pledge to maintain the refugees' present standard of living, comfort, and education, as well as freedom of speech, expression, and association. Nonetheless, the British Government should remain actively involved in the welfare and future well-being of these refugees, in consultation with Polish advisors, both in the field and in London, who would be funded by the British Government. Furthermore, UNRRA should be made to promise that no persons affiliated with the Warsaw or Soviet Government be entrusted with the refugees' care. Finally, only those refugees who wished to repatriate immediately should be required to register.[45]

London's reaction to Raczynski's petition was uniformly unsupportive. As the British Government had requested UNRRA do London a service, it was generally felt that one could hardly then start imposing terms. The consensus was that his demands went too far. London was satisfied that UNRRA would not forcibly repatriate the refugees, and that was sufficient reassurance for them. It was particularly concerned about Raczynski's suggestion regarding registration, as that would be tantamount to identifying some of the refugees as non-repatriable. This was something to be avoided at all costs, as it would put these refugees outside of UNRRA's mandate and, therefore, outside of UNRRA's care (perforce leaving them a British responsibility).

When the British Government and UNRRA met again, on March 21, 1946, Raczynski's demands were much watered down. London requested only that all refugees wishing to return to Poland be assisted in doing so immediately; that UNRRA should prevent any intimidation of the remaining refugees by either Communists, fellow-travellers, or by "irreconcilables from London" intended either to force their return or to prevent their return; that social and educational amenities should be maintained for those determined not to return until they could otherwise be accommodated and absorbed into civilian life; and that the camps should be disbanded as soon as possible, as camp life was not good for these people, who did not have to work, and because the camps were a considerable financial drain on the Exchequer and, if taken over by UNRRA, on UNRRA's reserves. None of these requirements would prove too serious an obstacle to negotiations.[46]

What did prove to be a key factor was the fact that UNRRA would soon shut down operations. The Director General was reluctant to take on the care and maintenance of these refugees with the whole organization winding down in anticipation of termination. It was UNRRA's legal counsel and its Repatriation and Welfare Division who changed his mind, arguing that UNRRA had a legal and moral duty to assist all eligible displaced persons until its resolutions were altered.[47] Thus, going into the final stages of negotiation, UNRRA was only reluctantly willing to take on the Poles in East Africa. This undoubtedly made Lehman's alternative even more appealing.

In a letter to the British Government dated August 7, 1946, Sir Humphrey N. Gale, Personal Representative of the Director General UNRRA, proposed that UNRRA accept financial responsibility for the Polish refugees in the Middle East, Africa, and India, as of August 1, 1946, but only under certain stipulations. The actual administration of the camps would continue to be the responsibility of the authorities currently doing so, but under UNRRA's general supervision and direction. UNRRA required that the appropriate administrative authorities in each area ensure that UNRRA's directives were carried out. UNRRA reserved the right to review the suitability of the staff involved in the care and maintenance of these displaced persons, and to have any who were considered unsatisfactory removed by the appropriate administrative authority. The British Government would arrange for the admission of authorized representatives from the Provisional Government of Poland to the areas where the refugees were located, and would assist the Administration in carrying out Resolution 92 and any other relevant UNRRA resolutions.[48] Crucially, the agreement limited UNRRA's financial responsibility for both repatriation and care and maintenance to a combined maximum of £1,700,000 — the amount budgeted for this project. Out of this sum, UNRRA agreed to pay the British Government the following per capita amounts for bona fide displaced persons: in India, £5 per month; in Palestine, £10 per month; and in East Africa, £4.15.0 (or four pounds and fifteen shillings) per month.[49] In each area, measures would be taken to certify the numbers of refugees receiving care and maintenance were displaced persons eligible for UNRRA assistance. UNRRA agreed to assume financial responsibility for those who wished to be repatriated, but would not be financially responsible for the removal of any displaced persons from their present country of location other than by way of repatriation. Finally, UNRRA insisted that the British Government assume responsibility for any displaced persons not repatriated at the moment of UNRRA's termination, which was expected to be December 31, 1946.[50]

There was a growing awareness in Whitehall that if it didn't accept this last proposal from UNRRA there was not likely to be another. It was also very clear that not accepting this offer would be a very expensive proposition, as "these refugees are costing ... an awful lot of money every day." London did not like the notion of re-assuming responsibility for the refugees upon UNRRA's termination, but the consensus was that the British Government should accept the offer anyway. P.J. Hancock suggested that one way of avoiding that scenario would be to have some other international agency assume this responsibility upon UNRRA's demise.[51] On September 4, 1946, G.J. Edmonds of the Foreign Office wrote Sir Humphrey Gale, accepting UNRRA's offer.

Of course, with UNRRA now providing the funding for the displaced persons' care, but with a very clear ceiling, and the British authorities still responsible for the administration of the camps, it was the British, not UNRRA, who had to bring the operating costs into line. It was a considerably smaller amount than the per capita costs that the British had incurred to date. H.H. Eggers of the Interim Treasury Committee was pleased with himself in November, when he was able to report to J.D. Bates of the Colonial Office that after a visit to Nairobi and a dramatic reorganization of the camps' administration, he had "swept away a large part of the existing staffs and drastically reduced the salaries of those remaining in employment. The cuts [had been applied] both inside and outside the camps." Not only had he been able to reduce the previous per capita expenditure from £4.16.3 per month, but he had brought it down to £4 per month, below the amount UNRRA was paying per person — £4.15.0.[52] Eggers' ultimate aim was to get the cost of operations in East Africa below the UNRRA per capita rate, because "any saving effected in East Africa might with advantage be applied to the Lebanon and Palestine, where conditions are very different and where UNRRA's monthly contribution might prove to be below subsistence level." This inevitably meant considerable scaling back, especially in the numbers and salaries of Polish staff, as well as the elimination of special allowances, most of which were in excess of UNRRA standards and had hitherto placed Polish refugees in a privileged position. There had been a growing suspicion that many of the Polish camp staff were redundant and could be eliminated anyway. The agreement with UNRRA provided the Treasury with the opportunity to address that, and establish identical standards of care in all of its territories, as much as possible — a goal of Whitehall.[53]

Thus, the shift in control to UNRRA brought both administrative and financial changes, which proved a shock to at least some of the Poles in the camps. They did not accept the shift passively. In late 1946, C.I. Burton of the Office of the Commissioner, East African Refugee Administration was hearing rumours that "the Polish leaders in East Africa and Rhodesia have received secret instructions passively to resist repatriation as much as possible." This was in direct contradiction with the late Polish Government-in-Exile's pledge not to oppose repatriation, and to allow individuals to make their own choice freely. Although the rumours were impossible to corroborate, he was convinced that there were grounds for suspicion. Burton felt that the educational staff were the worst culprits. He announced that the offices of the Polish Advisor to the Commissioner, EARA, and the Polish Educational Advisor to the Commissioner were to be abolished, as "they were no longer necessary." Instead, one or two subordinate Polish officials would be retained as staff in an advisory capacity. As an additional benefit, that meant a further cost-savings, which was always a welcome thing.[54]

This was enough to antagonize the Poles in East Africa, but it was not all. There was a minor altercation between UNRRA and the British Government over the indelicacy of one of its officials based in Cairo, a Mr. Curtis. Curtis had apparently written a British Member of Parliament, Mr. Crossman, expressing his unflattering opinion of the British Government's failure to encourage repatriation among the Poles in Africa, as well as the retention of London Poles in advisory and administrative positions. Curtis had apparently suggested to Crossman that London should "issue a strongly-worded instruction to Governments in Africa to oblige the majority of the refugees to go home." As a result, Crossman had enquired about repatriation policy and practice in East Africa.[55] Eggers (of ITC) took great exception to Curtis' hubris in commenting on British policy, arguing that if UNRRA objected to British policy, it was a matter to be discussed at the proper levels between the two administrations, not by minor officials. Eggers' fury was a reflection of a feeling common to the British administration, that the London Polish administrators could not be replaced with Warsaw Poles without causing considerable disturbance in the camps and, as UNRRA had no neutral staff with which to replace them (being so close to its own demise), the London Poles had to stay. The only alternative was no administration at all. The British Government didn't feel that it could, in all justice, advise the Poles to return to Poland, when it did not believe that the conditions there were good and when it refused to deliver the same message to Poles in Great Britain. Nor could the British Government require relatives of members of the Polish Armed Forces to repatriate, when their menfolk had already moved to Britain.

On the other hand, it had pledged to uphold UNRRA's mandate of repatriation. They were walking a fine line. Thus, as Eggers explained, the policy remained that "His Majesty's Government [would] continue to give every facility to any Poles who wish, and are able, to return to Poland, and indeed [would] use their influence with them to go back to their own country." However, London made it clear to Mr. Crossman that it also refused to do any more than that, and was not prepared to use compulsion on any Pole unwilling to return to his or her country.[56] In spite of these reassurances to Mr. Crossman, and UNRRA's pledge not to forcibly repatriate anyone, Mr. Curtis' hostility toward those Poles who were unwilling to repatriate may have been reflective of a rather common attitude within UNRRA in this region. Certainly it seems that the Poles believed it was.[57]

The reaction on the ground to these changes, both administrative and financial, was as predictable as it was vehement, and tensions boiled over by April 1947. The critical event was the abolition of the offices of the Polish Advisor and Polish Educational Advisor, key figures in the London Poles' continued influence over the management of the African camps. These Advisors acted as a conduit or liaison between the refugees and the British administration, with important communications functions in both directions — as the refugees' representatives to the British authorities, as well as using their "considerable influence" to ensure the refugees followed directives issued by the British authorities. They were especially important in the management of the educational system in the camps, a matter of vital importance to the London Poles. When the Government-in-Exile faced imminent de-recognition in June 1945, it had issued a declaration that it would continue in existence in order "to represent the true and enduring interests of Poland." It felt that its task was to continue the struggle for independence and to preserve the Polish character of its community, its sense of its own Polishness, through the encouragement of Polish political, cultural, and social organizations.[58] Of course, these would be pro-democratic, pro-London Pole, anti-Communist values being preserved. In the refugee camps, the educational system was crucial for inculcating these values in the youth. To lose control of the educational system would be to lose an important means of training the youth and maintaining influence within the refugee communities.

With protests against the dismissals came other grievances. Zygmunt Rusinek, Chairman of the Association of Polish War Emigrés based in Brussels, complained about the coercion he claimed was being applied to "encourage" repatriation. That coercion was taking the shape of steadily worsening conditions in the camps — reductions in food and clothing supplies, in allowances, and in the constant relocation of refugees to ever-larger and generally less comfortable camps. The reduction in supplies and allowances was a reflection of the changed funding sources for the camps, and the relocation was part of a British effort to reduce costs by consolidating refugees into larger, more economically efficient camps, but the Poles did not see it that way. They viewed the "often seemingly arbitrary measures affecting them," the provisional conditions in which they lived, as "an indirect application of undue pressure for their return to Poland." The refugees were especially concerned about the fate of the orphans among them. There had already been one attempt by the EARA and UNRRA to repatriate them to Poland, which had been foiled by the Attorney General of Tanganyika and the High Court-appointed Board of Guardians, who were the legal guardians of the Tanganyikan camps' orphans according to Tanganyikan law. It appeared that the British had abandoned them, and that UNRRA was determined to repatriate them.[59]

London recognized this for what it was, posturing, as much as it was a genuine reflection of the displaced persons' concerns. At least Eggers thought the Curtis incident and the complaints about the dismissal of the Polish advisors were all of a piece. UNRRA and the Polish displaced persons did not trust one another, and the tension that had always existed still remained. It would not have surprised him if Curtis, as the "man on the ground" in Africa, was doing "everything in his own power to make the life of the refugees uncomfortable, thereby, as he thinks, encouraging repatriation," in spite of UNRRA's pledge not to forcibly repatriate displaced persons. On the other hand, the Polish Government representative was also quite capable of "making mischief," according to Eggers. The loss of the two advisors, and the dramatic reductions in Polish camp staff, must have seriously undermined their control and authority in the camps. UNRRA's assumption of control of the camps would have sparked a passive resistance among the London Poles, who resented the Warsaw Poles' presence in UNRRA, and UNRRA's recognition, albeit mandated, of the Warsaw Government and the rights it claimed for its own. The London Poles remaining in office were fighting a rearguard action to defend what influence they still had from encroachment. In the end, London chose to ignore the complaints. There was little else it felt it could do.

So this was how things stood in mid-1947, when UNRRA finally terminated its operations. UNRRA had assumed financial responsibility for the East African camps, but not administrative. Britain continued to manage the camps on a daily basis. The situation for the Polish refugees became increasingly less comfortable, and their suspicions about what the authorities, British and international, intended for them only grew with time.

After a rather difficult transition period, the International Refugee Organization took over UNRRA's responsibilities, including that of administering the East African camps. There were two important differences between UNRRA and the IRO, which had an impact on the Polish displaced persons in Tengeru. The first important difference was in their respective memberships. While the Soviet Union and the various countries of the Soviet bloc had been members of UNRRA, and had increasingly used that membership to obstruct UNRRA's operations, these countries did not join the IRO. As the Cold War had hardened, UNRRA's councils and the camps had become sites of sometimes vicious, always disruptive proxy wars. With effectively two masters who were at loggerheads sitting on its General Council — the West, led by the United States, and the East, led by the U.S.S.R. — UNRRA had found itself often hamstrung, especially in the formulation of policy regarding displaced persons, who had become pawns in a much bigger game. While the Soviet bloc countries and the U.S.S.R. remained members of the United Nations and, in that way, able to monitor, comment upon, and create difficulties for IRO operations, their absence in the actual organization meant that the IRO had more freedom in its operations, especially in the field.

Second, the mandate of the two organizations was very different. UNRRA's purpose was to assist in the repatriation of the displaced persons, period. This worked well when dealing with displaced persons who actually wanted to return home. However, for those who did not, UNRRA's hands were tied. UNRRA was forbidden to pursue other alternatives for the resolution of the remaining displaced persons problem because the only solution it was authorized to promote was repatriation. The result was a stalemate with no end in sight. It was an untenable situation, as these displaced persons were never going to be persuaded to change their minds. By late 1946, it was clear that UNRRA had outlived its usefulness, even though the displaced persons problem had not yet been resolved. A new organization was needed to succeed UNRRA, one that would both care for the displaced persons and have the necessary authority to resolve the situation. That organization was the IRO. Its mission was, first, to promote repatriation where possible, but, second, to facilitate resettlement in countries other than a displaced person's homeland if repatriation was not possible. This made the IRO's task much easier, because it was given the flexibility to pursue a variety of options when trying to find a resolution to the situation. This change in mandate had important implications for the Poles in East Africa.

# 4 | Doors Closing

So in 1947, UNRRA was about to be terminated and the IRO was about to assume UNRRA's responsibilities. The British Government was providing care and maintenance for the Polish camps in East Africa and elsewhere, with UNRRA, then the IRO, financing it and arranging repatriation for those willing to return to their homeland. All displaced persons were expected to be settled once General Anders' army was demobilized. Operation Pole Jump had been created to move the dependants and close relatives of the demobilized Polish troops to England. This was thought to be the solution.

However, a closer examination of the individual refugees uncovered a problem. Less than 50 percent of the Poles dispersed through the various colonies and dominions qualified for Operation Pole Jump, as they did not fit any of the British Government's nineteen categories of close relatives. Still, the number of Poles in the camps throughout the Dominion decreased. Some returned to Poland; some emigrated to other countries when the opportunity arose; some settled where they were permanently, removing themselves from the camp system. As that number fell, the British authorities gradually concentrated the Poles. Palestine was emptied of Polish displaced persons in 1947. Those who had nowhere else to go were moved to the French Zone in Germany, and to Lebanon. India was evacuated in 1948, with the remnants in the camps moved to Uganda. Northern Rhodesia was emptied in December 1948, Southern Rhodesia in April 1949. The final residue of some 5,500 Poles was, by that time, concentrated in the three East African territories of Uganda, Tanganyika, and Kenya, as well as in Lebanon. The Poles there not only did not qualify for Operation Pole Jump, they also did not qualify for resettlement in the U.S., under the American Displaced Persons Act. There were few other opportunities for resettlement, as removed as they were from any embassies or missions of countries who might otherwise consider them. A few chose to resettle in Africa, and a few took advantage of another British resettlement scheme, known as Operation Westward Ho, but for the remainder there seemed few options.[1] For children without parents or legal guardian, minors too young to work, there appeared to be none. In the words of Sophia Wakulczyk, "We didn't have anybody anywhere," and so there was no one to sponsor their resettlement abroad.[2]

The Warsaw Government was adamant that these children should be repatriated to Poland. The London Poles were just as adamant that the children would not. The children proved to be a flashpoint in the ongoing battle between the London and the Warsaw Poles. There were at least two instances during those years, 1945 to 1948, when the London Poles attempted to remove groups of Polish children from UNRRA camps and take them to Italy or England, to keep them "safe" from repatriation to a Communist Poland. In each case, the Warsaw Government took great umbrage, demanding the return and repatriation of the children. Thus there was a history of tension over the treatment of orphaned Polish children even before the flap over Tengeru. Other than that, the African camps and the orphans slipped off the radar of the international relief agencies for the next few years, until about 1949. The camps, aside from the upheaval of consolidation, continued to enjoy what was, from their perspective, a state of splendid isolation, feeling little impact from the handover to the IRO or by the greater events of the world.

But certain things had changed significantly, and there were ramifications for these displaced persons, even if they were not aware of them yet. The IRO's mandate was different from UNRRA's. While UNRRA was restricted to repatriation only, the IRO was not. The IRO was first required to encourage voluntary repatriation, but was also permitted to pursue resettlement schemes for those displaced persons who could not, or would not, repatriate. This gave the IRO considerably more flexibility than UNRRA. The IRO also had a very clear mandate to clear out the camps. Like UNRRA, the IRO had only a limited life and budget. The countries funding the IRO fully expected that the displaced persons problem be settled by the time the IRO's operations were terminated, a process which was to begin in mid-1949, winding up definitively by June 1950. The organization's purpose was to bring closure to the matter. By mid-1948, the pressure on the IRO to settle the problem was mounting.

Another factor that ultimately shaped the IRO response to this pressure was the hardening Cold War. UNRRA had faced it already, when dealing with the tensions between the U.S. and the U.S.S.R., with Poland being one proxy in the battle. By 1948, the battle lines were drawn. But the IRO was spared the internal disputes, as neither Warsaw nor the Soviet regime were members. They were, however, very vocal members of the United Nations, the parent organization of the IRO. Thus, although the Soviets and the Communist Poles had little direct influence in the IRO, they had considerable influence via the public arena. Finally, by 1948, it was recognized that the Poles remaining in the camps were not willing to repatriate and, if the camps were to be shut down, this had to be addressed in whatever solution was found for them. Their ultimate fate was very uncertain.

In mid-1948, the IRO finally turned its attention to the Poles in East Africa, drawn to them by the Polish Civic Committee in Nairobi. That committee asked the IRO to petition the British Government to broaden the sweep of Operation Pole Jump. Sir Arthur Rucker, Director General of IRO operations in Europe, headquartered in Geneva, via his representatives in Nairobi, agreed and the IRO asked the British to consider taking in the widows and orphans of Polish soldiers who were killed during the war, but not under British Command. Apparently there were only approximately two hundred of them, and many had brothers and other relatives already in the U.K. who would be able and willing to fully support them. The IRO also asked that the British take in the orphans of Polish soldiers killed while not under British Command, and who had guardians in Great Britain who had been supporting them in Russia and then in East Africa. Those guardians wanted to bring the children to the United Kingdom. Finally, there were cases in which a whole family was eligible to go to the U.K., with the exception of one or two members. Typically, these were married daughters over twenty-one years of age whose husbands were missing. The families didn't want to leave their daughters behind and had turned down the opportunity to emigrate to the U.K. Surely, Rucker argued, this was wrong? Finally, he explained that there was "considerable local distress" because it appeared that fewer people were being allowed into the United Kingdom from East Africa than had been permitted from other parts of the world. Of the eleven thousand initially registered for transfer, only 1,500 had been removed. This was a cause of considerable upset among the Polish displaced persons in East Africa.[3] Rucker himself raised the issue with C.J. Edmonds of the Refugee Department of the Foreign Office in London in late June, passing on the Nairobi letter as a summary of the problem.[4]

This spurred considerable discussion in the Foreign Office. P.J. Hancock came up with the definitive response, which was resoundingly negative. He argued that Operation Pole Jump, when established, had forced the various departments involved to come up with a definition of "dependant," because of the ambiguity of the term. There had been considerable discussion, only after which they had drawn up a sort of table of "kindred and affinity" that defined "dependant" on what he considered really rather generous lines. The result, he argued, was the British Government "accepting responsibility for considerably more of the Polish civilian refugees than they [were] asking the IRO to look after. This is very advantageous to IRO and one certainly cannot imagine any other foreign Government being so generous." He pointed out that there was always going to be a problem with those cases on the borderline of the definition of dependant, no matter how the term was defined. And no matter how much more generously the British Government extended the definition, the IRO would inevitably ask for an even further extension. Hancock wrote, "[I]n general our view is that, having drawn the line, we have got to stick to it." He refused to consider making an exception to the principle that London's only obligation was to members of the Polish Armed Forces, and that it had none to non-members. "To make a breach in this principle would open us to innumerable and embarrassing requests all over the world."

Hancock was incensed by the accusation that Britain was in some way doing less for the East African Poles than had been done for Poles elsewhere. He pointed out that of the "extra" Poles allowed in from the Middle East, there were five hundred special visas issued to General Wiatr, head of the Polish Forces in the Middle East, to be used at his discretion to deal with the considerable number of Poles who had been discharged from the Polish Armed Forces due to various disabilities, and who it was thought cruel to leave behind. The East African Poles did not need this special category. Hancock was also still smarting over the way in which the British Government had been swindled, to use his word, when the Polish refugees from India had been selected for Operation Pole Jump. A Polish officer had been sent to India to draw up a list of those eligible, but when the refugees arrived in Great Britain, the British Government discovered that some two hundred widows and orphans who were not related to Polish soldiers who had died under British Command were included. However, by the time they were discovered they were already in Great Britain, and could hardly be returned to India, so there they remained. Hancock and his office were determined not to be tricked again. When it came time to consider Poles in East Africa for Operation Pole Jump, the rules were applied very stringently. A British officer was sent to East Africa to draw up the list of eligibles, ensuring that the list was compiled properly and without cheating. Of course, there were fewer categories and numbers being allowed into the United Kingdom from East Africa. This was as it should be, according to Hancock, because the cheating had been eliminated. What the East African Poles saw as a curtailment of Operation Pole Jump was, in Hancock's opinion, merely the successful application of the program's standards. They had nothing to complain about.

Hancock paid particular attention to the request to consider admitting orphans of Polish soldiers killed while not under British Command, and the married daughters with missing husbands. As far as the children went, he had several reasons to reject this proposal. First, admitting them would be inviting a flood of similar requests. There was also the problem of determining whether the individual in the U.K. who was identified as the guardian had ever possessed true guardianship. How could one prove that they had "in the past stood in any special relation to the child?" It was impossible. Furthermore, the War Office, which actually ran Operation Pole Jump, was unwilling to consider this suggestion.

However, Hancock did agree that excluding the widowed sister of a member of the Polish Resettlement Corps, while allowing the unmarried sister to participate in Operation Pole Jump, was unfair. He felt that the War Office might be persuaded to make an exception. He also thought that the War Office might consider, on compassionate grounds, cases where one member of a family would be left behind if the rest of the family moved to the United Kingdom. However, there was the problem of the "missing" husbands. There had been instances when the women claimed their husbands were missing, but the men subsequently turned up in Poland. Hancock concluded by arguing that the East African Poles were not being treated unfairly, and on July 13, 1948, he and others met with Sir Arthur Rucker to give him this answer.[5]

Hancock repeated the same forceful language in a letter to Rucker dated July 15.

> I realize that some 200 widows and orphans of Poles who were killed not under British Command were brought to the United Kingdom from India, but this was due to some shady work by a Polish officer sent out to India to draw up lists of Poles eligible to come to the United Kingdom. We were in fact swindled over this and are anxious not to be swindled again. This was the principal reason why Major Pett Ridge was sent to draw up the lists in East Africa.

He suggested, if Poles in the United Kingdom could make out a good case for guardianship, there was no reason why they couldn't apply to the Home Office for the child to come. That would be the more appropriate route, he suggested, than through Operation Pole Jump, as the Home Office could then evaluate each case based on its own merits.[6] The British Government clearly felt that it had done more than its share to alleviate the Poles' plight, and was not going to be talked into taking in more.

Meanwhile, the IRO, while preoccupied with the greater challenge of disposing of the tens of thousands of displaced persons still in camps in Europe, hadn't totally forgotten about the Poles in East Africa. The plan was to bring them to Europe, where the various resettlement missions of foreign countries could interview and screen them as possible immigrants. As long as they remained in East Africa, Lebanon, and India, that was not going to happen, as the missions refused to travel that far. If the refugees were going to be resettled, they had to be brought to the missions. So the scheme was to move them out to camps in the French occupation zone of Germany. By late March 1948, the IRO had already moved some 500 Poles from Palestine, and plans were to move the Poles from East Africa sometime soon.[7] It was all part and parcel of the overall scheme to settle all remaining displaced persons under the IRO's care, and was in keeping with the tactics used in Europe, where displaced persons were continually moved and consolidated into camps, to facilitate their care and resettlement.

Then the world caught up with the children in Tengeru. On August 3, 1948, the Canadian Government passed Order-in-Council PC 3396 authorizing the Catholic Immigrant Aid Society to bring one thousand orphan children into Canada. This was the usual device: a special immigration quota that could target a very specific group of immigrants, such as these orphan children. This allowed a country, such as Canada, to do its part in addressing the displaced persons problem in Europe in a carefully managed fashion. This particular Order-in-Council restricted the visas to children between the ages of five and sixteen, with the exception of a child under the minimum age accompanying an older sibling. All were required to undergo the usual medical examination required of potential immigrants — a check for ailments such as active tuberculosis, venereal diseases, physical deformities — which might result in the individual becoming a burden on the Canadian welfare system. The Society was expected to arrange their transportation with the necessary escort officers, and to supply a nominal roll of each group to the Government.

Upon their arrival, the Halifax office of the Immigration Service was asked to notify the Department of Immigration in Ottawa.[8] By "orphan," the Catholic Immigrant Aid Society meant, and confirmed with Ottawa, "a child bereaved of both parents."[9]

On September 30, 1948, the Immigration Service transferred 300 of the one thousand allotted visas to the Canadian Government Immigration Mission in Karlsruhe, Germany, where they were made available to Dorothy Sullivan, the Overseas Selection Officer for the Catholic Immigrant Aid Society.[10] Initially, these visas were expected to go to orphan children in Europe, but that proved impractical for a variety of reasons.

Meanwhile, the IRO's plans to clear out the Poles from East Africa were moving apace. On October 29, 1948, M.D. Lane, Chief of the Welfare Division of the Health, Care and Maintenance Department of IRO Geneva (Headquarters) decided to move a group of children from East Africa to Italy, where they could be repatriated or resettled from over the winter months.[11] The reasons for the transfer were straightforward and reflected IRO's overall strategy for resolving the displaced persons question. The world's eyes were fixed on Europe and the displaced persons in Africa were an unknown story. As a result, most of the resettlement schemes were specific to Europe. All the resettlement missions insisted on an interview with potential immigrants, including children, but few were willing to incur the expense of sending representatives to Africa to do so. With no shortage of resettlement missions in Europe, the interview and a medical examination, which were standard practice, would be quite simple to arrange if the children were there. Finally, if the Canadian or British resettlement plans fell through, there was more opportunity of finding the children alternatives if they were in Italy instead of Africa. Moving them to Europe seemed to make perfect sense.

Thus, in November 1948, F. Lorriman, the IRO's representative in Tengeru, suggested that the children in the orphanage be sent to Italy, where they would be cared for by a Catholic organization "in a Polish environment." However, when pressed for details, he was vague, which alarmed the Poles in the camp.[12] When the news reached Nairobi, there was panic and fury.

The reasons for the panic were manifold. It is important to note that in the ongoing dialogue about the children's move, the IRO had not once mentioned repatriation to Poland. Instead, the discussion was about making the children more accessible for resettlement missions from countries such as the United States. This made little difference. The displaced persons in the camp, both adults and children, were mostly survivors of Siberia and an inordinately suspicious group, as Jacobs had found, to his misfortune, in 1945. They had little love for the Soviet Union, or for Communism, and saw its machinations everywhere. They were very suspicious of UNRRA and its successor, the IRO. After all, it was an UNRRA representative, Jacobs, who had visited them in 1945, trying to register them and, from their perspective, to repatriate them to Poland. In fact, most of the displaced persons drew little distinction between UNRRA, the IRO, and the Communists. The three blended together into a clear threat from "the Communists"; anyone from outside, or in a position of authority, who spoke of repatriation seems to have been deemed a Communist. Earlier visits that were probably from UNRRA and IRO representatives were remembered as visits from the Polish Communists, because they were discussions about repatriation.

Most of the children had been completely oblivious to the repatriation drives, focused instead on school, the jungle, Tarzan, and swimming. However, some of the older children vaguely remember people they identify as Polish Communists coming to the camp to discuss the possibility of returning to Poland. Sophie Matusiewicz explained that Mrs. Grosicka had told them to attend a meeting where someone was going to talk about repatriation, and to listen to what the people had to say. If any of the children really wanted to go back to Poland, Mrs. Grosicka announced that she would not object. However, if they did not want to return they could simply refuse, which most children did. Sophia Wakulczyk recalls being asked to attend such a meeting as well, in order to report back to the other children what was said. She admits that she didn't really understand much, other than that the speakers were trying to persuade them to return to Poland. Krzysztofa Michniak remembers the Polish Communists visiting the children in Jamnagar. Very few Poles agreed to return, although some did because they had family there, or for other reasons.[13] Those who had returned to Poland were not reluctant to tell their compatriots back in Africa about the abysmal conditions in their homeland, stiffening the resolve not to repatriate.

What the reality was is less easy to discern. It is unclear whether the Polish Communist Government sent delegates to Africa or India in order to pursue displaced persons. The IRO had no record of any such visits, although that is not a definitive answer. The IRO's control over the camps was limited, as was their knowledge of them. On the other hand, UNRRA had actively pursued repatriation opportunities, and the IRO aggressively sought to either repatriate or resettle the remaining displaced persons. UNRRA's reputation was also badly tainted by the disastrous forced repatriation of Soviet prisoners of war and civilians from Germany to the U.S.S.R., in the summer of 1945 (as discussed in Chapter 3, "The Postwar Settlement"). Rumours about the repatriation and what had happened to those who had been forcibly repatriated had reached East Africa, and they were not pretty. While the Poles in East Africa were never in danger of being forcibly repatriated, they did not believe it. Even at the very moment that the IRO was talking of moving the children to Italy, rumours that Warsaw was "categorically demanding" the repatriation of all Polish children in New Zealand did little to allay the Tengeru Poles' fears.[14]

Whether those who visited Tengeru and spoke of repatriation were representatives of the Polish Government in Warsaw, Polish Communists working from within UNRRA and the IRO to advance Communist interests (which happened), or were UNRRA or IRO employees who genuinely believed it would be in the Poles' own best interests to return to Poland was, in one sense, immaterial. They were believed to be Communists and this shaped the Poles' response. It meant that these people would be viewed immediately with suspicion and any proposals they made would be dissected for hidden agendas. In the words of Father Krolikowski, whose opinion reflected that of many in the camp, "In Tengeru we had no proof that the IRO proposal was in any way connected with Polish Communist diplomatic maneuvers; nonetheless we questioned the intentions of the organization."[15]

These suspicions made the Poles very leery of any plans to remove the children from their control. Moving the children to Italy would do just that, and when Lorriman was unable to satisfactorily explain the IRO's plans for the children, their suspicions were heightened. That the children would be cared for by a Catholic organization "in a Polish environment" could be interpreted a number of ways. Given the de-recognition of the Polish Government-in-Exile, the recognition of the Communist Warsaw Government, and UNRRA's and the IRO's sympathies towards the Communist Poles, it could very well be that "a Polish environment" could mean a Communist environment.

The plans for the children had been foisted upon the Poles without consultation and without warning, which didn't help matters. The high-handed behaviour of the IRO, and its insensitivity to the concerns of the Polish elders and the needs of the children, were infuriating. There was a bona fide legal guardian already established for the children in the orphanage; the least that the IRO could have done was consult it. When the children had first arrived in Tanganyika, the High Court of Tanganyika, a British court, had appointed a Board of Guardians. The Board's membership was a mix of British Government officials, their wives, and Polish members. It was chaired by Bishop Edgar Maranta, from Dar es Salaam.[16] This Board, by Tanganyikan law, acted as the children's legal guardian. When the Board heard the news of the pending transfer, it objected strongly, arguing that its permission was needed to move the children. The Board members refused to consider the proposal unless a similar Board of Guardians was established for the children in Italy. The Board suggested that perhaps Mr. Papee, the ambassador to the Vatican of the former Polish Government-in-Exile, and a London Pole, could head it. The Board also demanded that it approve the full details of the system of care and education planned for the orphans.[17] The IRO was non-plussed by this, having not really understood the role or power of the Board of Guardians. There was some discussion within the IRO as to whether the Board of Guardians was even legal, and whether their permission was actually needed. No one wanted to play "the heavy," but it was unclear whether they wanted to allow the Board of Guardians to use the children for what clearly seemed to be their own political interests.[18]

Others were starting to take an interest in these children as well. In early December, Irene Dalgiewicz, Supervisor of Polish Projects of the War Relief Services, National Catholic Welfare Office (NCWC) in Washington DC, sent a list of Polish orphans in Africa to Monsignor Markle of the Canadian episcopate in Ottawa. She wrote hoping that the episcopate would consider sponsoring the children as immigrants to Canada, and offering him the aid of an IRO social worker, Josephine Powell, in the preliminary processing. NCWC had been considering the possibility of moving the children to Germany to facilitate their resettlement. East Africa was so far removed from regular lines of traffic, and therefore from the paths of the various national resettlement missions scouring the camps for potential immigrants, that it was highly unlikely that they would ever get picked up if they remained in East Africa. The NCWC had ultimately decided not to move them to Germany, for fear that representatives of the Warsaw Government would exert pressure to have the children returned to Poland. But the NCWC pledged to do what it could to assist the Canadians' Catholic Immigrant Aid Society, if they were interested in the children.[19]

Markle must have been persuaded because on December 9, 1948, Joseph Charbonneau, Archbishop of Montreal, wrote to Immigration Services in Ottawa requesting permission to bring these Polish children who were suffering "utter neglect" (and whom he mistakenly believed were in Kenya) to Montreal. He proposed that an organization of his Archdiocese, the Société de Protection de l'Enfance, would take care of the children and guide them in life. Apparently the Vatican itself supported the offer to alleviate this instance of human distress.[20]

Canada's Immigration Services was intrigued. Since the end of the war they had received numerous offers from various organizations and individuals to bring orphan children from Europe to Canada, most of which had come to naught. The department had a policy of examining each such application to determine whether the sponsoring organization was financially sound, and had the facilities to deal with such a movement of children. Few passed muster. However, one of the two applications that looked viable was that from the Archbishop and the Catholic Immigrant Aid Society. Of all the proposals that were reviewed, this one seemed promising.[21] Matters were greatly facilitated because the National Catholic Immigrant Society's application for one thousand visas for orphaned children had already been approved. Thus, when the Society approached Ottawa, Ottawa was cautiously interested. A.L. Jolliffe, Director of Immigration Services, spoke to the deputy minister and got his approval for the plan, if arrangements could be made to examine the children in Africa.[22]

The episcopate was keen to act on this project, trying to push matters along with a series of phone calls and polite letters of gratitude. Jolliffe responded at the end of the month that the department was exploring ways of arranging the examination of the children, and that he would be in touch when he had some news.[23] On January 10, 1949, Jolliffe contacted the IRO Mission in Ottawa, asking them whether the IRO would accept responsibility for the transportation of these children to Canada, should their application be approved, and what facilities could be made available for their preliminary examination.[24] J. Colley of IRO Canada replied that the IRO would be quite willing to arrange the children's transportation, if Canada approved their application. However, he was uncertain what facilities were available for examination of the children, explaining that the IRO itself was unable to provide such facilities. He pointed out that a large number of Poles had already come from East Africa to Canada, and arrangements for preliminary examinations had been worked out with the British Consul in those cases. Presumably similar arrangements could be made this time as well.[25]

There were two key parts to the process by which potential immigrants were reviewed: a screening, to ensure that they would be suitable candidates for life in Canada in terms of personality, probity, education, skills, et cetera; and a medical examination, to ensure that they had no physical problems that might render them dependent upon the state for support. Initially, Ottawa needed some way of doing the required medical examinations, including chest x-rays, to ensure that the children were free of tuberculosis. As the IRO was unable to arrange the medical examinations, the Department of External Affairs wrote the Chief Secretary of the Government of Tanganyika. The department asked what facilities were available for these examinations, explaining that it was necessary to determine the children's medical and physical health and fitness for immigration to Canada, before visas could be assigned to them.[26]

At the same time that the Canadian episcopate was talking to the IRO, another organization was also expressing interest in these children. On January 26, 1949, Mrs. N. Warrington of the Repatriates, Poles and EVWs Welfare Department of the Women's Voluntary Services (WVS) in London, paid a visit to the Home Office of the British Government. The WVS was a women's voluntary organization founded by Stella Isaacs, the Dowager Marchioness of Reading, in 1939, to provide support for the Air Raid Precaution services. Among many other services it had helped with the evacuation of children from British cities during the Blitz of September 1939. In the postwar period the WVS continued to operate, shifting its focus to children in need, among other things. The Polish orphans seemed to fit their mandate and Mrs. Warrington proposed the following plan to the Home Office: There were seventy-seven Polish children in an orphanage in Tengeru, facing a prickly situation. With the IRO in the process of winding up its operations in East Africa, the children's future was in question. The Poles in England were "very anxious that the children should be brought to England where ten of them are known to have some connections, and where they would find friendly Poles to welcome them." Warrington pointed out that the children were well brought up and would make "very useful citizens of any country which [would] receive them." Count Raczynski, of ITC fame, had already consulted with Lady Reading, a person of considerable connections and influence, who had approached the Lord Mayor's United Nations' Appeal for Children for support. That organization had granted the WVS £10,000, on the condition that the Home Office would admit the children to the United Kingdom, the IRO would pay their passage to the U.K., and the WVS would assume responsibility for the children. Warrington reported that the IRO appeared interested in the WVS proposal, as long as certain legal difficulties could be overcome. So she was asking Whitehall for permission to bring the children to Britain.

Of the seventy-seven children, approximately twenty could begin work at once, being aged sixteen to eighteen. Warrington estimated that within a year, another eight to ten would be of an age to work, and after two years, another ten to twelve. Thus, she argued, the scheme would be a bonus for the British economy —potentially gaining forty-two new productive workforce members. The WVS pledged to arrange their work placements and to have members supervising the children. The children wouldn't necessarily work in the vicinity of the camp, but wherever they could find employment and ensure that there was a WVS member nearby. The WVS had worked extensively with evacuee children and refugees from Europe, and with Poles in particular, so Warrington felt that the WVS could make this work.

The organization pledged to provide a small camp of approximately ten huts, eight for dormitories and two for recreation and dining. The camp would be located where there were WVS members with appropriate experience, as well as appropriate school and medical facilities. In the camp, the children would initially be supervised by a "very able Polish woman," whose salary might be paid by the Poles in the U.K. The WVS also realized that they would need a cook-caterer, but hoped that one or two of the older girls with younger siblings might be persuaded to remain in the camp to help supervise the young ones, with WVS assistance. The WVS also expected to get the following supplies for free: accommodation, medical and dental service, education, clothing, some food, hygiene products, livestock (hens and goats), furniture, cooking equipment, and holiday hospitality.[27] The Home Office agreed to consider the WVS' proposal. Thus, there were suddenly two potential solutions to the problem of the Polish orphans in Tengeru.

Meanwhile, the IRO's legal staff had concluded that the Board of Guardians was legal, according to Tanganyikan law, although its rule was limited to the children's sojourn in Tanganyika. Certainly the Tanganyikan Government, which was a British colonial Government, was of the opinion that the IRO needed the Board's approval before the children could be moved.[28] However, the IRO was determined that the Board would not be an impediment to it performing its task, which was to successfully resettle the children, and that meant moving them to Europe. The Organization began to put considerable pressure on the Board of Guardians. On February 23, even while these two resettlement schemes were taking shape, Myer Cohen, Assistant Director-General of the Health, Care and Maintenance Department of the IRO, informed the chief of IRO East Africa, H.A. Curtis, that:

> ... [U]nless the Board of Guardians can negotiate before April 1st, 1949 an agreement by which the British Government in East Africa authorises the permanent establishment of all the children and youth who wish to make their future in the territories where they are at present located, the date line for their transfer to Italy will be 1st May 1949.

A camp was being prepared for the children in Italy at Salerno.

> Salerno is situated right on the Mediterranean coast in a beautiful site, 40 km south of Naples, offers a mild climate and all the advantages of an outdoor life in a summer resort on a sandy beach. The children and youth will be able to pursue their studies and training during the period in Italy before they leave for their final destination. Final plans will be made for each on an individual basis, with full consideration of their wishes.[29]

Salerno was an impressive facility. It had originally been built by British troops upon the liberation of Italy, on the very spot where the American and British troops had landed in 1944. It was made up of double-roofed Nissen huts on concrete foundations. The centre had been converted into a Children's and Youth Centre in early 1949, and could accommodate 500 in barracks, with ten to twelve in each barrack, plus an adult leader.

> Special washrooms with showers had been added to the old installation by the Yugoslav displaced workers who have put all their energy and pride into the improvements the camp has to undergo before the arrival of the first inhabitants. A practical kitchen to which is

attached a huge dining room with large windows over-
looking the sea, and two attractive playrooms with open
fireplaces and nicely decorated walls, complete with the
isolation ward and first aid hut, the premises on which
the Rome office is placing all its attention. Salerno
camp and beach are not unknown to the displaced children in the vicinity, who last year spent their best summer vacations there....[30]

As the details for the transfer were worked out, Cohen seemed well
aware of some of the potential pitfalls of such a move. He insisted that
any decisions or plans for reuniting children with parents or relatives be
worked out before the children left East Africa, and that the decisions
be recorded in their files, which would accompany them to Italy. He
also insisted that care be taken not to separate siblings. Any children
with relatives in New Zealand, South Africa, or Australia should be
transferred there immediately. He wanted some of the Polish teachers
from the camp to accompany the children to Salerno, for continuity and
to ensure their continued education.[31] And he wanted all the children in
Mombasa, the nearest port, by April 15, in preparation for shipping out
to Salerno.[32] In early March, the IRO informed both the camp administration and the Board of Guardians of the plans. The Board communicated that it would consider the proposal, and would meet with the IRO
representatives (Curtis and Lorriman) on March 21, to discuss it.

While all this high-level negotiation was going on, rumours were
flying in the camp. While the children remained largely oblivious to the
politics, the Poles in charge of the children and the camp were becoming
increasingly distraught, and the tension mounted.[33] From the children's
perspective, what they "knew" was that the Communists were trying to
get at them, but that the Polish elders in the camp would protect them.
Nonetheless, this unrelenting pressure resulted in some mild panic in
Tengeru, and in Nairobi. A.L. Pennington, Director of Refugees for the
Tanganyikan Government, acting on behalf of the Acting Secretary of
the Tanganyika Territory, wrote both Mrs. Warrington of the WVS, and
the Canadian Department of External Affairs, urging them both to push

their schemes forward quickly. By this time, the number of available orphans had mushroomed from seventy-eight to 132, due to an influx from India and the Rhodesias, where the Polish refugee camps had recently been liquidated. In both cases, Pennington expressed the hope that the schemes could be expanded to accommodate the full 132, but stated that he would be very grateful, as would the Board of Guardians, if they would at least take the original seventy-eight. He explained that the IRO had just informed him they intended moving the children to an IRO camp in Italy, on May 1, unless a firm offer came up that would move them directly from East Africa.[34]

While he didn't explain to the Canadians why this was important, he did to Mrs. Warrington. Well aware of the WVS's sympathies for the London Poles, he wrote that it would:

> ... [S]ave the children concerned a great deal of anxiety. The fact must be faced that, no matter how good the arrangements which it may be possible for IRO to make for them in Italy, the children (and their guardians) will be very alarmed at the idea of their leaving an area under British control, especially for a country where, they feel there is always a possibility of a successful communist 'coup d'etat.' They are all aware of the promise made some years ago by the British government that no Pole (excluding, of course, ordinary criminals) in a British territory should be sent back to Poland against his or her will; and although it has been explained to them over and over again that IRO also will not repatriate refugees or displaced persons against their own wishes, the fact remains that they fear that, once outside a British territory, they may be in some danger of forced repatriation.[35]

His appeal to Ottawa took a slightly different tone, as Canada's position regarding the London Poles was not as clear. Instead, Pennington reassured the Canadians that it was possible to do full medical examinations, and that the children were all good candidates for resettlement in Canada. Thus, there was no need to move the children to Europe.[36]

A quick resolution was not in the near future, however, as both schemes hit snags about this time. By mid-March 1949, the Home Office had finally evaluated the WVS proposal. It was not terribly favourable. W. Storr of the Home Office was skeptical about the scheme's viability. He thought that very few of the children or youths would be able to work. At best, perhaps thirteen of them might be eligible. He was also very skeptical of the scheme's financial viability, given its very small capital of £10,000. Relying on the Polish community in Britain was a mistake, for he well knew that the Poles in England were "not well stocked with funds, and that for even such a necessary and useful work as the provision of an employment bureau they had to approach Government Departments for financial assistance, which was not forthcoming." Furthermore, if the Secretary of State granted visas for these children, he was accepting responsibility for their well-being, no matter what the WVS said. Finally, he argued, Britain had already offered "the maximum amount of assistance in solving the problem of Displaced Persons in the Middle East," and so would not grant permission to this extra batch of people to come into Britain.[37]

The Canadians had their own concerns about the project, when in March the people in Karlsruhe discovered that there were some illegitimate children among the orphans being considered for the movement.[38] When Karlsruhe contacted Ottawa, there was some debate as to whether this made a difference or not. Jolliffe was reluctant to include them in the scheme because he feared "a bad background mean[t] the possibility of accepting an unmanageable or incorrigible child." The acceptance of illegitimate children materially increased the risk, he argued. There was the further questionable point as to whether or not the child was really an orphan.[39] His superior, the Deputy Minister for Mines and Resources , the department responsible for immigration affairs, was not convinced by Jolliffe's arguments, nor was the Minister. Both felt that the illegitimate children should be accepted, as there was no evidence that they were any greater risk than others. What was key was their upbringing. The skilled investigators reviewing the cases would be able to determine both whether the children were truly orphaned or not, and whether they were suitable candidates or not. Excluding illegitimate children en masse, because they may or may not truly be orphans, would be a mistake. Instead, they should be admitted, if they met the admission criteria.[40] A cable was sent to Karlsruhe notifying them that illegitimate children could be included in the Catholic orphans movement.[41]

Meanwhile, the international climate was souring. The Canadian Delegation to the United Nations wrote the Secretary of State for External Affairs in Ottawa in early March, warning that the representative for Poland in the United Nations' General Assembly had attacked the IRO for focusing its efforts on resettlement, rather than repatriation. This, of course, was true, as most of the remaining Polish displaced persons were generally hostile to the notion of returning home and forcible repatriation was not an option. As the IRO's overarching mandate was to empty the camps, it sensibly emphasized resettlement for these particular displaced persons. It was, nonetheless, an embarrassing and misleading accusation. What was even more damning was when the Polish representative protested that the IRO was "a gigantic help-wanted agency selling cheap labour to the Marshallized countries of Europe," and made a specific reference to labour camps in western Canada.[42]

In a meeting of the Social Committee of the United Nations, the Polish representative, Mr. Katz-Suchy, accused Canada of working its Polish displaced persons long hours for poor pay, making them live in miserable conditions, and threatening to deport any who protested. He cited one instance in particular, that of a number of the Polish women hired by Mr. Dionne, a Canadian Member of Parliament and owner of a textile mill in Quebec. Katz-Suchy accused him of being:

> ... [E]ager to take his share in the humanitarian work undertaken by the International Refugee Organization and recruited a hundred girls from camps for displaced persons in Germany; he compelled them to sign two-year contracts, cloistered them in a nunnery and restricted their freedom of movement. Tired of working for almost no pay, eighty-four of them ran away. That

transaction was effected with the full knowledge of the IRO.[43]

The Canadian Department of External Affairs was quick to provide the Canadian U.N. Delegation with a response, should the challenge arise again. One hundred Polish women had been admitted to Canada to work for Dionne. Each signed a two-year contract to work under normal conditions for normal rates of pay. Part of their pay was deducted and held in a savings account for them, but the money was freely accessible. In fact, forty-seven of them dipped into their savings in October 1947, to purchase winter clothing. They were accommodated in a hostel run by nuns, not a convent, and while there was a curfew, their movements were not otherwise restricted. Indeed, by December 1948, only eight remained at the Dionne mills. It was hardly the slave labour camp described by the Polish representative.[44]

The Byelorussian representative, Mr. Stepanenko, had also taken up the attack, claiming that the Canadian press had reported that the displaced persons were much more productive than Canadian workers. The real reason these people had been brought to Canada was not humanitarian, but economic. They were "imported" in order to do the work Canadians refused to do. The Soviet U.N. representative, Mr. Maevsky, also complained that there were hundreds of children in German displaced persons camps being sent to countries other than their homelands, and accused the IRO of recruiting cheap labour for capitalist enterprises in the United States, Great Britain, France, Canada, and certain Latin American countries, where they worked as forced labour without any rights.

In fact, Canada was not the chief target of this attack — far from it. The Poles' chief targets were the United Kingdom in particular, as well as the United States, with Canada caught in the crossfire. Belgium, France, and various Latin American countries had been subjected to marked and repeated criticism as well.[45] The Polish Government was engaged in an ongoing, low-level assault against all Western countries, accusing them of preventing the repatriation of hundreds of thousands of Poles "for the political purpose of obstructing the people's-democratic countries and for the economic purpose of supplying cheap labor to

the US, the Marshall Plan countries and to countries beyond the seas."
According to at least some observers, it was "a moot point as to whether
the Polish Government was more interested in obtaining the return of
the Poles ... or in exploiting for propaganda purposes another instance of
Western 'intransigence'."[46] Still, the accusations were embarrassing. And
the Polish Government kept up the diatribe throughout the spring.[47]

Pressure was mounting on all sides, and the tension was building both
in Nairobi and Tengeru. On March 21, as arranged, the IRO's Curtis and
Lorriman arrived in Tengeru to meet with the Board of Guardians to
discuss the pending move to Italy. However, when Curtis and Lorriman
arrived at the camp, they discovered that their appointment at noon had
been superseded by a visit from the Acting Governor of Tanganyika, who
had arrived at 10:00 a.m. The Board had pre-empted them. In a private
meeting with the governor at the camp, the Board presented him with a
letter of appeal, written on March 16, but hand-delivered that day. In it,
the Board objected to the hasty decision made by the IRO to remove the
children. They argued that there were at least two possible resettlement
schemes in the works — the British and the Canadian. Both were well-
advanced, but needed more time to come to fruition. The Board was
fearful because they were aware that Warsaw was pressing New Zealand
to repatriate the Polish orphans in that country and, while they knew
that there was no connection between the two instances, now that the
IRO was going to remove these children from East Africa, who knew
what that could mean? So the Board appealed to the governor to uphold
Tanganyikan law and demand that the IRO postpone its move for three
months, until July 15, while still continuing to support the children
financially. This would allow the schemes to mature.[48]

While Curtis and Lorriman cooled their heels, waiting for a meeting with the Board that would never happen, the governor read the letter.
He, rather than the Board, then met with Curtis, and informed him that
he believed a three-month delay was a reasonable request and so supported it. He also stated that he would strongly recommend this position
both to Pennington, his Director of Refugees, and, if necessary, even to
the Secretary of State for the Colonies in London. The governor has-
tened to explain that he was not trying to thwart the IRO, as he agreed

that the move to Italy was probably in the children's best interests, but explained that it was a matter of principle. The Board of Guardians was a legal body, with ultimate authority over the children. It had "every right to consideration of its wishes and opinions on the subject of the future of the children under their care."

Curtis was quite annoyed. He didn't believe either of the schemes were going to amount to anything, as they had been in the works for eighteen months and nothing had happened yet. He figured this was just a political game being played by the Board of Guardians, and that every member of the Board knew their fear of forced repatriation was "nonsense." Curtis wanted closure on this matter quickly, both because it was in the children's best interests, to his mind, and because if the IRO backed down now any future orders for movements would be ignored, and IRO's "prestige [would] have sunk to zero."

The whole affair had become a game of brinksmanship. Ignoring the Board and the governor, Curtis issued the orders to move the children to Mombasa by April 15. Mr. Lorriman again asked the camp commandant to approach suitable teachers to act as escorts to Italy (no one had accepted as yet). Officially, the move was still going forward. Curtis was not optimistic that it would happen on time, but he was also not ready to abandon the effort as he felt it was vital that the move happen quickly. So he asked his superior, Myer Cohen, to approach the Secretary of State for Colonies in London, the governor's superior and, in the stilted language of the cables of the day, "to convince them patent reasonableness of long term move, inform them Guardians are obstructing and induce them cable instructions Tanganyika Government to facilitate move as planned." He also asked Cohen for permission to cut off funding for any children remaining in Tengeru after May 1. Without that kind of weight behind IRO's order, Cohen was certain the move wouldn't happen by the deadline.[49]

The Board of Guardians reiterated its objections in a communication to Curtis on March 23. In it, the Board repeated its request for the three-month delay, to allow time for the two applications (to Canada and Great Britain) to produce results. The Board expressed great alarm at the prospect of moving the children out from under their care and from the British Commonwealth, without a more definite resettlement program in place. "In Italy, as you know," wrote the Board,

> ... there is a very strong communist influence so much so that the communist leader has stated in the Italian Parliament that if the Soviets attacked Italy the communists would welcome the entry of the Russian Army and in view of the repeated efforts of the Warsaw communist dominated Government's efforts to have the orphans repatriated, it is our considered opinion that the proposed move to Italy is not in the best interests of these children and we as their Guardians will resist this move by every means in our power.[50]

As Lorriman pointed out to Curtis, the concern about the Italian Communists got to the heart of the Board's true fears — the fear that the children would be forcibly repatriated to Poland. That same day, Curtis warned the Commissioner of the East Africa Refugees Administration and the IRO representative in Nairobi to expect delays in the children's transfer.[51] Meanwhile, his staff continued to compile nominal rolls of the children's names and personal data. By the end of March, there were 141 children and youths for transfer.[52]

On March 26, 1949, the request for a three-month delay became official with a cable from the Director of Refugees in Dar es Salaam, on behalf of the Governor of Tanganyika. That was closely followed by a more detailed letter from Pennington. In it, he described the state of negotiations, both with the WVS and with the Canadian Department of External Affairs and his optimism that one of them would bear fruit.[53]

At this moment, the London Poles waded into the chaos. K. Papee, the Ambassador for Poland to the Vatican, and an appointee of the former Polish Government-in-Exile, wrote IRO East Africa to inform them that the Canadian episcopate had indeed offered to take in the Polish orphans from the Tengeru camp, and that negotiations had begun with the Canadian Government for admission. He argued that, in light of this, "sending the children to Italy would be quite useless and unnecessary."[54]

Everything hinged on the results of the two appeals — the British and the Canadian — and pressure was mounting back in the potential recipient countries. In Britain, the WVS was not only being pushed by Pennington, but by the Lord Mayor's Fund, who was anxious to know what was being done with its £10,000. In late March, Lady Reading contacted Mrs. Warrington to find out the state of the proposal, as the Home Office had not yet communicated its decision. Mrs. Warrington put her in touch with Mr. Storr.[55] When Lady Reading met with Mr. Storr she was informed that the scheme had not been approved.

He offered her several reasons for the denial. It had always been a principle of the IRO that unaccompanied children should be encouraged to return to their country of origin and, in fact, the Warsaw Government already had been protesting that "we [the British were] snatching Polish children away from their own country." The Home Office saw no point in stirring up trouble when it didn't really want to bring in these children anyway. Second, Mr. Storr explained, past experience with the Polish refugees suggested that if these orphans were brought to the U.K. either their parents or other relatives would suddenly appear and would then qualify for entry into the U.K. as well, because of their relationship to the supposed orphans! Third, he argued that it was not clear there had been any attempts made yet to resettle these children elsewhere, and the Home Office was a bit perturbed that no other alternatives had even been explored. Furthermore, the Home Office's experience with recent Ukrainian immigrants was that it would cost between £6,000 and £8,000 annually to maintain these children with appropriate supervision, a budget that the WVS patently did not have, and a cost the British Government was not willing to incur. Finally, Mr. Storr argued that Britain had already done more than its fair share of providing for the displaced persons, and especially the Poles, and "until the other nations in the IRO [had] assumed a burden more commensurate with that of the United Kingdom, the Home Secretary [felt] bound to scrutinise most carefully any schemes of immigration for further classes of displaced persons."[56]

The WVS continued to push and the Home Office, in the end, reluctantly offered to admit five children who were found to qualify under Operation Pole Jump, and three who were found to have relatives who had come to Britain under the European Voluntary Workers Scheme (even though the scheme had been explicitly intended only for those displaced persons with no dependents).[57] To admit more would be impossible "without exposing [the Home Office] to a flood of fresh applications from Poles in East Africa who are not qualified to come here under present policy." The WVS would be financially responsible for the maintenance and education of the children, as they would not be eligible for support through the Polish Resettlement Act. Nor could this concession be construed to mean, in any way, that the British Government was "prepared to accept any further liabilities in respect of Polish refugees remaining in Africa."[58] In view of the changed circumstances, the Lord Mayor's Fund, without whose funding the WVS could not care for the children, decided against the scheme and, on May 18, the WVS informed both the Home Office and the Poles of their decision to abandon the project.[59] The Home Office thanked Lady Reading and the WVS for having saved the British Government considerable embarrassment.[60] Now the children's only hope was the Canadian proposal.

# 5 | Confrontation

With the British Government's refusal of the Women's Voluntary Services' proposal, the Canadian proposal became the only likely solution for the orphans, although neither the IRO nor the Board of Governors knew that yet. Meanwhile, the IRO was increasing the pressure in Dar es Salaam to permit the children's movement. By April 1, 1949, Curtis had heard from IRO Geneva that, while Canada was a definite possibility, it was not yet a probability. As no proposal was firm, contingency plans had to be made. All that was known at that point was that the episcopate was keen to have the children, but no one wanted to make assumptions. Curtis' instructions were to stand firm and insist on the May 1 deadline for moving the children to Mombasa, and then Salerno. While he was willing to do everything possible to make it happen, Curtis was also skeptical of what he considered to be an optimistic deadline.

The opinion in Geneva was that the children would be in Salerno for about three months, and undergo a proper screening there. Most were expected to go to Canada, although nothing was certain. In Salerno, not only would the children be screened, but they would be taught about the new Poland, so that they could make an informed decision about whether to repatriate or not. The IRO would provide a comprehensive educational and cultural program.[1] Of course, such long-term planning for the children suggested that they were going to be in Italy for a while, which ran contrary to the Board of Guardians' wishes that they be resettled quickly. Too long a delay in Italy would only heighten the distress and suspicions in Tengeru, and IRO East Africa knew that. Curtis pressed his superiors to make every effort to get either Canada or the U.K. to approve the children. Brigadier Lush, of the Resettlement Division in Geneva, promised that he would communicate with both Canada and the U.K. in an effort to expedite the children's reception.[2]

Meanwhile, the IRO informed the Secretariat in Tanganyika that, although everything was being done to facilitate the proposal for the children's resettlement in Canada, the children were going to have to pass through Italy for a final tracing check for possible relatives "because of … international commitments," a polite, if vague euphemism for the political realities of the IRO's situation, and the anticipated protests that would erupt from Warsaw.[3] The wish to do a final tracing check was not unusual. Whenever an unaccompanied child was discovered, the IRO's procedure was the same. The child's particulars were collected — their original home, names and addresses of any family members the children knew about, the children's history, et cetera. This information was forwarded to the IRO's International Tracing Service, who sought to track down any family members, their key objective being to reunite families. Until the tracing exercise was completed, the IRO was reluctant to let a child move. It only seemed proper to do one last tracing check before allowing any resettlement mission to speak with them.

There was no way to ignore the politics of the situation. Although Warsaw did not sit on the General Council of the IRO, it did have a delegation to the U.N., and it could create considerable embarrassment for the IRO at that level. Furthermore, the IRO was required by its constitution to explore the possibility of repatriation with any displaced person first, and only when that alternative did not appear viable could they explore resettlement possibilities. The IRO could not be seen as avoiding this obligation, especially in this particular case. Then there was the thorny issue of the children's age. Generally it was accepted that children who were not of the age of majority were not able to make decisions for themselves. In those cases the IRO's and the American military Government's regulations stipulated that any unaccompanied child was to be "repatriated or resettled in accord with the wishes of the government of the established country of nationality."[4] Although there was still a certain degree of bickering over whether the age of majority was sixteen, seventeen, eighteen, or even twenty-one (as the Poles insisted), the policy created a sticky situation for the IRO. Warsaw, as the recognized government of the established country of nationality, legally had the final say in the children's disposition. Thus, Warsaw's wishes could not be simply ignored or dismissed out of hand. On the other hand, the IRO also had a policy of not forcibly repatriating anyone, not even an individual who was legally a child, but old enough to comprehend and contribute to the decisions made as to its disposition. These were the very real constraints within which the IRO was operating, constraints that the Tengeru Poles were ignoring. The IRO concluded by pointing out to the Secretariat that, in view of the short life left to it, any further delay could mean it might be forced to withdraw financial support from these displaced persons.[5]

In Dar es Salaam, Governor Surridge obfuscated, cabling back to the IRO that they didn't understand why the children needed a final tracing check, as all available information about the orphans' missing relatives had been in the IRO's possession for months, and neither the orphans nor the orphanage staff could add anything more, whether they were located in Tanganyika or in Italy. The Secretariat suggested again that it seemed reasonable to delay their transfer to Italy for three months, until there was a final answer concerning the applications to the U.K. and Canada.[6]

Brigadier Lush immediately responded, explaining to Governor Surridge that neither the Canadian nor the U.K. scheme was at all certain, so the IRO had to pursue other alternatives as well — such as resettlement in Australia or New Zealand. As selection missions would not visit Africa, the children had to be moved to Italy so that they could more easily be interviewed by selection missions, whether it was the Canadian mission or another. Lush pleaded with Surridge to realize that the IRO was "really working in the best interests of the children and to persuade the Board of Guardians likewise."[7]

Lush's pleas were followed up by a letter from Sir Arthur Rucker himself, directed to the U.K. Delegate to the IRO, and sent on the same day that Lush sent the second cable to Surridge. In it, Sir Arthur hit hard, pushing London to pressure the Tanganyikan Government, which ultimately reported to Whitehall, and to make Tanganyika cooperate in the IRO's transfer of the children. He explained:

> IRO has given careful consideration to the move of these children and has decided to adhere to its original plan to move them to Italy for the following reasons:
>
> i) Neither the Canadian nor U.K. projects are in their final form.
> ii) Both the above may fail and in this case it is essential that the children should be available for interview by Australian and New Zealand Selection Missions.
> iii) If the Canadian project succeeded, it would be necessary for a member of the Canadian Selection Team to see the children. He would not go to East Africa.
> iv) Final tracing can be conducted more expeditiously from Italy than from Mombasa.
> v) It is essential to liquidate the East African refugee problem.
>
> IRO Geneva has also come to the regretful decision that if the move of these children is made impossible by the obstruction of the Board or Boards of Guardians in East Africa, IRO will be compelled to treat the case as one of refugees refusing to avail themselves of reasonable offers of resettlement and to withdraw its assistance. This has been communicated to the Board of Guardians and to the Governor's Deputy.[8]

If the children refused to move, the IRO was going to cut off their funding. And the IRO continued to make its plans, drawing up the nominal rolls of the children to be moved to Salerno on May 1 and arranging for Charlotte Babinski, a tracing officer from the International Tracing

Service, to be sent to Salerno to work with the children. She was selected because of her skill in the Polish language, as well as her experience in interviewing and casework.[9]

In the face of this pressure, the camp's inhabitants fought back. The next salvo was a letter from the Camp Commandant, Captain Williams, addressed to Curtis (Williams had replaced Colonel Minnery at some point). Its ostensible purpose was to confirm the discussions that Curtis had had with the Board of Guardians on April 8 about the situation. Williams' real purpose was to correct an apparent misconception of Curtis'. He explained that Curtis was mistaken if he believed the Poles in Tengeru opposed resettling the children. Rather, they were driven by "well founded fears of Italy as a selection area." Their fears were based on several factors: the political conditions in Eastern Europe; and the fact that Italy was under "great communist influence" and if there was a Communist coup there, "no organization in the world would be able to dictate the destiny of these children," especially as the Communist Warsaw Government had already and repeatedly demanded the children's repatriation. They had even received a warning recently from the Polish Ambassador to the Vatican, Papee, suggesting it was inadvisable to send the children to Italy. He argued, as did the Board, that only a very quick movement through Italy would ensure the children's safety and that could only happen if the children were already visaed before entering Italy.

The fear of Italy was grounded in the tremendous strength of the Italian Communist Party. In the April 1948 election in that country, there had been considerable concern, both domestically and internationally, that the Italian Communists, as part of a Marxist Popular Front coalition with the Italian Socialist Party, might actually win the election and take the country into the Communist bloc. The Pope himself had interceded in the electoral campaign to tell the Italians that to vote for the Popular Front would be to vote against Christ. Washington had taken a close interest in the election's outcome and had made clear both its grave concern about the Communist threat and its own preference for victor. It was an election about ideology, rather than issues. While the Christian Democrats won a solid victory, the Communist Party sat in opposition, having won 31 percent of the vote.[10] Thus, from the perspective of the Tengeru Poles, the Italian Communist threat may have been defeated in the election, but it hardly appeared vanquished.

No one, Williams declared, objected to the children going to Canada, but as well, no one understood why the children had to go to Italy, and especially for three months or more. The children themselves were becoming a handful, as "the children cannot see that they are any different as human beings to those children who have parents and they therefore reproach the Board with throwing them away and doing nothing about the other children who have parents." Many families in the camp were offering to "absorb into their families" these orphans, rather than see them abandoned in this fashion. The atmosphere in the camp was deteriorating badly.

Williams reminded Curtis that the Poles had requested he try to get Canada to send a selection mission to East Africa to screen the children. It would not be the first time they had sent such a team, and it wouldn't cost any more than the previous trips had. (This would have been news to Curtis and Lush, who knew of no such selection missions visiting Africa.) At the same time, the team could also interview the adult population for positions as farmworkers or domestics. Perhaps, even, as the IRO representative at Tengeru was Canadian, he could be approved by the Canadian Government as an official representative who could screen the children? Williams pointed out that Curtis had also promised to cable Geneva, requesting a selection team be sent to East Africa; to inform Geneva there had been no organized obstruction in the camp; and to obtain authorization to visa the children before they left Tengeru. All the Board of Guardians was asking was the children be accepted either to the United Kingdom or to Canada and fully visaed before leaving.[11]

It was all a bit disingenuous. The crux of the problem, according to Curtis, lay with the attitude prevalent in the camp. From his perspective, the Poles were not keen to resettle and the camp's staff, both Polish and British, shared that reluctance. Curtis had even heard Captain Williams say several times that he didn't know why the IRO was there at all, "always pestering people to go places where they don't want to go." Although Curtis acknowledged Williams to be "an excellent and able fellow, though old," and an excellent commandant for a small camp of hardcore displaced persons, he just did not and would not understand the resettlement policy. Nor did he understand that it was the IRO, not the British Government, who ran the camp. Thus, although it was a good, as in well-run, camp, it was not "movement-minded." The combination of a well-established facility with farm, educational system, cinema, and out-of-camp employment, with the attitude of the staff and inhabitants and a deep-seated belief that Tengeru would not close, meant they were not inclined to cooperate with the IRO on this particular project. Williams' appeal to Curtis to delay was to no avail. Curtis soon informed Pennington, Director of Refugees, that IRO Headquarters in Geneva had not agreed to postpone the children's transfer to Italy.[12]

When he broke the news to Captain Williams and the Board of Guardians, he tried to couch it in as sympathetic a language as he could.

> I really do appreciate the anxieties of the Board....
> I do not think the guardians genuinely fear forced
> repatriation to Poland, since this is clearly not even
> a remote possibility, and I think their fears of com-
> munism in Italy are exaggerated. The real fear, with
> which I have much sympathy, is that some, if not all,
> of the children may be in Italy for a considerable time
> and not accepted for any country. Having seen the
> children, I think this is very unlikely.... It is clearly
> most desirable, if possible, that the children should
> have visas for a final destination before they leave. At
> the request of the Board, I have sent a strong appeal
> to Lush asking him to do his best to persuade a
> Canadian Immigration Officer to come here as soon
> as possible...."[13]

Although Curtis was not optimistic that this would happen, his promise raised false expectations among the Poles, as well as reinforced their determination to fight the children's removal.

In Ottawa, the episcopate was getting increasingly anxious, pressing Jolliffe's department for an answer. Pennington's letter informing the

Canadians that the medical examinations could be performed in East Africa and requesting the Canadians to accelerate the process appears to have gone astray, at least temporarily, as Jolliffe informed the episcopate that nothing could be decided until they had heard from Tanganyika. In fact, the letter had been received by E.H. Gilmour, Under-Secretary of State for External Affairs, but not yet passed on to Jolliffe. The episcopate began to pester Immigration, pushing for a quick decision. The information about the medical examinations finally reached the Department of Immigration. This resolved one obstacle, only to be replaced by another. The increase in number, from seventy-nine to 132, required both a written acknowledgement from the Archbishop accepting responsibility for the additional children and that notice be sent to Dar es Salaam of the increased number. All of this was settled within a week, and the episcopate again pressed that the process to bring the children to Canada start right away. By this time, however, Ottawa had also been informed of the IRO's plan to move the children to a camp in Italy unless there was some likelihood that they could be accepted for immigration directly from East Africa to Canada or some other country.[14]

At the same time, Immigration came up with yet another hurdle for the episcopate to jump, informing the Archbishop that he needed permission for the children's admission in writing from the Ontario and Quebec provincial governments. "Upon production of these documents," wrote Jolliffe, "further consideration will be given to this matter." He also mentioned that he understood the IRO was keen to move the children to Italy, to facilitate their screening. Immigration found this an appealing prospect, as it meant that Canadian officers could then do the medical examinations and screening themselves, without having to travel to East Africa.[15]

Unbeknownst to any outside of Ottawa, Canada had actually been considering establishing a special mission to East Africa to screen the children. However, before the decision was made, news had arrived that the IRO had made arrangements to move the children to Italy. With that news, the proposed East African mission was abandoned.[16] There was a brief flurry of communications between IRO Canada and the Immigration Branch confirming that the Canadians were both interested in all 132 children (which indeed they were) and preferred to have the children moved to Italy for screening. Then Canadian External Affairs sent a cable to Dar es Salaam, informing them that the Immigration Branch was considering the admission of all 132 Polish orphans located in Tengeru, but that the children should be moved to Italy by May 1, where Canadian immigration officials could examine them, as there was no Canadian Immigration Officer in East Africa.[17] Unfortunately, this news didn't reach Nairobi until April 21.[18]

Things continued to get increasingly tense in Tengeru, as the deadline for departure neared. Brigadier Lush warned Curtis that the Board of Guardians was still hostile to the whole plan, contrary to Curtis' hope that at least Pennington had been brought onside. Although disappointed, Curtis decided that they "would proceed with arrangements for the move, [as] everything possible has been done which could be done by us to ensure that it will take place." He wrote Lush, "I refuse even to consider at the moment what action will be necessary if the children do not entrain on the appointed day."[19]

The case for moving the children to Italy was considerably strengthened at this point when the American Government announced that it was going to allow an additional two thousand Polish orphans, up to the age of nineteen, into the United States, a jump from three thousand to five thousand. However, the new regulations did not apply to Africa. The regulations instead stated specifically that, in order to qualify, the orphans had to be in Italy or in the Western occupation zones of Germany or Austria. The selection was expected to begin in about two months. This meant, then, if the children currently in East Africa were transferred to the camp in Italy, they would qualify for this new programme and those who did not get accepted by Canada would be entitled to be admitted to the United States.[20]

It is unclear whether news of this latest development ever reached Tengeru. News of another development did, however, and it galvanized the camp. By April 4, rumour had reached Tengeru that the IRO was threatening to cut off funding for the children if they didn't leave for Italy by the deadline of April 28. On the heels of that rumour, news arrived from the Vatican that the Canadians had agreed to take the Polish orphans under the care of the episcopate in Montreal (they hadn't), and that the episcopate was negotiating with the Canadian Government to have the medical examinations and the screening for the visas done in Tanganyika (it wasn't). Ambassador Papee wrote, "Under those conditions, the transfer of the children to Italy is now, more than ever, pointless; therefore, steps have been taken to prevail upon the IRO to abandon the project."[21]

With this hopeful news in hand, the Board of Guardians continued in its opposition. Word soon reached the camp that special carriages had been arranged to transport the children from Tengeru to Mombasa, en route to Italy. The Board of Guardians met on April 20, and was unanimous in its decision to withhold their approval of the move. They continued to fear that without visas in hand upon leaving many of the children would not reach British territory, and would find themselves repatriated, voluntarily or not. They had word secondhand from Count Raczynski that the negotiations with the Women's Voluntary Services had been "progressing well" until Warsaw interfered, which had put a stop to those negotiations, a damaging misrepresentation of what had actually transpired, but serving to heighten the Board's fears. They had also received a letter from Reverend Father Maciaszek, a former Tengeru inhabitant, who had gone to Turin, Italy, to await transit to Argentina. His letter complained about the unpleasant and cold weather, the crowded accommodations, the food (which was of sufficient quantity, but poor quality), the high price of everything, and the interminable wait. Maciaszek warned that the Italian Communist Party worked quite openly and effectively in Italy, and he had been told that "the population of this suburb of Turyn (*sic*) [were] communists." His advice was that "anyhow do what they can to avoid Italy."[22]

Then the bad news hit the camp in a double blow. The telegram from the Canadian Department of External Affairs finally arrived on April 21, reporting that the Canadian Immigration authorities were quite willing to consider admitting all 132 orphans to Canada, but that they "would be quite satisfied if orphans were to be moved on May 1 to Italy where Canadian Immigration officials could examine them as there is no Canadian Immigration Officer in East Africa."[23] A second cable arrived at the same time from Mrs. Warrington, informing the Poles that she "bitterly regret[ted] to inform [that] Home Office will not agree to take any orphans except possible the fourteen with sisters or brothers ... in England."

The bad news did little to change the Board's mind, however, as Lorriman warned Curtis. "I am asked to explain to you that the fears and objection of the Board of Guardians are not lessened by the news, as the Warsaw Government is evidently now aware of the impending move and may demand of the Italian Government that the children be handed over."[24]

Indeed, the Board's response was even more blunt. On April 22, immediately upon receipt of these telegrams, the Board sent a cable to the Director of Refugees announcing that its opposition to the move was even more adamant now that it was clear that Canada might refuse to admit some children if they didn't pass inspection in Italy. This was unacceptable, as it would endanger those children and put them in peril of repatriation. The Board announced that it would oppose the move until Canada agreed to have the medicals done and visas issued in Tengeru, before the children left the camp. It advised the Director of Refugees to cancel the railway coaches that had been booked for April 28, and carbon copied the cable to the IRO offices in Nairobi.[25]

The EARA tried to reassure the Board, arguing that there was every possible indication, short of an actual guarantee, that Canada would accept all 132 orphans as soon as they were inspected in Italy. Refusing to let the children go to Italy, when even the IRO representative in Ottawa recommended the move, would "seriously jeopardize" the children's future. In any case, it explained, those children not under the Board's guardianship (that is, those who had been moved into the camp recently as a result of the consolidation of the IRO camps) would still be moved to Mombasa, so that they might be considered for the Canadian and other resettlement programmes.[26] And on April 23, the camp commandant received a cable informing him of the details of the pending transfer.

> Orphans and unaccompanied children en route to Canada, via Italy, will leave Tengeru Camp for the Tengeru railway station at 7.00 hours on Thursday

28th April for English Point Camp, Mombasa. Embussing will take place at the orphanage, entraining will be completed by 08.30 hours, the train will leave at 08.45 hours.[27]

The atmosphere in the camp had turned extremely sour by this time. Lorriman vented his frustration to Curtis, sending him "a sample of the kind of tripe that is going on here." The camp had been planning a couple of dances, to which Lorriman, as the local IRO representative, normally would have been invited. On April 24, however, he received two short notes. One was from the Polish Culture Officer of the camp, who wrote, "I am sorry to inform you that the dance party announced tonight will not take place. On account of the move of orphans ordered by the IRO the people of the Camp do not feel like enjoying themselves to-day." The second was from the director of the school who informed Lorriman that the high school dance that was to happen that night was also cancelled, "as an expression of sympathy towards the orphans." Lorriman explained, frustrated, that "this change of plans took place right after church to-day. Perhaps that is not significant. These dances had been arranged for some time marking the end of Lent. Don't mind me, I didn't want to dance anyway."[28]

Pressure was also being brought to bear in London, where rumours were flying. Mr. Jordan of the Polish Combatants Association in London visited A.W. Wilkinson of the Refugees Department of the Foreign Office on 25 April, to find out what exactly the IRO was planning. Among several questions he raised about the status of Polish displaced persons, he told Wilkinson that the Poles in East Africa had informed him that the Polish unaccompanied children there were being sent to Europe for repatriation to Poland. He claimed to have dismissed it as a rumour, but when he asked the IRO for confirmation of his belief, he had received a rather noncommittal reply to the effect that the report could be neither confirmed nor denied, but that the children's wishes would be taken into account. It was a disturbing response for someone seeking a clear and definitive answer. Wilkinson explained that the IRO was being cagey because "they could not guarantee that every child would be resettled and could not give a written guarantee that none would be repatriated, since the former would raise false hopes and the latter might lead to international friction." It was also his belief that the IRO would succeed in resettling them all, and that it really was in the children's best interests to move to Italy, as they stood no chance of resettlement if they stayed in Africa. He further warned that, if they refused to move, they would probably lose out on any schemes to resettle hardcore displaced persons, and "that they could expect to face grim privations and possible deportation to Poland...." The British Government felt that by refusing to cooperate with the IRO, the Tengeru Poles were doing a considerable disservice to the other Polish displaced persons by unnecessarily using up precious funds that could be used to assist others in their resettlement. Mr. Jordan seemed to accept this, but pointed out that the rumours were very damaging. In a letter to Sir Arthur Rucker, warning him of this conversation, Mr. Boothby of the Foreign Office cautioned Sir Arthur to "make sure that these Poles are handled with the necessary tact and firmness. Careful study of their rather peculiar psychology may result in a breakdown of their present resistance."[29] The implication was that if this wasn't done, disaster loomed on the horizon.

By now it was clear that the British Government had withdrawn its support for the Board, and on April 25, Curtis sent a telegram to Geneva telling his superiors at IRO Headquarters that the Tanganyikan Government had informed Tengeru the previous day that "it now consider[ed] IRO's present proposals reasonable and for orphans' benefit it [could] no longer support Guardians' application for delay departure."[30]

Undaunted and desperate, on April 26, the camp population threw down the gauntlet. In a general meeting, the camp population formally passed a set of resolutions demanding that the Canadian Government be asked to visa the children before they left Tengeru, and that the children not be moved before that happened. The children would not be allowed to leave without Polish supervisors, who would accompany them until the moment when they were turned over to the appropriate people in Canada.[31]

Unaware of the brewing crisis, or in spite of it, Marie Lane, Chief of the Health, Care and Maintenance Department for IRO Geneva, sent on the children's particulars to Admiral Mentz, Chief of Mission for IRO Rome, so he could prepare for the children's arrival. She stressed in her letter to him that "this group will need to be handled with more than usual care," as he should be able to tell from the report she had included. The most recent news that she had was the movement was supposed to have started on April 28, but they expected great resistance. Hopefully, she wrote, the delay wouldn't be too great.

The report was revealing, and hinted at the growing challenge and frustration that the IRO was feeling in dealing with this particular group. Lane provided Mentz with a statistical breakdown of the children, but warned him that the numbers kept changing. Sixty-one of the now 163 children stated that England was their destination of choice. Ninety-one preferred Canada, ten preferred to remain in Africa, and one preferred Australia, for a total of 163, including the ten who preferred Africa. Of the 163, fifty were male children; thirty-three were male youths; forty-six were female children, and thirty-four were female youths.

The numbers and names, however, changed constantly. Some children were suddenly claimed by relatives who appeared from nowhere. Some had become over age in the interim, or were found to be older than originally reported. Some older siblings intended to remove their younger siblings from the group, as soon as they themselves had found a permanent residence and were able to support their younger brothers and/or sisters. Lane warned Mentz that there was little accurate information available about the children. Many didn't know where they were born, their age, or even their parents' Christian names. The records were also very unreliable and incomplete. Mrs. Grosicka, who was head of the orphanage, had her own records, but there appeared to be serious errors in the ages recorded and there was no way of knowing which was correct. Lane recommended to Mentz that if the tracing officers in Salerno were unable to sort this out, it might make sense to have a physician determine their physical age and a psychologist determine their mental age, combine the results and come up with a proper age for each child whose birthdate was in doubt, and issue them certificates to that effect. This was crucial for eventual placement in schools, as well as determining their status for employment, marriage, and legal responsibilities, among other things. According to the records, the ages ranged from ten to twenty-one years, with some exceptions: a two-year-old illegitimate child, whose mother was deceased, and five youths aged twenty-one to twenty-four years old, with younger siblings in the camp whom they were unable to support. Forty-three of the younger children had thirty-two older siblings, who were unaccompanied youths, in the camp. The older siblings were being included in the move because the IRO didn't want to break up the family groups.

Lane further warned Mentz to take the information on the attached nominal roll with a grain of salt. While it listed what was known of the children's relatives, she advised that the relationships were not be taken too literally. She suspected that many of the "aunts" and "uncles" were actually unrelated sponsors and friends. It also seemed that twenty-four of the children (fourteen family groups in total) had either a father or mother in Poland, although none had both parents there. These children claimed to have letters from their parents telling them not to return to Poland, and the IRO staff had actually seen a few of these letters. In one case, the mother of two of the girls, Czeslawa and Bronislawa Morawska, had been traced recently in Poland and she had requested that the girls be returned to her. Czeslawa was already twenty-two years old and working in Dar es Salaam, but she didn't have permanent residence there so she was unable to provide for her sister, who was still in the orphanage. The IRO had suggested to Czeslawa that she return to the camp and accompany her sister to Italy, where the two of them could decide where they wanted to go. They hadn't yet shown her the letter from her mother, figuring she wouldn't believe it was really from her. In fact, it might just strengthen her resistance to the notion of repatriation. "Besides," as Lane wrote, "raising the question of repatriation at this time in Tengeru, we feel, might prove fatal to the proposed move." Better that she receive a letter directly from her mother, asking her to return.

According to Lane, all of the children listed for either Canada or the U.K. seemed willing to go to either. They had been allocated as they had because so far Canada had only agreed to take seventy-nine. Lane explained that while they had listed ninety-one for Canada, they expected some of the older ones to drop out of the move eventually. As well, some on the list for Canada had relatives or sponsors in the United States, who they hoped to eventually join. Meanwhile, Canada was a significant step forward. In other cases, the children had relatives elsewhere, including East Africa, who were incapable of supporting them. In these cases, the IRO had contacted the relatives and assessed their ability to support the children. That information would be included in the files that would accompany the children on their trip to Italy.[32]

Then the fateful day arrived, April 28, the day the children were to be moved from Tengeru camp to Mombasa, in preparation for shipment to Italy. As the camp commandant reported it, the trucks arrived at the camp at 6:35 a.m. to transport the children to Arusha's train station. As they stood there, not a single child emerged from the barracks of the camp, not a single piece of baggage was deposited with the baggage master. The camp commandant himself drove around the camp to check if the children were mustering, but not a single person on the lists was to be seen. The train sat in the station at Arusha all morning, waiting for the children. When it was clear that they were not going to show, the transport was cancelled.[33]

The children didn't really understand the intricacies of the politics swirling around them, but they understood that someone was trying to take them away from the camp and that the adults in charge of them, particularly Mrs. Grosicka and Father Krolikowski, were determined that they would not be taken. Rumour had it that it was the Polish Communists, coming to take them back to Poland. That galvanized the children. None really understood what was going on, but having finally escaped Siberia, the Communists, and the Soviet system, they were not about to return. In the small hours of the morning that the trucks were due to arrive, all the children were roused from bed, suddenly, by their supervisors. Some, like Stan Studzinski, were taken to the church, where they stayed until midday. Others, like Sophie Matusiewicz, were rounded up and taken into the bush.[34] A few of the older children living in the camp, but in smaller houses rather than in the barracks, also ran to the church. It was a dramatic moment that brought back memories of the deportations and of Russia, and they didn't need any special encouragement to run. It was almost an instinctive reaction to hide. As Krzysztofa Michniak explained,

Over there, nobody has to say nothing. Over there, nobody has to tell you what to do. Your instincts! Because when you go through Russia and when you are hiding so often, no matter what, and you live always scared.... So it comes naturally to you. When the children heard they would be coming with trucks, the first thing, because we were raised Catholic, we go to church. Because old ladies go to church, nobody was even thinking the children would be at church.[35]

Curtis and his superiors were furious, but not surprised. They held the Board of Guardians responsible for the fiasco and accused them of instructing the children not to cooperate. As a result, Curtis informed Pennington on April 29, IRO Geneva had instructed him to withdraw all financial assistance for those children who had refused to move. They were "no longer considered admissible to care and maintenance at the Organization's expense as long as they remain[ed] in Tengeru camp." As far as the IRO was concerned, this was on the heads of the guardians, and Curtis wasted no time telling them so.[36] Brigadier Lush raised another potentially serious concern, that their intransigence might have harmed their chances of being accepted into Canada.[37] Canada did not have to take in the children, and if the children proved uncooperative, Canada could easily wash its hands of them.

Meanwhile, the camp commandant received a scathing letter from Pennington, condemning the Board of Guardians for its decision. While he had been sympathetic to the Board's concerns earlier, the withdrawal of the children's funding clearly hit a nerve. Pennington condemned the results as deplorable, but understandable on the IRO's part, given the complete lack of co-operation on the part of all concerned. He had tried to take the Board's concerns into consideration, but could not "avoid the conclusion that they are approaching this matter in a completely unrealistic manner." Enough was enough. One could not expect Canada to issue visas for the children without first examining them, and one could not expect Canada to send officials to Tengeru to do so. With the Canadian Government expressing the willingness to take the whole group, subject to screening, Pennington felt the Board was taking a huge risk of losing this opportunity by not co-operating. After all, an earlier attempt to get them to Canada had failed just because the children were not in Europe and could not be examined by Canadian officials. He was now dismissive of their fears, arguing that the IRO had given its "most solemn assurances" that no child would be repatriated to Poland against his or her will. Even in the cases that the Board cited as examples of the IRO failing to carry out a specific undertaking, there was not a single case of someone being repatriated unwillingly to Poland.

Pennington discounted their fears of a Communist coup in Italy. The fear might have been more viable two years earlier, but he felt that now, with the formation of NATO and the Western Union, and the rift between Yugoslavia and the Comintern, as well as the strengthening of American forces in Western Europe, a coup was not likely to happen. Italy was firmly in the American camp and on the pro-democracy side of the Cold War. He was also upset at the way in which the Board had overstepped its authority by instructing children who were not under its authority to disobey the order to proceed to Mombasa. As a result, these children's future had been placed in jeopardy, and they now faced possible expulsion from the camp (as the IRO controlled the camp). Pennington further pointed out that issuing visas for a large group was very different from doing it for individual refugees with individual sponsors in Canada.

The whole situation was a fiasco and he asked the Tengeru Poles to consider the implications if they should lose this opportunity in Canada, especially now that the IRO had cut off their financial support. It was not clear that either the Tanganyikan or the British Government would be willing to pick up the shortfall. Furthermore, if the children remained in Tengeru for any length of time, the IRO might wash their hands of them altogether, and then who would arrange their passage to any country, even if one would consider taking them? The letter, which was carbon copied to the Commissioner of the EARA, as well as Curtis and Lorriman, concluded by saying, "I would be very glad if you could do all possible to persuade the Board of Guardians to change its decision," reiterating that, if they lost this chance, he had no idea when the next one might come.[38]

Of course, Pennington was being a bit disingenuous when speaking about the funding problem. In reality, if the IRO withdrew funding for the children, the expense for their care and maintenance fell to the British authorities, as it always had in the past. The IRO had maintained the same payment system as UNRRA had implemented. It paid the British Government a certain monthly amount for each displaced person who fell within its mandate, and the British paid the bills. Ultimately, the British Treasury had always been accountable for the expenses incurred, not the IRO. Thus, Pennington's ire was the result of being faced with bearing the cost of these displaced persons at a time when the British Government was determined to be rid of those expenses. To have the Board of Guardians mess up an opportunity to reduce that expense by over one hundred mouths was galling enough. To then lose the IRO allowance for these children was absolutely infuriating.

Pennington's letter gave Curtis cause for celebration, as it was clear that the British authorities were now supportive of the move. On May 2, the same day that Pennington so thoroughly dressed down the camp commandant, Curtis felt optimistic enough to write IRO Italy, informing them that the movement was going to happen after all. The expectation was that they would move from Mombasa on June 4. Clearly, the impression was that the British authorities would make the Board of Guardians come to heel.

He pleaded with IRO Italy to treat these children with kid gloves when they arrived.

> You've been so helpful in the past, I hate to ask another favour. But this comparatively insignificant move of a few adolescents has become a thing of such great local importance, watched with tremendous interest by almost every refugee in Africa, that it has become rather a vital issue for the future work of IRO in these parts.

The success of future moves of this type through Italy depended a great deal on what the children reported back to Tengeru,

... [A]ccordingly..., it would be a good investment for IRO as a whole to make a real fuss of these children to ensure good reports being sent back. As Uganda phrased it in a recent letter, we should descend even to balloons and flowers, teddy bears and sugarplums, if that is what it takes to make them write cheerful letters back to the camp population. They are our ambassadors of good-will, after all, and are the subject of enormous speculation about futures and about the good intentions of IRO.

He ended with the appeal that they please do what they could.[39]

Meanwhile, Geneva confirmed that the Tanganyikan Government was in:

... [C]omplete sympathy and support [for the] IRO proposal and has firmly indicated consequences likely to devolve on Guardians if children remain Tengeru and has instructed camp administration make every effort persuade Guardians change unreasonable and reprehensible attitude.

Curtis was also instructed to inform Pennington that, should it change its attitude, the IRO would be pleased to once again assume full responsibility for the children as of their date of departure from Tengeru.[40] He did so, immediately.[41] Curtis was sure that, finally, the Board would be made to see reason. He firmly believed that this was the best solution for the children.[42]

However, Curtis' optimism was premature. The Board was unapologetic and intransigent in its belief that the move was a rushed mistake. As the camp commandant reported to Pennington, there was nothing that he, Pennington, or the EARA Commissioner could have said that would have swayed the Board of Guardians from their opinion, either then or earlier. While he believed that the Board had not explicitly ordered the children not to report for the transport, he did believe that the children knew that the Board disapproved, and acted accordingly and with the Board's acquiescence. The intransigence was not just on the children's part. The whole of the staff who were ostensibly to accompany the transport, as well as many of the children from outside the orphanage, had failed to get their documentation in order in time. Even the orphanage's supervisor, Mrs. Grosicka, had been uncooperative, intially deciding that she would not accompany the children to Italy, but would instead wait for an entry permit for herself and one child, Teresa Bllowas, for the U.K. The only leader prepared to participate in the move was Mr. J. Hoffman, but even he only agreed to do so if the Board of Guardians approved of the move and if he was admitted to Canada as a conducting officer.

The Board was still unconvinced that the move was safe for the children. It was all well and good if others felt willing to take such risks with the children, but the Board did not. While there were several resettlement schemes available to the children if they were in Europe, there was no guarantee that they would be accepted by any of them, leaving those not accepted beyond the Board's protection. Even the expansion of the U.S. quota from three to five thousand orphans was not sufficient, because there was no guarantee that these children would be included. Thus, the move to Europe and away from its control and protection was an unacceptable risk in the Board's opinion. They reiterated their position that their appeal was a reasonable one and that a decision should be delayed until they had heard from Canada. The Board also refused to accept responsibility for the loss of maintenance payments for the children, and dismissed that as a matter to be settled between the Government of Tanganyika and IRO Geneva.[43]

On May 4, the Board of Guardians took the battle directly to the IRO. Their letter to Curtis seethed with distrust of the IRO, fear of the Warsaw Government, and with a sense of righteous indignation. It painstakingly rehearsed the chain of events that had led to the present impasse and concluded by summarizing their position.

> ... The adults as well as children fear to leave this territory
> with no guarantee as to their future. They are afraid they
> will be stuck in one of the camps in Italy or Germany

without any hope for the future. They say: "Younger and stronger people were rejected by the Canadian Selection Missions, how can we hope to be accepted."

On account of all the points raised above the orphans' Board of Guardians still maintains its decision: we do not agree to the orphan children leaving Tengeru Camp unless fully documented and visaed for Canada.[44]

Needless to say, their intransigence did not endear them to either the EARA or the IRO. Within two days, Pennington had written the camp commandant again, passing on the text of the cable from the IRO, in which the organization offered to reassume full responsibility for the children if the Board of Guardians changed its decision and allowed the movement to proceed. His patience was wearing thin and he pointed out to the commandant that the Board only had authority over thirty of the children on the list of those who were to have been moved. This meant, he explained bluntly, that the remaining ninety-six children on the nominal roll, because of their refusal to move, had now been rendered outside of the IRO mandate and were therefore liable for deportation. Although he hoped it would not come to that, he made it clear that the Tanganyikan Government felt no obligation to keep the children in the camp indefinitely. Furthermore,

... [I]f arrangements for their resettlement, which the Government considers reasonable are made and come to nought because of the non-cooperation of the refugees concerned the Government may feel itself compelled to take the necessary steps to ensure that its orders are not flouted.[45]

On May 17, Curtis responded, reiterating the IRO position. He insisted that the move to Italy was still the best solution for the children. Now that Italy had formally joined the IRO, the Italian Government was bound by the IRO Constitution and, thus, had pledged not to repatriate anyone against their will. He expressed the utmost confidence that

Canada would look favourably upon the group, but also confidence that Canada would not commit itself to taking on the children without seeing them in person. He hoped that the Board would "see their way to withdraw their opposition to the move" and that if they did they would put it in writing. "Geneva Headquarters [IRO]," he wrote, "will require some assurance that, if train and shipping arrangements are firmly booked, there will not be further money wasted."[46]

Meanwhile, the Board of Guardians had taken it upon themselves to contact the Department of External Affairs in Ottawa, pushing to know what the Canadian Government's decision was, or at a minimum, whether it agreed in principle to the children's admittance to Canada.[47] In response, External Affairs cabled the Board of Guardians, informing them that discussions were still proceeding between the Canadian Government, the IRO, and the Roman Catholic Church.[48] External Affairs also told the IRO that no final decision could be reached until Immigration had received certain documents from the episcopate, the still-outstanding provincial approvals of the admission.[49]

How much impact the news from Canada had on the Board of Guardians is not known, but it certainly strengthened the IRO's and the Government of Tanganyika's positions. The Tanganyikan Government had put considerable pressure on the members of the Board, and on the staff at the orphanage, in order to induce them to withdraw their opposition. And it worked, because on May 19, Pennington notified Sir Arthur that the children who had failed to move on April 28, would now be leaving Tengeru for Mombasa on June 1, and embarking for Italy on June 4. He did ask Rucker if he could provide some kind of reassurances as to the conditions at the camp in Salerno, as the rumours were flying around the camp about lice-infested blankets, poor food, et cetera. He thought the reassurances might help allay some of the fears.[50]

The trip was set. The children were scheduled to depart from Mombasa on the SS *Jerusalemme* on June 3, arriving at Bari, Italy, on June 19. They would proceed from there to Salerno by train. The trip went smoothly. Mrs. Grosicka was appointed head of the transport, with several other adults from the camp accompanying her to manage the children, including Father Krolikowski, who came along in the role of chaplain.[51]

This time, the children's reaction was decidedly different. With Father Krolikowski and Mrs. Grosicka appearing to consent to the move, no matter how begrudgingly, the children felt safe in the move. By that time they were very used to being told on a moment's notice to pack and get ready to move on to another camp. This had become a natural rhythm in their lives. A few had heard a rumour that they were eventually going to be taken to Canada, others were oblivious. For them, it was yet another adventure. And Mombasa, the port from which they would leave Africa, was a grand start to the journey. They were there for several days, which meant no school, but a chance to explore the town and the beach. As Michal Bortkiewicz explained,

> Me? I didn't even know we were going to Italy! I was going on a trip somewhere, going somewhere was all that was interesting to me! I didn't think about where we were going. When we went to Mombasa, I said, "Wow! Swimming in the ocean!" So I used to sneak out of the camp where we were staying, and we'd swim to the bazaars. We'd dive in and swim across the bay to Mombasa! And Mombasa was different! It was like going to Arusha, but in Arusha there was no water. And Mombasa, the ocean! It was fantastic! A new adventure![52]

Marian Kacpura laughs when he remembers climbing coconut trees to get the fruit.[53] Those who had swimsuits went swimming on the beach and there were regular excursions into the old city to explore the bazaar and winding streets. To get across the bay to the old town from the camp where they were housed, the children were taken in small, light sailboats.[54] Released from the routine of the camp, the sojourn in Mombasa seemed a seaside holiday, and the children relished the beach, the town, the freedom. It was idyllic.

The journey to Italy lasted about two weeks, working its way up the African coast, through the Suez Canal, and on to Italy. The *Jerusalemme* was an Italian passenger ship and, from the children's perspective, quite comfortable, even though they were in the cheapest cabins. As they remember it, the voyage was uneventful. Helena Koscielniak recalls that some of the children put on performances for the tourists on the ship, for which Mrs. Grosicka was paid (what happened to those proceeds is unknown). What made the trip memorable for many of the boys was their first taste of wine. This was an Italian ship, after all, and at meals everyone was served wine, rather than water. As Marian Kacpura remembers, as one bottle was finished the waiter matter-of-factly replaced it with another, and the boys got roaring drunk. When they reached the high seas, the results were quite dramatic. When Mrs. Grosicka and Father Krolikowski discovered what was happening, they asked the ship's staff to dilute the wine with water.[55]

While the children remember the voyage as a pleasant and comfortable trip, Father Krolikowski's recollections were more troubled. A few of the older boys and girls were "undisciplined, arrogant, and rude, [and] they began to have a bad influence on the younger ones." Discipline issues became increasingly common and he found the immodest behaviour of some of the older girls to be distressing. Some of the older boys began smoking cigarettes on the sly and wearing large hats that made them look like gangsters, as he described it. He was conscious of the reactions of the other passengers to these unruly teenagers. Those who refused to pack away their hats had them thrown overboard. For a priest in his early thirties, being responsible for an intractable crowd of over 140 children, aged ten to twenty, was an enormous challenge.[56] Despite all of that, from the perspective of the IRO the trip went well. At the port of Bari, the children faced a fourteen-hour train ride to Salerno. On June 20, the group, healthy but tired, finally arrived in Salerno. The children settled into the camp for what was supposed to be a relatively short stay of several months.[57]

There was still one thing left outstanding for the Government of Tanganyika, the sticky question of the children's financial support for the months of April and May, which the IRO had stopped when the children had refused to move. It was not a small sum and the British authorities would have liked to avoid paying it, if possible. So, upon the departure of the children from Tengeru, the Governor of Tanganyika approached the Secretary of State for the Colonies, pleading with him to intercede with the IRO on his behalf. He protested that while he had initially supported the Board of Guardians' demand for a three-month delay, that changed when he heard the Home Office did not support the WVS's proposal and the Canadian Government was willing to consider accepting all the children, but preferred they be moved to Italy where Canadian immigration officials could examine them. At that point, "although the Board of Guardians and the others concerned were still most reluctant for the children to proceed to Italy in the absence of definite confirmation from the Canadian Government that it would accept all the children, I withdrew my request for any further postponement of the move." (This was not quite what had happened, for he had not supported the IRO until losing the children's funding after the fiasco of April 28, but it sounded better than the unvarnished truth.) Strenuous efforts had been made by the officials of the Refugees Department to persuade the Board of Guardians and others concerned to withdraw their opposition to the transfer, with the result that the children were now on their way. He concluded, "I hope that in the circumstances IRO will reconsider their decision to withdraw financial support from the children in the question for the month of April; in the meantime the matter is being taken up with their local representatives."[58] It took the IRO a month to decide, but on July 20, one month after the children had arrived in Salerno, the IRO replied. It had agreed, now that the children were "happily installed in a camp near Salerno," to restore the maintenance allowance for the children for the month of April.[59]

# 6 | Warsaw Strikes

G etting the children to Italy had been a nerve-wracking experience. Their safe arrival on June 20, 1949, was distinctly, and perhaps thankfully, anticlimactic, given the intensity of the negotiations in the preceding months. With the children finally in Italy, it seemed that the crisis had passed. The children quickly settled in, thrilled at the beautiful beach where they could swim to their hearts' content, pleased with the excellent food and friendly people, resigned to the classes which soon began. Some of the older children enrolled in a local agricultural school. Krzysztofa Michniak was one of two girls who volunteered to take classes there. She was taught how to raise angora rabbits and chickens for profit. Some of the others laughed at her for cleaning up after rabbits, but at least she didn't have to work in the dining room or peel potatoes. Michal Bortkiewicz also took classes there, as he was interested in one day getting back to some type of farming.[1] Those who had finished school in Tengeru did odd jobs around the camp, such as tending the chapel, looking after the younger children, teaching classes, and working in the office or kitchen.[2] Of course, very soon the boys were getting into trouble. Marian Kacpura remembers that the beach was littered with live ammunition left over from the Allied landing. The boys would twist a bullet out of its casing, pour the powder in a line on a piece of wood, and set it alight. If they were careful, they could etch their names into the wood permanently.[3] Stefan Kozlowski remembers that one guy in his barracks got the bright idea for a practical joke — he pulled a wire from the wiring inside the barrack and dropped it into a puddle. When someone stepped in the puddle, they got a rude shock.[4] Everyone was impressed with the food. Of course, there was a lot of pasta, something new to them, but the fruit was both different and delicious — apples, plums, lemons. There were even occasional excursions to historical sites.[5]

While the affair seemed to be winding down, in fact, things were far from settled. The Board of Guardians may have agreed to let the children go, but only with great reluctance and under duress. Their fears had not been allayed. They were watching very closely, especially as the IRO still didn't have a concrete plan for the children. The Canadian Government had still not agreed to issue visas for the children, in spite of repeated queries from Tengeru, the IRO, and even the Polish Ambassador to Rome.[6] There were apparently several impediments in the way that had to be addressed.

First, it was still unclear whether the children actually could be included in the thousand visas allotted to the Catholic Immigrant Aid Society. Those visas were supposed to be for children from Germany and Austria, so there was some confusion about whether or not the children from East Africa, even though they were now located in Italy, could be included.[7] Furthermore, the episcopate still hadn't received the provincial permissions that Canadian Immigration required, which meant that nothing could proceed anyway.[8] In spite of pressure from the IRO, the Canadian Immigration Officer in Rome, and the Polish Ambassador to the Holy See, Immigration refused to make a decision until it had received the necessary documentation from the Archbishop.[9]

Then the Archbishop reported back to Immigration, explaining that the documentation was not forthcoming, and would never be forthcoming, because the Quebec Government claimed to have no authority to issue such a permission. There was apparently no legislation in the province that placed orphan children's welfare under the jurisdiction of provincial institutions. Instead, it was left up to the individual welfare organizations, which were generally religious organizations in Quebec. If Immigration was waiting for Quebec's permission, nothing would ever get done, as it would never come. Once again the Archbishop pledged to accept full responsibility for the children, and that none would become a public charge. He explained that arrangements were now in place to put every one of the orphans in institutions where they would be boarded, fed, and educated, and where they would be taught a trade that suited their aptitudes. He urged Immigration to act quickly on the matter.[10]

This was almost the last hurdle. The Ministry of Labour was quickly consulted, to ensure that the older orphans would be able to find employment. Once that was confirmed, Immigration approved the children's screening.[11] Fortier wrote to G.G. Congdon, Superintendent of European Immigration (Canada), London, on June 22, to inform him that the children now in Italy were to be charged against Dorothy Sullivan's quota of one thousand, subject to the same medical and civil examinations that all displaced persons applying to Canada underwent. He asked Congdon to inform the Canadian officer in Rome, J.B. Potvin, of what visa numbers to use. The Canadian Government Immigration Bureau in Karlsruhe was also notified that permission had been granted for the admission of 132 orphans from the Salerno camp.[12] Fortier assumed that the IRO would also contact the Canadian officer in Rome so he could make the appropriate arrangements for the examinations.[13] On the same day, Fortier also confirmed with IRO Canada that it would arrange and pay for the children's and their escorts' transport to Canada.[14] Finally, he informed the Archbishop and the Catholic Immigrant Aid Society that the orphans' admission to Canada had been approved, provided they were in good health and met the requirements of the immigration regulations. With the children now in Italy, he told the Archbishop, the Canadian officers in Rome had been instructed to begin the civil and medical examinations as soon as possible.[15] The IRO moved quickly, confirming that they would arrange the transportation and the escort, and contact the Catholic Immigrant Aid Society to arrange the orphans' reception in Canada.[16] Dorothy Sullivan was asked to proceed to Italy to make the selection.[17] This should have meant that all was in order, although somehow, in all the communications flowing back and forth, it appears that neither the Department of Foreign Affairs nor, more importantly, the Board of Guardians in Arusha, was ever informed that a decision had been made.[18]

Then the plans ran into a glitch. Miss Sullivan arrived in Geneva for briefing, before going on to Italy for the actual selection. No one had realized that her quota of one thousand was restricted to children under the age of sixteen, which meant that many of the children didn't qualify.[19] Also, at that point Ottawa was told that there were some 150 orphans, not the expected 132. An additional eighteen had been moved in from Uganda and Southern Rhodesia. IRO Geneva expressed its hope that the additional children could be included in Miss Sullivan's quota. The Archbishop of Montreal stepped up to the challenge and offered to take the additional children, if they met the visa requirements. With that assurance, Jolliffe approved the increase.[20]

That resolved the issue of numbers, but not the problem with the children's ages. The IRO, in a deft manipulation of the situation and a burst of creativity born of desperate necessity, offered up a solution for consideration by the Canadians. Geneva argued that, of the 146 children and youths presumably going to Canada, eighty-eight did fit within Sullivan's mandate. A further twenty-nine were older siblings of the children who were within her mandate. Another sixteen boys had only reached the age of sixteen while in the orphanage, and one young man, aged twenty-four, had younger siblings in the proper age range. In this way, the IRO argued, each of these children had a claim to admission to Canada, unless Canada wished to break up what remained of already devastated families. Surely Canada would not be so cruel? Geneva asked IRO Canada to take this interpretation to the National Catholic Welfare Society, the Canadian Government, and the Archbishop and persuade them to accept those who fell outside the strict boundaries of Sullivan's mandate, assuming they met Canada's normal immigration requirements.[21]

Meanwhile the IRO had its own plans for the children. The IRO had a well-established protocol surrounding the disposition of "unaccompanied children," the name given to children in its care who were either orphaned or separated from their legal guardians by events of war. This protocol, it felt, had to be implemented, even given the special circumstances of these children. Essentially, the protocol consisted of two steps: First, the children had to be "traced," that is, an attempt had to be made to track down the children's families. IRO gave first priority to reuniting children with their families whenever possible, as this was deemed in the children's best interests. Second, and simultaneously, before any child could be resettled (i.e., settled in a country other than their homeland), they had to be given the opportunity to consider the possibility of repatriation to their homeland, in this case, Poland, free from undue influence. In this way, the child would be able to make an informed decision. No child would be repatriated against their will, but they had to be presented with the option of returning home.[22] Before the children could be given Canadian visas, the IRO was determined to ensure that the proper procedures were abided by.

The International Tracing Service, a branch of the IRO responsible for identifying and reuniting displaced persons with their families, had already agreed to send Charlotte Babinski, a tracing officer, to Salerno to assist in interviewing the children, beginning about two weeks after their arrival.[23] IRO's Repatriation Division also informed IRO Rome that they would be sending a repatriation officer, Pierre Krycz, to Salerno for two weeks, to talk to the children about Poland. He spoke Polish and had visited postwar Poland, so he could give the children a good sense of the state of the country. His purpose was not to mount a "repatriation propaganda campaign," but to "give the children as objective information as possible with a view to counteracting the propaganda to which they have been subjected since 1943."[24] The general consensus in Geneva was that the IRO had a "moral obligation" to ensure that these children had every opportunity in a neutral setting to "freely come to a decision regarding repatriation and resettlement before going to their final destination," wherever that might be. Geneva assumed that the children's reluctance to repatriate to Poland was the result of their long indoctrination by the adults in Tengeru, and that, once removed from that influence, they might be able to make a properly informed decision. The assumption was utterly incorrect, and one that would undermine their relations with the children and their escorts.

Cognizant of the sensitivity of the children, as well as their escorts, to the question of repatriation, Geneva decided to send Miss J. Powell to Italy, to get to know the children and to assess the situation. Upon her arrival in late June, four days after the children, she discovered that while the children's physical needs were well taken care of, IRO Rome was ill-equipped to deal with the planning side. This mission had done very little in the way of repatriation over its lifetime, and had no in-house repatriation staff. No one seemed to know much about the children, or even if they had Canadian visas yet.

Powell quickly realized that the Polish escorts, while nominally co-operating, were extremely suspicious of the IRO and its motives. She hadn't realized that a Catholic priest (not Father Krolikowski) had joined the children en route and was now at Salerno. His primary concern seemed to be the plans being made for the children and she got the impression that "he was not quite satisfied of the intentions of IRO and felt that our [the IRO's] policy was to brutally separate families and indiscriminately send workers to countries of resettlement as cheap labour." He was less of a problem, because he soon left the camp, but Mrs. Grosicka, the former director of the orphanage who also had accompanied the children to Salerno, was potentially a serious obstacle. She had considerable influence with the children and so could not be ignored. Grosicka's main concern was to get the children's resettlement sorted out as quickly as possible. In that instance, she and the IRO were in accord, and Powell suggested to her seniors that this could be a way in which the IRO would be able to work with her. It would be a challenge, as Grosicka was very suspicious of the IRO and of the IRO staff members with whom she had had to work (perhaps with some justification, Powell thought), and strongly believed the children would be better off in a Western country, free of the influence of the U.S.S.R. In spite of this, Powell concluded that she could still be useful. More importantly, any attempt to remove her from the camp, whatever her attitude, would make a difficult situation disastrous and would "precipitate unnecessary crisis." Powell spoke to Grosicka about the possibility of repatriating the children with families in Poland, as it appeared there were some children who had family there. Grosicka agreed that if the relatives were willing to take the children, she would try to persuade them to go. But she also told Powell that all the relatives had already written the children, telling them to remain in the orphanage as they could not afford to care for them in Poland.

Powell's recommendation was to proceed as planned. Tracing should be started immediately and attempts should be made, by IRO Warsaw if possible, to track down and interview the children's relatives in Poland, so that parents could make valid plans for their children. The children also should be given whatever materials were currently available on conditions in Poland. Those youths over the age of eighteen, without younger siblings, who didn't want to be repatriated should be presented to the various resettlement missions operating in Italy. However, she warned, in light of the very tense and potentially explosive atmosphere, both of these exercises had to be implemented by a person chosen "on the basis of their tact and unbiased attitude." All of this had to be carefully coordinated in order to avoid a crisis. Any misstep could result in an unmitigated disaster.[25]

Not long after Powell's visit, Yvonne de Jong of Child Welfare, IRO Geneva, arrived in Salerno for a week's stay, to check on the children and their processing. De Jong was even more adamant the children be put through the proper screening and tracing when it became clear to her that few of the children met the definition of "unaccompanied children." According to PCIRO Provisional Order No. 33, an unaccompanied child was sixteen years of age or under; outside of their country of origin; an orphan, or a child whose parents had disappeared or who had abandoned them; without a legal guardian; and not accompanied by a close relative.[26] This was patently not true of most of these children. Three already had visas for the U.K. and a further sixteen had either relatives or sponsors in that country. Another fifty-eight of the children were over the age of sixteen, although twenty-nine of those had younger siblings in the group. A few of the children had relatives in Argentina, France, and Australia. About twenty-eight of them had at least one parent in Poland. A further twenty had applied for emigration visas to the U.S. through the U.S. Consul General in Nairobi. This was not a group of orphans, she concluded, as there was little evidence of the death of their parents in general, and at least 10 percent of the group had at least one parent alive. Only eighty-eight of the children could truly be called "unaccompanied." This was especially disturbing as the wording of the Canadian resettlement scheme clearly stated that it was for "orphaned children," and no one knew how the Canadians would react when they discovered the children's true family status. Ideally, each child's case history would have to be individually examined by a Child Welfare officer in conjunction with the repatriation officer and ITS before any final recommendation could be made on the child's final disposition.

A proper tracing was going to be impossible. De Jong was appalled at the state of the children's records, which were in abysmal shape. Properly documenting the children would have taken an impossibly long time, so she recommended relying on personal interviews, correspondence from relatives that the children might have in their possession, and any information that Tracing was able to provide to complete each case history and allow each child or youth "a happy conclusion for his final establishment." She expected it would take at least two weeks to do even this cursory tracing exercise.[27]

From the IRO's perspective, that was not such a bad thing, as it had also decided the children needed to be given an opportunity to reconsider their decision against repatriation in an environment less hostile to the new Poland. As de Jong explained to Mrs. Grosicka and Father Krolikowski:

> ... [I]t was normal human duty to unite children with their parents wherever they might be, and that since, through emigration, the children were going to acquire another nationality, their short stay in Salerno offered the last opportunity to make these facts quite clear to them. In order to fulfill their duties in this respect, the Re-establishment Officer (Krycz) had brought with him quantities of films which are now to be projected in the camp with recreational movies and posters and pictures of Poland.[28]

This was the task given to Pierre Krycz, the IRO repatriation officer assigned to these children. This would have taken time even if all the paperwork had been in order. When Babinski and Krycz arrived in Salerno, they were shocked by the conditions under which they would have to work. Not only were the children's files in abysmal condition, but a lack of transportation, clerical assistance, even a simple typewriter, made it doubly hard for the two to bring any order to the records.

To complicate matters further, Babinski and Krycz faced a particularly tough crowd. These children were a tight-knit group. The orphanage was the children's family. Their real families, if any were still alive, were only vague memories who had little claim to the children's affection or loyalty. The older siblings had been acting in *loco parentis* for the younger children for years, and the group as a whole was united against any outside threats. They were fiercely devoted to each other and especially their siblings. They had been raised in an environment that was vehemently anti-Communist and anti-Warsaw, and deeply suspicious of anyone who might try to deport them to Poland. The hysteria of the previous months in Tengeru had to have merely heightened their fears and reinforced their suspicions. This made Babinski's and Krycz's tasks especially difficult, as they had already been cast as the enemy who might try to send them to Poland. They could expect little co-operation from either the children or their Polish escorts.

When Babinski looked at these children's files, it was clear that no effort had been made to trace the children's families. A nominal roll had been sent to the IRO representative in Warsaw, Mr. Widdicombe, to check against his records and for his use in handling queries at his end, but nothing more had been done at that end either. None of the information reported on the parents' or relatives' fates had been verified; there was no background provided on the children or their family, let alone the story of the children's displacement or their separation from their parents. Not one child had a proper birth certificate and, for those children under the ages of fourteen or fifteen, the birthdate used was considered unreliable. In Babinski's mind, the most important task was to prepare registration forms and social histories for all the children in Salerno, and to begin the process of tracing relatives, including any in Poland. This would be in keeping with IRO standard procedure, but it was going to take time.

Babinski and Krycz decided that they would interview the children as a team, in an effort to get as clear a picture of each child's situation as possible. The children proved singularly uncooperative. From the children's perspective, Babinski and Krycz were the enemy. None of the children could later recall their names, not surprisingly, as they were just two more administrators in a sea of authority figures who had been bouncing them from camp to camp to camp. None of the children recognized that they were from the IRO. What they remember is being interviewed by Polish Communists who claimed to have found relatives of theirs in Poland and who were trying to persuade them to return there. Krzysztofa Michniak was not in the camp when the interviews occurred, but her sister was, and she reported to Krzysztofa the essence of what happened. When the "communists" interviewed her sister, they told her that her grandmother and uncle were both in Poland. Her sister, much affronted, replied that she didn't know that and didn't believe it. When the interviewers pushed her, telling her she should return to Poland, she said, point blank and very determined, "No, I'm not going." Krzysztofa was rather glad she wasn't there for the interview, because she is certain she would have dissolved into tears under the pressure.[29]

Michal Bortkiewicz had a similar experience. When they interviewed him and his brother, they told them they had uncles and cousins in Poland and they should return to be with them. Michal and Piotr were suspicious because they had made no mention of their brother and so the two boys replied that it couldn't be the same family because they knew their father was dead and that their brother was not there. When the interviewer insisted that there were at least cousins, and therefore family, the Bortkiewicz boys dismissed this, saying that there were lots of cousins but they weren't the same family, and they did not want to go to Poland. Instead, Michal announced that he intended to go to Canada to be a cowboy.[30]

Al Kunicki's conversation went a little differently, insofar as the interviewers tried to play on any possible fears about how he would fit into Canada or wherever he resettled. They argued that he would have to learn yet another language and he would inevitably be treated as a second-class citizen wherever he went. They asked Al whether he might not prefer to return to Poland. Al played with them a bit, but finally said, "Oh yeah, but I want to go back to where I was born. And you guys gave it to Moscow!" Al recalls that the man looked at him long and hard, and then called for the next child.[31]

As Stan Paluch put it, reflecting the sentiments of almost all the children,

I said, "No, I don't want to go to Poland." I was just in
Russia. For me, Communists were ... I lost all my fam-
ily [to them]. For me, I would never agree [to return] ....
I would never go back to Communist countries![32]

Even so, the interviews confirmed the officers' suspicions about the
unreliability of the files. It came out in some of the interviews that the
children had the addresses of relatives in Poland, although that information was not recorded anywhere. Babinski was convinced that a number
of the children had lied in the interviews about their family in Poland.[33]
Her suspicions were well-founded. By that time, many of the children
had re-established contact with family members who were now back
in Poland. Kazimiera Mazur had been in touch with her mother and
her two sisters, who had worked their way back to Poland by 1946. Her
mother was insistent that Kazimiera and her brother and sister not return
to Poland, in spite of pressure from the Polish Government for her to
write to her children and tell them to do so. Her mother's argument was
that she could offer them nothing in Poland. The rough cabin in which
they lived had broken windows, she couldn't afford boots for herself. How
could she support another three children? And Kazimiera and her siblings were as determined to not return. They saw no future in Poland, but
tremendous opportunity elsewhere.[34] Other children had similar stories
of parents or relatives in Poland, with whom they may or may not have re-
established contact.[35] None wished to return to Poland. A large number
of them displayed no interest in having their parents traced or clues about
relatives pursued — much to Babinski's surprise and frustration. Her
explanation was that the "palpable indoctrination against repatriation and
against the present regime in Poland during the past several years most
certainly [had] affected the reliability and completeness of the information obtained from the children." Of the 121 children interviewed over
the course of those three weeks, Babinski concluded that only twenty-
nine did not require further tracing. The remainder needed further investigation, preferably before they were moved yet again.[36]

Krycz's task was especially difficult. Of all the children, only two
were willing to return to Poland; most indicated that they wished to

resettle in Canada. The reasons they offered were myriad: they had relatives in countries other than Poland, who they would prefer to join; their
parents or relatives in Poland were incapable of supporting them; they
feared being drafted into the Polish Army; they didn't like the present
political regime in Poland; and so on. Krycz remarked that none of these
reasons were considered valid reasons for not repatriating, but it was
difficult to promote repatriation to a group so deeply suspicious.[37] He
and Babinski clearly misunderstood the source of the children's antipa-
thy toward Poland and anything Communist. They both blamed the
adults for indoctrinating the children. In fact, the children had arrived
in Tengeru vehemently anti-Soviet and anti-Communist. They had
required no indoctrination; Siberia had been enough.

The tension in East Africa was not lessened by Krycz and
Babinski's efforts. In a letter back to Tengeru, Mrs. Grosicka complained vociferously about the two IRO representatives. She was angry
because they had initially hidden the fact that they spoke Polish. Even
moreso, she was furious because it was clear to her that their objective
was to coerce the children to return to Poland, under the ostensible
goal of reuniting them with their families. When the children were
examined it was done individually, and none of the Polish guardians
were permitted to be present. They told the children that they had
recently visited Poland and had liked what they had seen, and everything that was said abroad about Poland was a lie. The children were
very upset, she reported, and defiant.

Some of them bluntly denied it when they were told about freedom,
good schools, and happiness in Poland. Others wept so bitterly that
Grosicka could hardly calm them. When Wandzi Wyrzykowska was
told that she had a father in Poland, she laughed and said she knew from
good friends that both her parents died in Russia and she even mentioned the place. When they further tried to persuade her that her father
was definitely in Poland, and that his name was Kazimierz, the little girl
replied: "This is not true because my father was Wladyslaw." When they
said that she had been too small to remember, the girl replied: "I know
and I will not go to Poland."

They found a father of a big boy, and when he firmly denied this, said it might be a grandfather and that he, as an almost grown up boy, should go to Poland. Then the boy said that, had he wanted to go to Poland, he would have gone straight from Africa and wouldn't need any mediators to do this. Then the man of the Mission got excited and told the boy to keep quiet, but did not frighten him. The boy replied for himself and the others: "We came here to get our visas for Canada and to proceed there where we shall work in the profession we learnt in Africa and the small children will be looked after by the Canadian Bishops." I could quote very many of such examples.[38]

In spite of the hostility, Babinski and Krycz found two sisters who were willing to return to Poland, Czeslawa and Bronislawa Morawska. Their mother was alive and in Poland, something the girls had known. However, when they moved to Salerno with the group they had been determined to go to Canada rather than rejoin their mother. The older sister, Czeslawa, aged twenty-one or twenty-two, explained to Babinski that their mother had written them advising them not to return to Poland, as her living conditions were not very good and she couldn't support them. However, they had since received another letter from her, asking them to come home, and they had decided that they would do so. In fact, Father Krolikowski and Mrs. Grosicka both knew of the letter and had duly informed the IRO representatives of the girls' change of heart. Some of the other children were not sympathetic. Al Kunicki looked on it as a betrayal of the "tribe," because they had broken ranks. There was, he explains, a tacit understanding that no one would give in to the pressure in this war against the Russians, which is how he and others saw this ongoing pressure from the Communists, and the Morawska sisters had caved in.[39]

The girls were transferred to Cinecetta Camp, a transit camp, on Monday, July 18, so that the IRO could begin making arrangements for their transportation to Poland. There, the repatriation officer for IRO

Rome interviewed the girls and began the necessary paperwork. Krycz pushed him to expedite their repatriation so that they wouldn't have to wait too long. Miss Palau, the camp director, agreed to keep an eye on the two girls. Unfortunately, the girls' departure was delayed because there was no suitable escort, so there they waited, in the camp. Then the cauldron erupted.

That Saturday, Czeslawa went into Rome with two others from the Tengeru group: Mr. Papuga, an escort from Tengeru, and Olga Gnyp, one of the children. They had visas to the United Kingdom and were trying to arrange their transportation. Neither of them spoke English, so they had asked Czeslawa to act as their interpreter. Olga's younger sister, Helena, stayed to play with Bronislawa while Olga went into Rome. When they left Cinecitta Camp, Czeslawa promised her sister that she would be back by noon. When she got back to the camp, however, Bronislawa had gone missing! Helena said that a tall, thin, grey-haired man had approached the two girls as they played together outside. She had never seen him before and she didn't know his name. In fluent Polish, he had asked Bronislawa if she remembered him, to which she replied that she wasn't sure. He took her by the hand and asked her to go with him, saying that she was wanted at the Polish Embassy. And so she had left with him. This the camp director reported immediately to Irene Page, the IRO representative responsible for the girls.

Later, Krycz found out from Bronislawa what had happened. When they got to the Embassy in Rome, yet another man interrogated her, asking all sorts of questions: how many Polish children were there in Africa? When and where the deportees of 1940 were dispersed? Who were their leaders? Did the leaders or teachers turn the children against repatriation? Did they talk unfavourably about Poland? How many IRO officials from Geneva were working in the camp? What were they doing there? And so on. She had answered the questions as best a thirteen-year-old could, and after the interview was finished, they had fed her lunch and taken her back to the camp. Of course, no one at Cinecetta knew this yet.

No one at IRO Rome was keen to phone the Polish Embassy, for fear of unnecessarily spreading alarm. By this time, it was after 1:00 p.m.

and most people had left for the day anyway, it being Saturday. The duty officer was not due in until 2:00 p.m. However, when Page contacted Krycz and told him what had happened, he urged her to contact both the Polish Embassy and the police right away. She tried the Legal Advisor at home, but got no answer. Page decided to try the camp one more time and finally got Czeslawa on the phone. Czeslawa explained that her sister had just returned with the man who had taken her away and now he wanted her to go with him.

Page told Czeslawa to stay put and that she would be out to the camp as quickly as possible. Meanwhile, she asked her to find out the man's name and where he came from. Page phoned the Legal Advisor again, this time successfully, and told him the situation. When she couldn't get the duty car, she jumped in a taxicab and rushed to the camp. When she got there, she was told that Czeslawa had left with "someone from the diplomatic corps." Bronislawa was now back, very upset that her sister had left with that man. Page took Bronislawa with her back to IRO Headquarters in Rome. There, the Legal Advisor tried to ask her questions about the morning's escapade, but he didn't speak any Polish and couldn't communicate with her. The Legal Advisor phoned the Polish Legation and requested an interpreter, but was told that no one worked Saturday afternoons. Undoubtedly frustrated and confused, the Legal Advisor informed the Cinecetta Camp Director that Bronislawa would be staying with Irene Page that night, and that if Czeslawa showed up she should also be brought to Page's hotel right away. That evening, Czeslawa showed up at the hotel, escorted by the camp police.

When she was asked what had happened, she explained that she had told the man that she didn't want to go with him. She had finally recognized the man. He was the Polish Red Cross official who had issued the repatriation certificates for herself and her sister just a few days earlier. The man had retorted that "the English have nothing to do with her now, that she belonged to the Polish Government and must accompany him to the Polish Embassy." When she had still hesitated, he threatened her, telling her that she would have to live with the consequences of not co-operating. Afraid of what would happen if she refused, she left with him. After waiting some time at the embassy, another man had appeared and asked her all sorts of questions: the same questions they had asked of Bronislawa. When she told them that she had been well-treated and no one had turned the children against repatriation, they appeared not to believe her. They kept telling her to speak the truth and that they would know when she did, because of what her sister had told them. She said she was not mistreated at the embassy, but that she was frightened by the questioning and that they did not seem to believe her. When they asked her if she wanted to repatriate, she said that she wanted to wait for another letter from her mother before deciding. In fact, by the time she got to the Victoria Hotel that evening, Czeslawa and Bronislawa both were determined not to repatriate. As Czeslawa argued, if they didn't believe her that day, they would never believe her in Poland. The whole day's experience had been too unnerving and frightening.[40] Irene Page kept them at the hotel overnight and then returned them to Salerno promptly the next morning. Inevitably, the story of what happened to them flew around the camp, further hardening the children against repatriation, as well as panicking and infuriating the adults who were their escorts from Africa.

Krycz was furious. Three weeks of careful work trying to present what he maintained was as even-handed a picture of Poland as possible, to these very suspicious children, had been undone in a few disastrous hours. Besides the individual interviews, Krycz had met with large groups of the children to argue the merits of repatriation, provided an exhibit of photos of Poland taken by IRO officers on a visit there, shown colour films and Polish newsreels, and distributed a Polish newspaper for the children to see what it was really like in their homeland. The ITS had also been working very hard to trace the children's remaining families and relatives, and were continuously in contact with IRO Warsaw. This one escapade had destroyed all of the tenuous goodwill and interest that he had been able to generate. Krycz estimated that about fifteen of the children might have opted for repatriation until the Morawska fiasco and the "skillfully indoctrinated propaganda" of the London Poles. He lashed out at IRO Rome for not having better security at Cinecetta, and demanded that someone confront the Polish Legation about the untoward and improper methods that they used to get information about the children.[41]

The Poles in Salerno were quick to report the fiasco back to Tengeru. Grosicka had panicked after the Morawska sisters returned to the camp, especially when she heard that the Polish Government was insisting it had jurisdiction over the children and was determined to repatriate them all. She cabled Arusha, asking the Board of Guardians there for help protecting the children. As a result, an angry crowd invaded the house of the IRO representatives in Tengeru on August 4, demanding action. If they had foreseen the danger to the children in moving them to Italy, why hadn't the IRO? A midnight mass was held for the children, and the next day a representative of the Board of Guardians arrived in Nairobi, to demand that the IRO do something to prevent the children's repatriation. Curtis, although assuming all of this to be nonsense, cabled Geneva requesting their immediate assurance that no child would be repatriated unwillingly and any such demands from Warsaw would be refused. He closed the cable requesting that IRO Rome might want to ensure that any future communications from Grosicka to Tengeru "cause less alarm." He also suggested that the sooner the children were resettled the better, as it was impossible for him to do his job effectively in the present poisoned climate.[42]

IRO Geneva was livid. The heightened suspicions of the Poles, both in Salerno and in Tengeru, made their task almost impossible.[43] Geneva sent instructions to immediately disperse the teachers who had accompanied the children to Italy, reflecting the commonly held, but mistaken, belief among the IRO personnel that the children were being used and corrupted by their Polish supervisors, and that their removal would make the children more tractable.[44]

Meanwhile, Warsaw's representatives in Rome were not idle. The next morning, July 27, Warsaw's Embassy in Rome phoned Brigadier Daly (IRO Rome), requesting interviews with all the children. Ominously, as Mrs. Grosicka had feared, the Warsaw Embassy raised concerns about the legal guardianship of the whole group and intimated that it believed that the children should not be resettled unless the plans had been approved by the embassy. Uncertain what to tell them, Daly phoned Geneva. Jacobsen, Assistant Director General, Repatriation and Resettlement, IRO Geneva, told him he should make "all reasonable facilities" available to the representative of the Polish Embassy to meet with the children, but the meeting had to be in the presence of an IRO repatriation officer and a child welfare officer. He also instructed Daly to ensure all measures be taken to prevent a repetition of the Morawska incident. And he reminded Daly that IRO policy was to give repatriation priority over resettlement and, if circumstances warranted it, Geneva was willing to change the plans for the movement of these children to Canada.[45]

Daly, although himself not particularly in favour of the children's repatriation, duly contacted the Polish Embassy and made arrangements for a delegation to visit the children. The Poles made it clear that their intention was to repatriate these Polish citizens, and that they believed only the Polish Government had the authority to determine the disposition of these citizens who, because of their age, were not able to decide for themselves.[46] On July 29, a delegation from the Polish Embassy arrived in the camp, where the children were gathered en masse in the recreation hall. The IRO representatives, Father Krolikowski, and Mrs. Grosicka were also in attendance, with Father Krolikowski presiding. He introduced the visitors and then gave them the floor. They spoke for a mere fifteen minutes, silenced by the children's smirks and marked indifference. When the speech was over, the children were invited to meet with the Polish representatives individually, if they wished. Not a single child did so, until Father Krolikowski prevailed on two of the older children to at least explain why they did not want to return to Poland. From the perspective of the Communists, the meeting was a disaster and they soon left, angry and belligerent.[47] Daly, on the other hand, was pleased. Warsaw's representatives had had an opportunity to meet with the children, as he had been instructed to arrange, but to little effect.[48]

The pressure on the IRO continued to mount from all sides. On August 2, Count Czapski, chair of the newly created Polish Orphans Board of Guardians in Italy, and a London Pole, protested to Assistant Director General Jacobsen about the way the children were being treated. Czapski complained that Krycz had spent days promoting repatriation and submitting the children to interrogations that often reduced them to tears. His heavy-handed approach had created a feeling of "unacceptable impressment." Krycz had been allowed to remove official documents from the children's files, as well as the nominal rolls, and to take them to his hotel outside the camp. Then, after the "long and disruptive" efforts of Krycz, the children were subjected to a visit from the Polish Legation in Rome — the Communist Poles. These men also had tried to persuade the children to repatriate. Given the frightening experience of the Morawska sisters, Czapski argued, you must understand the Poles' suspicion and fear. In response to Czapski's point-blank questions, Jacobsen promised that the children would not be repatriated to Poland unless they wished to do so, and that they would be moved to Canada as quickly as possible. Those children who might be found unable to go to Canada for reasons of health would be redirected to other resettlement schemes in other countries in the West, with the first choice being Britain.[49]

The Polish Government in Warsaw now became directly involved in the fray, demanding an explanation from Widdicombe (IRO Warsaw), and a nominal roll listing all the children. Widdicombe obfuscated, explaining that while he had a nominal roll, it was only for his office's use and he could not give it to the Polish Government without Geneva's permission. He did, however, give Warsaw a breakdown of the group by age. He also explained the results of the tracing efforts made to date. According to Widdicombe, a number of the children were found to have relatives alive in Poland — thirteen with a mother, two with a father, ten with other relatives. Seventeen had relatives in the United Kingdom, and four had relatives in other parts of the world. He reassured Warsaw that efforts were being made to persuade the children to consider repatriation.[50]

The next day, Widdicombe spoke to Mr. Youdin, Chief of the Repatriation Division for IRO Geneva. Only then did he find out about the Morawska incident. It was Widdicombe who had to explain to the Polish Minister of Foreign Affairs the consequences of his people's actions. He explained that, contrary to Warsaw's suspicions, the repatriation officer, Pierre Krycz, had been chosen to counsel the children as he had been in Poland the preceding October, and was "known to be heartily in favour of repatriation as the best solution for Polish Displaced Persons." Krycz had worked hard to persuade the children to repatriate. In fact, two of the children, the Morawska sisters, had decided to return home after receiving a letter from their mother. As Widdicombe explained it to the Polish Minister, they were then moved to a transit camp near Rome, documented, and waiting for transport. During the few days' wait, the girls were taken by someone from the Polish Embassy in Rome and "intensively interrogated." Now neither girl wished to return to Poland; both were very upset and had absolutely refused.

> Most unfortunate of all, when this information became known to the [rest of the] group, there was a general refusal to consider repatriation and further efforts on the part of IRO Repatriation Officers were of no avail. When Mr. Krycz, personally distressed at the frustration of all his efforts to persuade children to decide to return to Poland, paid a visit to the Polish Embassy to express his regret over what seemed ill-advised procedure, the person or persons with whom he talked at the Embassy agreed that what had been done had been a mistake.

As if that were not enough, Widdicombe explained, the IRO had just been informed by the Italian Government that the Polish Embassy had requested the extradition of the entire group. As a consequence,

> …[I]t appears that the Italian Government, anxious not to become involved in any dispute over these children, suggested to IRO that it would be convenient if they left Italy at once. Since the chances of voluntary repatriation seemed at that point nil, it was decided to move the children to Germany.

He reassured the Polish Minister that, although chances were now very slim, the IRO's Repatriation Division was going to continue to try to persuade at least the children with parents in Poland to return home, and that Mr. Krycz was going to follow the children to Germany and continue counselling the group. Widdicombe ended the note by expressing his own personal distress at the unfortunate turn of events.[51]

# 7 | The Scramble for Canada

The situation in Italy had quickly become untenable. The Warsaw Government was demanding that the children be turned over to them for repatriation, and the Italian Government quietly was asking the IRO to get the children out of the country before it faced an international incident that it would rather avoid. The IRO felt it strategic to move the children out of Italy, to Bremerhaven in northern Germany, as quickly as possible, in spite of the fact that they still hadn't been screened nor had any Canadian officials even laid eyes on any of them. It was all a bit of a mess.

The Bremen enclave, a small chunk of American-occupied territory surrounded by the British occupation zone, was the port from which all ships taking displaced persons to the western hemisphere sailed. Discretion being the better part of valour, the IRO had decided that Italy was no longer a secure place to keep the children while they were being screened. They had drawn too much attention, and the situation with the Polish Embassy was too sensitive. Menacingly, the Polish Embassy in Rome had formally petitioned the Italian Government to prevent their removal from Italy, save for repatriation to Poland. The Italian Government chose to ignore the Polish note and made no move to stop the children's transfer.[1] Indeed, as a member of the IRO, they could not have complied. However, Italy was also sensitive to the fact that it looked like a major international incident was about to develop, and it did not want to be involved. To avoid putting Italy in a difficult position, the IRO felt obliged to move the children out of the country quickly.[2]

During the evening of August 1, 1949, the IRO summoned Father Krolikowski and Mrs. Grosicka to Salerno, to tell them of Warsaw's demands and their plan to thwart the Communists. They argued that Bremerhaven would be much safer for the children, as it was an American enclave inside the British occupation zone in Germany, and would be safe from Communist interference. They asked Father Krolikowski and Mrs. Grosicka to return to the camp and get the children packed, ready to leave at dawn the next day. The children were to be told that they were moving to another camp, but really they would be put on a special train for Germany. Father Krolikowski and Mrs. Grosicka didn't know what to say, so were relieved when Mr. Czapski of the Guardianship Committee arrived and agreed with the IRO. Mr. Czapski, Father Krolikowski, and Mrs. Grosicka returned to the camp. The children were gathered in the recreation hall and told to pack right away. However, by the next morning all three were having serious misgivings, uncertain that Germany would be any safer for the children. When the IRO arrived to take the children to the train, they refused to let them go until they received a guarantee of their safety. Father Krolikowski even considered seeking sanctuary for the children in Vatican City, but the idea was rejected because of the even bigger international incident it would ultimately cause. Finally, Admiral Mentz, Director of IRO Rome, gave them a written guarantee that no repatriation commission would have access to the children, they would be treated as applicants for Canadian visas, and they would be accompanied by both their guardians and a representative of the Vatican (Monsignor Meysztowicz) until they left for Canada. With that in hand, Father Krolikowski and Mrs. Grosicka allowed the children to leave for Germany.[3] So on August 3, the same day that the Warsaw Government demanded an explanation from the IRO's Widdicombe, the children were moved out of Italy to Tirpitz, a transit camp in Bremerhaven, still on temporary transit visas (which was stretching the rules, as transit visas were intended to be used by displaced persons with proper visas in hand who were "transiting" through American-controlled territory, en route to their new home).

The children themselves knew little about the machinations behind the scene. For them, it was yet another mad scramble in the middle of the night, once again fleeing the Communists. Rumours had been flying around the camp the whole day — that they were going to Germany, that they were going to the Vatican City, that the Communists were trying to get them — but no one was telling them much, just to pack their bags and get ready to move at a moment's notice. It was two days of considerable confusion, anxiety, and resignation for the children. Used to being told nothing and being shunted around according to the whims of some administrator or entity, the children made increasingly wild plans. Some became concerned when they realized that the train, on the way to Bremerhaven, would pass very close to Poland and they feared that the Communists might suddenly divert their train into enemy territory. If that happened, some of the boys planned to leap off the train before it crossed the border and demand sanctuary in Germany.[4]

Their rapid departure left Charlotte Babinski and Pierre Krycz scrambling as well. They were still in the midst of their review of the children and the tracing process was not nearly complete. Krycz was particularly concerned about the position in which the IRO was putting itself by not returning the children to their next of kin, which was certainly IRO policy. Of the 148 youth and children brought to Italy from Tengeru, he had identified a possible twenty-seven as having relatives in Poland or elsewhere. Of those twenty-seven, he believed only one had the right to determine her own destiny, Czeslawa Morawska, because she was twenty-one years old and so of a legal majority. He was also deeply disturbed with the "complete disinterest in parental or family care" on the part of many of the children. He was convinced that the children had been briefed or prepared for the interviews ahead of time, and told how to answer the questions they would be asked. "If these cases are not handled with the greatest care," he cautioned, "IRO may in future, have to face serious allegations in the event of eventual legal action taken by parents who explicitly had expressed their wish that their children be reunited with them."[5]

So Krycz and Page followed the children to Bremerhaven, where Krycz continued his review. The children were horrified to see him again.[6] The adults accompanying them were incensed, as they believed they had been promised that this would not happen. Both Admiral Mentz and Jacobsen had promised it. So when Krycz began the interviews anew in

Bremerhaven, Czpaski and Monsignor Meysztowicz sent scathing letters to Sir Arthur, Jacobsen, and Mentz, accusing them of either duplicity or incompetence.[7]

The Canadians were also scrambling to stay on top of the situation. Back in Immigration Services in Ottawa, Fortier cabled his people in Rome to forward what little documentation they had to the Immigration staff in Karlsruhe, Germany. There wasn't much time for screening and processing the children, as the Canadians had just been told that the IRO intended to move the children out of Germany by August 29. It was going to be a challenge. None of the children had yet been interviewed or had had a medical examination, and their number had risen by twenty-six from the original 132 approved in June. There was also the problem of the children's ages, as the visa officers still hadn't been informed whether the age restrictions could be waived.[8]

When Warsaw heard that the children had been moved to Germany, it launched an aggressive and multi-pronged attack, both through diplomatic channels and the media, intended to prevent the children's movement and embarrass the IRO, Canada, and anyone else who could be tarred with that brush. The first salvo had the Polish Government's representative in Berlin meet with the Polish Liaison Officer seconded to the American military Government in the American Zone of Germany, who then approached both the Canadian Government Immigration Mission in Karlsruhe and the Canadian Military Mission in Berlin, for a list of the children's names.[9]

At the same time, W.W. Schott of the Office of the United States Political Adviser (POLAD) in Frankfurt received a hand-delivered letter from Major Kjanowski, the Polish Consul in Frankfurt. In it, Kjanowski expressed surprise and indignation that this group of Polish children had been taken to an embarkation centre in Bremerhaven, rather than to a repatriation centre, as was the normal procedure. He argued that, in light of existing Polish and international laws, unaccompanied children were subject to the care of their home authorities, and that he knew that the U.S. Military and upper echelons of the IRO shared this opinion. Given the repeated demands by the Polish Government for the children's repatriation, he insisted that the American authorities should take immediate steps to prevent the children's intended emigration and to arrange their immediate transfer to a repatriation centre. The Poles also approached the British authorities on the same day, and registered the same protests and demands.[10]

Finally, General Wikto Gross of the Polish Foreign Ministry gave a rather damning interview to the *New York Herald Tribune Paris*. He condemned the IRO as "nothing but a recruiting center for cheap labour for some European countries and some overseas countries," as well as the Italian Government for allowing the children to be moved without the Polish Government's permission. He raised the alarm about the children's age, pointing out that most of these children were girls, and two-thirds were under seventeen years of age. Finally, he accused the IRO of preventing two of the children (Bronislawa and Czeslawa) from returning to their widowed mother in Poland, against their wishes.[11]

The Canadian response was to politely refer the Polish Government to the IRO in Geneva, as the children were still their responsibility, not the Canadians' (which was technically true as they had not yet been visaed). The Americans and British, on the other hand, were caught off guard, so they obfuscated until they could find out exactly what was going on. When they each finally got an explanation from the IRO, it was a bit disingenuous. They were told that the children had been part of a larger group taken from Poland in 1940, by the British Near East Resettlement and Rehabilitation Organization, which was or became part of UNRRA, nicely missing a crucial part of their story — their forced deportation to Siberia — which would have explained to the American and British the children's hostility to all things Communist or Soviet. These Poles had been settled in various corners of the Near East and Africa, including Tanganyika. They had just been processed recently by the IRO for resettlement in Canada (also not quite accurate). Since their initial departure from Poland and their movement to East Africa, the Polish Government had, at no time, made any effort to contact these children, nor had it ever made any claims on them. Most importantly, this was a regular IRO transport, meaning that the American and the British responsibility was limited to granting safe conduct through their respective zones, and accommodation while the children awaited embarkation.[12]

This, the Americans and the British both explained to the Poles. The Polish retort to POLAD was as sharp as it was dismissive. The Polish Mission complained that no Polish consular office, or any other Polish representative in Germany for that matter, had been apprised of the plans to send Polish children to foreign countries instead of being repatriated. The Polish Government was "convinced that this act of clandestine violence which is contrary to all established rules of international practice has not been brought to the notice of the Office of the Political Adviser" — POLAD could never have known what was happening, or it would have surely prevented this heinous crime. The Poles demanded that POLAD prevent the children's embarkation for Canada and "from their being deprived once more of their home and country;" provide a list of the children's names, and inform the Polish authorities when they might be able to make arrangements for the children's repatriation.[13] The Americans' response was as prompt, but noncommittal, basically repeating their earlier disavowal of all knowledge or responsibility, and referring the Poles to either the IRO Headquarters in Geneva or the Canadian Government.[14]

In frustration, the Polish Mission in Berlin confronted the Canadians again, in the person of P.T. Molson, Acting Head of the Canadian Military Mission, demanding the children not be permitted to sail and that the Poles be allowed to visit the children in order to arrange their repatriation.[15] Molson promised to convey the Poles' concerns to the Secretary of State for External Affairs in Ottawa, which he did, as well as copies of the Poles' representations to the American authorities and the Americans' response, which the Americans had obligingly given him.[16]

The next day, Warsaw continued its attack, this time directing its attention at the IRO. In Warsaw, John Widdicombe's assistant, Mrs. Gardiner, was summoned to the Polish Ministry of Foreign Affairs (Widdicombe was in Germany at the moment, leaving Mrs. Gardiner as the most senior IRO representative available). The Ministry's spokesman, Mr. Szeminski, protested the IRO's refusal to cooperate and warned that if the children left for Canada before clarification "had been arrived at," his government would consider lodging "a vigorous official protest." He also warned that the American authorities had assured the Polish that the children would not be permitted to leave until their position was clarified.[17] On the same day, J. Bikart, the Senior Representative of the Polish Red Cross, visited P.E. Ryan, Chief of Operations, IRO U.S. Zone in Germany. Bikart requested that Ryan immediately stop the transport of the children; that he provide him with a list of their names, ages, and birthplaces for tracing purposes; and that a representative of the Polish Red Cross be allowed to see the children and assume control of them. Bikart reiterated the by now well-honed Polish argument, that only legitimate Polish authorities in the U.S. Zone were authorized to make decisions about these children's future.[18] On August 13, the Senior Representative of the Polish Red Cross in the British occupied zone in Germany, Z. Radomski, sent a letter to the Zone Welfare Officer for the IRO, British Zone, in which he echoed Bikart closely.[19] The two Zone Directors for the IRO, American and British, were equally noncommittal in their responses to the Polish demands. Ryan promised to take the Polish Government's concerns under advisement, and the British argued that as the children were not in the British Zone, there was nothing they could do.[20]

By this point, IRO Geneva was getting quite concerned, and not just because of the Polish threats. Rumours were flying that, in the end, the Canadians might not accept many of the children, as they were reluctant to take any over the age of sixteen. There was also some concern about what position the Americans had decided to take on the matter, given what Gardiner had been told in Poland.[21] On August 13, the Deputy Director-General of IRO contacted Ryan to get a sense of his understanding of the situation. Ryan replied that, as far as he knew, both the IRO and EUCOM (European Command, U.S. Army) regarded the children as in transit, which meant that they were the IRO's responsibility, not the U.S. Military Government's. Ryan knew nothing of any promise by any American authorities that the children would not be allowed to move until the situation was clarified, but warned that there was a chance that the American Government might intervene due to the pressure from Poland. It appeared to him that the Poles were not going to let the matter drop.[22]

At the same time, the Polish Military Mission had, once again, asked Molson for a response to their questions.[23] Finally, on August 16, Ottawa gave him their response:

Movement of these children to Canada has been arranged by Catholic authorities in Quebec and the IRO. Immigration is satisfied that the children will be properly cared for and has therefore authorized their entry. The children are, of course, under the jurisdiction of the IRO until they are landed in Canada, but the Canadian Government has no objection to their entry and does not intend to interfere with the present arrangements.[24]

By this time, Krycz had finished his interviews. He was not pleased with the results. Of the 132 children he interviewed, only "a certain number" appeared to be truly orphaned. Twenty-seven certainly had relatives, if not parents, still alive and in Poland or elsewhere, and the International Tracing Service was now trying to contact the relatives. A small number had relatives in the U.S., Argentina, South Africa, and Australia, and efforts were underway to contact them as well. Krycz wanted time to follow through with those investigations because he firmly maintained that the children should be reunited with their relatives.[25]

The Canadians were also taken aback by what they found, now that they had finally had a chance to interview the group. The rumours had been true, as it wasn't clear from the initial review whether all the children would be successfully visaed. First, there was considerable confusion about which children were actually approved by Ottawa, as there were some notable discrepancies between the nominal roll provided to the Canadian visa officers dated June 22, and the actual children in Tirpitz, based on a nominal roll dated August 10. The list from which they were working was missing forty names. P.W. Bird, the chief visa officer, wondered whether they had, indeed, been approved by Ottawa, but somehow omitted from his nominal roll. So IRO Geneva contacted IRO Ottawa to see if Immigration could cable Bird at Tirpitz, authorizing visa action for the forty. Immigration Branch in Ottawa responded promptly on August 17, granting approval in principle for the extra forty names, pending screening.[26]

A more serious snag developed, however, as the screening began in earnest. There were a number of children who, it appeared, couldn't pass the medical examination. A panicked cable was sent by Monsignor

Meysztowicz and Dorothy Sullivan to the Archbishop of Montreal, and then passed on to the Immigration Branch, pleading with Ottawa to grant these children special permission to enter Canada for humanitarian and practical reasons. The children who had been identified as questionable were Wladislaw Nerka, Bronislawa Paluch, Wiktor Drabowicz, Boleslaw Kacpura, and Franciszka Woyniak. Wladislaw was twenty years old and slightly lame, but a trained mechanic and reported to be an excellent worker. Bronislawa, aged eleven, had a slight curvature of the spine and was accompanied by her older brother, aged sixteen, who was listed as a trained mechanic. Boleslaw, aged thirteen, was deaf and dumb, but trained as a tailor and was with a sister, aged fourteen, and a twelve-year-old brother, both of whom were in fine health. Franciszka, aged twenty, had a partially paralyzed right arm and leg.

It was also becoming clear that there were children in the group who did have parents in Poland. Sullivan and Meysztowicz argued that these children's parents insisted that the children should not return to Poland, but should remain outside the Communist bloc. Their plea was heartfelt.

> Please urge the Government to allow them to enter also. Kindly obtain for all these victims of persecution special consideration so that we may not be forced to leave them to the mercy of those who have fought bitterly to repatriate them.[27]

For the children, their stay in Tirpitz was a blur of medical examinations, vaccinations, x-rays, doctors, meetings with a myriad of officials — exactly who they were and which organizations they were from, the children had no idea. None of them paid much attention to what was going on around them; this was just another transit camp on the route to somewhere else. None of them paid much attention to Krycz. All were focused on getting to Canada. And Sophia Wakulczyk fell in love.

It all happened innocently. One day, Sophia, now eighteen, was asked if she would help out in the IRO office at the camp. A shipment of goods had come in and all of the paperwork was in Polish. No one in the office read Polish, but the German supply officer, Robert Schreiber, did speak English. Because of the eight months Sophia had spent with the Ramseys, her English was good enough to act as translator, so she agreed to help out. When she entered the office the first time, Robert rose to his feet and very elegantly bowed to her. He had had a very proper upbringing, being from an upper middle class, and very prosperous, merchant's family. She was quite taken aback and very flattered. The second time she came to the office, he had peaches for her and she was swept off her feet. Unbeknownst to her, Robert soon announced to his mother that he had met the woman he was going to marry. Sophia continued on to Canada with her two brothers, but the two of them kept up a close correspondence. Robert followed her to Canada within two years, and the two settled in Kitchener, Ontario.[28]

Meanwhile, the Polish Government persisted in its attack. The Polish Military Mission in Berlin finally issued a formal note verbale to the Canadian Military Mission there, repeating its demands that the movement of the children be stopped and a list of the children's names be provided. The Canadians reiterated their argument that the children were not their responsibility until they entered Canada, but that the Canadian Government had no objection to their entry, nor did it intend to interfere with the arrangements made.[29]

On August 16, Cecil Lyon of the American Embassy in Warsaw was called into the Foreign Office of the Polish Government by the Acting Director of Department III (American-British), Mr. Krzeminski. Krzeminski began by stating that he hoped he was addressing the right person, but with so many different authorities involved, all of whom were avoiding assuming responsibility, he was at a loss as to whom he should be speaking. He told Lyon that he objected to the pending movement of the children to Canada, which the Polish Government regarded as tantamount to kidnapping. He protested that the IRO was preventing the children from talking to Polish officials, and had put the children under the direct charge of an émigré priest who was acting on behalf of the London Poles, and therefore undermining the legitimate Polish Government. The Polish Government had already taken up the matter with the IRO, the British authorities, and the Italian Government, getting nowhere. When Lyon protested that this was not an American affair, Krezminski insisted it was, because the children were in American territory. He warned that the United States didn't want to be involved in such a sordid affair, "without making proper investigation and assuring themselves that these children are being moved in accordance with international law."

Meanwhile, the Polish press was having a field day.[30] It had begun on August 14, a few days before Lyons' meeting, with an article in the official newspaper of the Polish Workers' Party, the *Tybuna Ludu*, with a piece entitled, "On the Trail of Kidnappers. Whereabouts of Polish Children from Tanganyika Discovered." The article echoed the Polish Government's demands. It also condemned the United States, asking rhetorically,

> Is it possible that American authorities, when granting visas to Polish children, do not know that they are assisting kidnappers? Are they perhaps unaware of a violation of international law, of violating IRO's statute, so carefully prepared by themselves and then pressed upon other countries? Perhaps they have completely forgotten that they are members of this organization?

A second article appeared in the same newspaper on August 19, entitled "Slave Dealers," accusing Canada of caring nothing about the welfare of the displaced persons, but only seeing them as a source of cheap labour.[31]

It was not just the Polish press either. In Italy, an Italian Communist paper condemned the Italian Government for failing to respond to the Polish request that it be permitted to arrange the children's repatriation, especially since many parents had requested it. Not only had it failed to reply to the Polish Embassy, but it had also allowed the children to be moved to Germany. This was especially serious, the article argued, because at least two of the children had told the Polish Embassy that they wished to repatriate, but were still moved to Germany, in spite of the fact that their mother, who was in Poland, very much wanted them back.[32]

The negative press in Poland had not gone unnoticed by the Canadian Legation in Warsaw. K.P. Kirkwood, the Chargé d'Affaires of the Canadian Legation, reported what he knew to his superiors in External Affairs, Ottawa, on August 18. Interestingly, the Warsaw

Government had yet to approach either the Canadian Legation or the British Embassy. This meant he had to rely on what Lyons told him of his meeting with the Polish Foreign Ministry, and on the press. He warned them of the hostile reports in the Polish press and that matters were not helped by John Widdicombe (IRO Warsaw). Widdicombe was very pro-Polish and he had openly expressed regret that the children were not returning to Poland. Kirkwood suggested that Canada should expect some kind of protest and that much would be made of it in the press, in the same manner as the Dionne case.[33]

By this point, EUCOM and Washington were becoming increasingly worried about the situation and about possible physical interference by the Poles. They wanted to ensure that the movement went through "without disorder" and promised to supply the IRO with whatever forces were necessary to ensure that the ship left on time.[34] Washington was also concerned about ensuring that it had all the facts of the case at hand. On August 19, the State Department in Washington DC directed its people in Geneva, Berlin, Heidelberg, Warsaw, and Rome to "report soonest" all information that they had about these children. The State Department expected that it was soon going to have answer some hard questions. It was also concerned, as a member of the IRO, that this group be treated in accordance with American policy. That policy required that a child's best interests be the principal factor in determining whether they be repatriated or resettled, and that repatriation should be considered in the child's best interest only when both child and parents desired it.[35] The American occupation government (the Occupied Military Government United States or OMGUS) in Berlin quickly reminded Washington that the children had been moved through American-controlled territory on transit visas, and as such were not an American responsibility. The implication was that this was not a matter for the State Department.[36]

By this time, IRO Geneva was no longer able to ignore the situation. On August 17, five days after Mrs. Gardiner had been called into the Polish Foreign Office in Warsaw and lambasted for the IRO's actions, R.J. Youdin invited a Polish Government representative to visit the Director General in Geneva "if you [Poland] wish further discussion this matter."[37]

Meanwhile, a flurry of cables flew back and forth between Sir

Arthur and P. Jacobsen, Assistant Director-General for Repatriation and Resettlement. There was considerable debate about whether to let Warsaw meet the children, as Jacobsen was concerned it would be setting a precedent. The Poles had already been given ample opportunity to meet the children in Salerno, he argued, although they had chosen not to. He was concerned, and rightly so, that the Vatican and the Catholic authorities would take great exception to a third attempt at what they would inevitably call "forcible repatriation." Jacobsen was in the awkward position, after all, of having already faced the wrath of the Tengeru and Vatican Poles once, over the repatriation efforts of Krycz. He had long promised Count Czapski, of the Polish Orphans Board of Guardians in Italy, that the children would not be forcibly repatriated. Yet another round of interviews intended to persuade the children to consider repatriation would not go over well.

J.D. Kingsley, Director General of the IRO (and Sir Arthur Rucker's superior), disagreed, arguing that this was a special situation. The Polish Red Cross had never had an opportunity to speak to the children, having had no representatives working in either East Africa or Italy, so this last chance should not be denied them. Realistically, he felt that no minds would be changed by their visit, so there was little risk of incurring the wrath of the Vatican or anyone else, but perhaps there was some opportunity to placate the Warsaw Poles. He realized that it was somewhat of a gamble, but he thought the risk was minimal. Jacobsen begrudgingly acquiesced, but pressed that the Canadians and the Vatican both be warned before the visit. The decision was that the Polish Government would not be given permission to see the children, but Widdicombe was instructed to inform the Polish Red Cross privately that if they asked to see the children, their request would be granted. However, it would be clear this would not affect the children's transit status. Widdicombe was also instructed to speak to the Catholic authorities involved to discuss those cases where there seemed to be a strong possibility for voluntary repatriation. His task was to gain their acquiescence to the repatriation of these particular children, a tricky proposition.[38]

The Polish Red Cross leapt at the chance. On August 19, Jacobsen cabled Tirpitz camp to warn them to prepare for the visit. He also asked

Mr. Grohn, the camp director, to tell the Canadian Selection Mission and Monsigneur Meysztowicz of the plans and to explain that it was at the Director-General's request. He told Grohn that he wanted him in Tirpitz during the visit, or at least a senior international employee directly subordinate to him, as he did not expect this to go smoothly.[39]

Fortier reported to Ottawa that the Poles were being given access to the children for two days, during which time neither Miss Sullivan nor the escort officers were allowed to see them. Amazingly, the visit came to nothing, as the one Polish Red Cross representative who did visit the camp refused to interview a single child until the IRO produced a nominal roll. The IRO steadfastly refused to do so, arguing that it would contravene policy as established by the IRO's General Council, and based on decisions made by both the Economic and Social Council and the General Assembly of the United Nations.[40] In the end, the Polish Red Cross withdrew in a huff, without talking to a single child.[41]

Meanwhile, the protests continued. The Demokratischer Frauenbund Deutschlands (DFD), a German women's organization, passed a resolution on August 19, protesting the "planned deportation of 150 Polish children to Canada through the IRO," and sent it to the IRO Headquarters in Bad Kissingen.[42]

By this time, Washington was becoming increasingly concerned. Dean Acheson, Secretary of State, contacted Alvin Roseman, the U.S. Representative for Specialized Agency Affairs in Geneva, asking him to send a report "soonest" on the Polish children.[43] He had become concerned because of a press clipping from the Warsaw Overseas Press Service dated August 10, that spoke of the IRO kidnapping children, and referred specifically to the two Morawska sisters who wished to repatriate. Acheson expected that he would eventually have to deal with the charges and, as a member of the IRO, wanted to be sure that the IRO had acted (in the stilted language of cables), "consistent with U.S. policy that best interests of the child should be principal factor in determining whether to repatriate or resettle and that repatriation should take place as serving best interest in any case in which both child and parents desire it."[44]

Meanwhile the children's processing was more or less complete. Of the 147 examined, the Canadian visa officers granted 123 of them permission to enter Canada. Of the remaining twenty-four, fourteen were rejected outright, four were held back for further review, and six were held back for further medical examination — either an investigation for venereal disease or a chest examination. Three of the children — Teresa Bialowas, Olga Gnyp and her sister, Helena Gnyp — had been granted visas to the United Kingdom. The Gnyps had already left Rome. Of the four cases held back for further review, three were siblings — the Kacpura family. The oldest was Boleslaw Kacpura, the tailor. His younger brother and sister refused to continue on to Canada without him. The fourth case held back for further review was that of Franciska Wozniak, the child with a slight, but permanent paralysis in her right arm. The Canadian officials felt that, although she might be a risk on the general labour market, she would only be a fair risk if she was steered towards an appropriate occupation. But before the visa officers at Tirpitz would make a decision they wanted some feedback from their superiors.[45]

From the Canadians' perspective the review had not gone well. P.W. Bird was incredibly frustrated by the whole exercise. Part of the problem was the various nominal lists floating about, none of which agreed with the other. It was all well and good to be told to adhere to the lists, but which one? And how could anyone have faith that either was correct? The lists he had did not match those of either Sullivan or the IRO. Further, Bird and his staff had been led to believe that all of the documentation would be completed before they saw the children, which was patently not the case. He complained that it appeared as though the IRO was doctoring the files overnight. Some important documents seen one day had disappeared by the next.

He also faced considerable pressure from the Polish authorities, who repeatedly demanded that he halt the screening process. The position Bird had taken with the Poles so far was straightforward: his task was to process those cases of individuals who wished to emigrate to Canada and, if they met the requirements, issue visas. His only concern was whether they met Canada's requirements, not whether they should be going to Canada or some other country. This had become his mantra, but clearly he was very uncomfortable. It had been absolutely necessary to maintain the utmost care and secrecy while examining the children and was still necessary to do so, as "the Polish Repatriation Mission appear[ed] to be prepared to go to any length to insist on their repatriation to Poland." It was also clear that Bird had no confidence in the IRO, so much so that whenever he phoned his superiors, he did so from a hotel in Bremen, because he was convinced there was a leak to the Polish authorities somewhere.[46]

Also, because the family history of each child had not been forwarded with them from Rome, things had been slowed down considerably. The documents had had to be prepared on the spot in Tirpitz, which took some time. A big part of the problem facing the visa officers in trying to construct the children's family histories was the tortuous route they had travelled to Bremerhaven, making it impossible to get definite proof of their parents' deaths. Bird worried because, "[i]n most instances there was some inference that the children might not be bona fide orphans." In fact, three cases were refused because it was definitely established that one child had a father in France and two others had a mother in Africa. In some instances, the children admitted that one parent, usually their mother, might be alive in Siberia or Poland, "but as they were behind the Iron Curtain, I [Bird] took the liberty of assuming that to all intents and purposes, and in the absence of proof to the contrary, that the children might be considered orphans." Bird had the definite sense that he and his staff had been the victims of a degree of obstruction and that, in at least two cases, the documentation appeared to have been altered.

Finally, he explained, other children were ultimately rejected because they were found to have either tuberculosis or a physical disability, although in one case, a girl was found to be pregnant and, in two others, they were suspected of having a venereal disease. So it was probably with some relief when, on August 20, Bird reported that the processing was completed. Having begun on August 15, the marathon finished at midnight on August 18, after Bird had examined a total of 147 children. He believed that all the visaed cases would "go forward" on the SS *General Heintzelman* on August 29.[47]

Miss Sullivan of the Catholic Immigrant Aid Society was determined to appeal some of the rejections. One group of three siblings — Helena, Krystyna, and Tadeuz Kropa — had been rejected because they were apparently not orphans. Sullivan explained that their mother had died in

Tehran and their father was unable to look after them, being an invalid, and so had put them in the orphanage. He had stayed with the group, however, performing odd tasks for the orphanage, including serving as the shoemaker, so he could keep an eye on his children. Neither the children nor the orphanage's director, Mrs. Grosicka, knew exactly what was wrong with him, other than he suffered from a kidney condition and had seriously impaired vision in one eye. Sullivan explained that, prior to the children's departure with the orphanage, both the Camp Leader and Mr. Lorrimer, the Camp IRO Officer, had talked at length with the children's father, who was hospitalized at the time. The father felt he was unable to support his children due to his ill health, and that they should emigrate. While some of the details of this story were at variance with what the children told the Canadian visa officers, the fact was that the children could not be returned to Tengeru. The oldest, Helena, was found to have tuberculosis, which meant that she needed to remain in a sanatorium in Europe. The younger two were considered to be "in danger if placed in a Children's Centre in Germany," presumably of being forcibly repatriated to Poland. Sullivan argued that these children, along with the others, had been:

> ... [S]ubject to exhausting and nerve wracking pressure
> aimed to lead toward repatriation since the 20th of June
> when they came happily off the boat in Italy, believing
> the assurances which had been given that they would be
> on the boat going to Canada very quickly.

For these reasons, Sullivan and the Catholic Immigrant Aid Society asked that they be allowed to continue on to Canada, pledging that the children would never become public charges and that every protection would be given to them. This seemed to carry little weight with the Canadian visa officers, who instead wanted to know the state of the father's health before reconsidering their decision. Dorothy Sullivan assured the officers that the father was dying, and that she could get medical evidence from Africa to that effect. The officers agreed that if she could produce the medical evidence, they would reconsider the case — but only then.[48] Apparently she was persuasive, at least in some cases, as on August 23, Immigration Ottawa notified Congdon that the Catholic Immigrant Aid Society had expressed its willingness to assume full responsibility for the public charge liability of the children rejected because of minor physical disabilities.[49]

Predictably, the Polish Government and its representatives continued to press for the children's repatriation. On August 23, the Polish Ministry of Foreign Affairs, under the guise of confirming the August 16 conversation with Lyon, reiterated its demands in a formal note delivered to the American Embassy in Warsaw.[50] Lyon was quite perplexed that Warsaw insisted on complaining to him, but had not yet approached Kirkwood at the Canadian Legation in Warsaw.[51] Kirkwood was also perplexed. He was also still rather in the dark about the matter and wrote the Department of External Affairs requesting a summation of the situation and Canada's position on the matter (which they promptly sent him[52]). He did warn Ottawa that the Polish press was continuing to have a field day, with numerous articles condemning the IRO for having kidnapped these children to work as slave labour in Canadian factories or on Canadian farms, while their families waited in vain for their return to Poland. He reported that, rather damagingly, an IRO representative, a Miss Page, was quoted as having said she doubted if the children were even Polish any more, as they may have become British subjects while in Tanganyika, although the Polish Government might still be able to claim they were Polish by parentage or birth. It didn't help that she herself was a Canadian.[53]

While the propaganda campaign in Poland had begun in early August, with articles full of condemnation and outrage, demanding the children's return, the vitriol was even thicker by the month's end. The quantity of articles was voluminous, all with titles such as "To Save Polish Children Abducted by IRO"; "Grim Spectre of Deportation to Canada. Return our children to us, Appeal the Families of Poles Detained By IRO"; "The Children Must Return to Poland. The Appeal of Families Menaced With Deportation to Canada"; "Families of Children, Abducted By IRO, Demand the Return of Their Sons and Daughters"; "123 Polish Children Deported By IRO to Canada"; "A Crime Under IRO 'Care'."[54]

Lyon was also reporting the explosion of hostile press to his superiors in Washington. He was as dismayed as Kirkwood, as the press was attacking the United States as much as Canada. He sent one article in particular, entitled "Slave Dealers," as an example. In it, Canada was accused of not much caring about the emigrants' welfare. Canada needed them:

> ...[F]or hard work, from which we [i.e., Canada] shall draw our profits and we verify their health, as we would army horses, to make sure they are strong.... Reports have been received about Polish girls' slave work in Canadian plants, about "Polish Negroes" deprived of care, working on Canadian farms.... The determining factor in IRO policy are persons having nothing in common with care for children and for emigrants in general. They are, on the other hand, strongly interested in supplying Canadian plants and farm owners with cheap manpower.[55]

At the same time, another genre of articles began to emerge. What made these articles different were the testimonies from individual families who claimed that they had children in the group from Tanganyika. In "Families of Kidnapped Polish Children Indignant with IRO's Conduct," Jadwiga Szypnicka was reported to be waiting impatiently for her youngest son's return, eleven-year-old Bohdan. Her "whole life [was] devoted to awaiting [her] youngest son." Disconcertingly for Lyon, who decided to investigate the veracity of these articles' claims, according to the nominal roll and Krycz's interview, Bohan was actually born in 1932, making him approximately eighteen years old. Furthermore, according to Krycz's interview with the boy, Bohdan had adamantly refused to repatriate because he wanted to finish his studies, but not in Poland. He was resolutely determined not to become a "communist," rather he wanted to join his older brother in England. The article also mentioned two sisters with an uncle and aunt looking for them. According to the relatives, these two girls, aged nineteen and twelve, were "an unceasing topic of ... conversation." However, according to the IRO's nominal roll, they were aged nineteen and fifteen, above the age of discretion at which they were considered mature enough to make decisions for themselves. A third example cited in the article was just as confusing. Halina Jurman was an orphan whose parents had died during the war, but according to the article she had relatives in Poland who were shocked and indignant at the IRO's actions, as they wanted her to return. According to the nominal roll, she was twenty years old, and accompanying a younger sister, Marija, who was nineteen years old and never mentioned in the article.[56] In all honesty, Lyon didn't know what to make of the information.[57] If nothing else, it was evidence of the wild rumours that were circulating in Warsaw. It also suggested that perhaps Warsaw was less interested in the children than in the discomfort and embarrassment it could cause the Western powers with its accusations.

Indeed, the language of the articles was increasingly rote. There were two interlinked themes. First was that the capitalist West, in this case Canada, was exploiting the IRO as a vehicle for getting cheap labour for its factories and farms. In the process, it was robbing Poland of its future labour force. Every displaced person who failed to return to Poland was a grievous loss to the Polish economy, as well as an insult to Poland's wartime suffering and postwar recovery. The second theme was that returning these children to Poland was in their best interests, as they had families in Poland. Failing to reunite the children with their families flew in the face of the IRO's mandate and continued the gross injustices of the war. The children would not be properly appreciated in Canada, argued the Poles. In Poland, they would be.

Circumstances threw that conclusion into doubt. The lack of convincing evidence of any family seeking their children's return, the errors in the press accounts about the children who were supposedly being sought by their families in Poland, raised questions. Furthermore, if Warsaw was set on having the children return to Poland, one would expect the Poles to take full advantage of any opportunity to meet with them and persuade them to return. Instead, when opportunities arose, they were wasted. Warsaw should have been hounding the IRO and the Canadian Government, not the British, American, and Italian Governments, if it truly wanted to halt the children's movement. After all, it was the IRO and the Canadian Government who controlled the children and could quash the movement the quickest. Instead, the visits to see the children were perfunctory exercises, a demonstration of the principle that the Poles had access to the children, rather than a serious, concerted effort to win them over. Warsaw's focus seemed more on embarrassing the major powers and scoring points at home than on saving the children. If the children's best interests were truly the issue, Poland had an odd way of pursuing it.

Nonetheless, the Polish representatives in Germany did not give up. On August 22, after having visited the children in Tirpitz, Dr. Kalmannowicz of the Polish Red Cross spoke to Sir Arthur Rucker and requested that the transport to Canada be postponed. Rucker explained to Kalmannowicz that he had already consulted with Mr. Kingsley, Director General of the IRO, about the matter and that he had been instructed that the IRO would not release a nominal roll to the Polish authorities. Any child who wished to repatriate would be assisted in doing so, those not willing to be repatriated would be resettled, and the IRO would not postpone their departure on a ship for which arrangements had already been made. As none of the children had opted for repatriation, their departure would go ahead on August 29.[58]

By August 22, it seemed that the list had been finalized. One hundred twenty-three children had been processed for Canada, and one for the United Kingdom. Fourteen had been rejected, largely for medical reasons, mostly tuberculosis. Four had been set aside for further review, although three of them, in all likelihood, would be rejected because one of the three siblings was the twenty-year-old deaf mute (the Kacpura siblings). His brother and sister were acceptable, but it was not clear that they would go on to Canada without him. Another six, some of whom were suspected of having VD, were "furthered," meaning that the decision had been delayed pending further investigation. The plan was to put the children who were rejected into an IRO center in Germany. The children who were going to Canada would embark the USAT *Heintzelman* and leave for Halifax, Nova Scotia, on August 29.[59]

At this point the IRO decided the moment was ripe to launch its own counterattack in the press. IRO Rome issued a press release on August 23, dismissing the Polish Government's statement that the children were being deported by the IRO. IRO Rome made it clear that the IRO had no power to deport anyone, and that these children "had freely elected to take advantage of a generous offer from Canada where they [would] be found foster homes and work." Indeed, it stated that a delegation of three representatives from the Polish Embassy in Rome had visited the children in the IRO Children's Centre in Salerno, to determine if any wanted to repatriate. The representatives had been accorded every hospitality and courtesy, and the children were, in accordance with IRO statutory policy, invited to present themselves to the Polish visitors to discuss the possibility of repatriation. The IRO did acknowledge that two of the children had originally declared their willingness to be repatriated, but they had changed their minds. The group had since been transferred to Germany, in the ordinary course of IRO shipping procedure, as all IRO ships going to Canada sailed from Germany. The Italian Government had no involvement or authority in the transfer. The press release concluded by stating that simply being in Germany did not mean that any children who, at that late moment, suddenly decided they wanted to repatriate could not do so. Rather, the IRO would happily assist them and provide them with the same facilities as they would have received if they had decided to repatriate while in Italy.[60]

The press release had, predictably, little impact. The next day, the Director of the Department of Press and Information for the Polish Government made his own press release, announcing that the Polish Government had requested permission from the American Government for access to the camp in order to make the necessary arrangements for the children's repatriation. He pointed out that the U.S. authorities could not avoid responsibility for what happened to the Polish children while under their jurisdiction. Upon receiving the press release, Lyon fired off a telegram to Washington, asking for quick advice on how to handle the increasingly prickly situation.[61]

Secretary of State Acheson panicked and ordered the departure be delayed until he was certain that U.S. policies regarding repatriation had been abided by, although he also ordered that the Polish Government not be told this.[62] Lyon complied, reporting that he had left the Polish Foreign Office with the understanding that the ship was still expected to sail on August 29.[63]

The response from the Department's counterparts in the field was immediate and adamant. Both Riddleberger of the U.S. Office of the Political Advisor in Heidelberg, and Alvin Roseman insisted that Washington had neither the authority nor the grounds on which to delay departure. This was a movement that had originated outside of Germany, and outside of American jurisdiction. The Polish Government had had opportunities to interview the children, the children had been properly screened, and the IRO had presented the children with ample opportunity to choose repatriation if they wished. None chose to. As Roseman argued, the IRO had complied reasonably with its constitution and Provisional Order No. 75. As Riddleberger put it, "…it seems to us here that the Embassy is in a position to point out that the Polish authorities, in protesting the departure of these children, are not really motivated by any solicitude for the children's welfare but rather are acting and airing the matter in the press for propaganda reasons."[64]

# 8 | Canada — A Home at Last

On August 29, the *Heintzelman* sailed for Canada with the children on board. The voyage itself was uneventful, if less comfortable. According to the children, the *Heintzelman* was no *Jerusalemme*. If the Canadians needed any further confirmation that the Poles had not lost interest in the children, however, they got it when the children's ship docked in Halifax. There, according to a local newspaper, *The Ensign*, "Soviet Polish representatives" met the children as they came off the ship. The children were carefully shepherded past the "Soviet Poles" and onto a train bound for Montreal, accompanied by several priests and nuns, as well as Father Brosseau of the sponsoring agency, the Catholic Immigrant Aid Society.

Just before the train reached Montreal, it stopped at Drummondville, Quebec, where most of the children alighted. There, the children were transferred to buses and taken to Contrecoeur, a summer resort on the banks of the St. Lawrence River. The boys were installed in the summer camp of the Frères du Sacré Coeur, Saint Vincent, and the girls, in that of the Sœurs de Notre Dame du Bon-Conseil, Saint Hyacinth.[1] This was meant as a temporary way station for them, before moving to their final destinations. It was also as a way of hiding the children from the Communists.

It was just as well that most got off in Drummondville, as the small group of children who continued on to Montreal were met by a "reception committee" of Communist Poles armed with candies. According to *The Ensign*, "the young Poles were furious even at the sight of these agents of a hated regime." The majority of the children, the ones who had been taken to the summer camps, settled in comfortably. However, in spite of the subterfuge, within a few days, the Warsaw Poles had found them. In the words of *The Ensign*,

> The priest who had been with the children [Father Brosseau] was in Montreal, actually at lunch at the Archbishop's Palace, when a much frightened call came from the girls' camp. He immediately jumped into a car and with a Canadian priest rushed back. The nuns [who were supervising the girls' camp] had received a visit from some unknown people who had come to see the children and demanded [to be] admitted. Word had also passed to the police and to the boys' camp. It was there that the excitement was the biggest. The older lads rushed off to defend the girls and their truculence was hard to restrain. However, police arrived on the spot and the "visitors" beat a hasty retreat. Since that time special precautionary measures have had to be taken lest the emissaries of the Polish legation in Ottawa repeat their visit.[2]

Neither Sophia Wakulczyk nor Bronislawa Kusa remember the boys driving off the Communists, but they do remember the Communists showing up. Sophia recalls watching through a cabin window as one of the nuns confronted them in the yard. It was a nasty scene, and she recalls that one of the men slapped the nun on the face before leaving.[3] Bronislawa never actually saw the Communists, but she remembers being outside, playing with some friends, when a nun yelled at them to run to the river immediately and not talk to anyone.[4]

Meanwhile, there were still some twenty-five children who had not been allowed to go to Canada. With the confusion and acrimony that had erupted over the *Heintzelman* move, the remaining children had almost been forgotten. Nonetheless, Irene Page continued to plead their cases. She had written to Paul Martin, Minister of National Health and Welfare and clearly a friend, to ask him to petition on behalf of the remaining children. Of the twenty-five, she pointed out, five cases were not a concern — four were visaed for the United Kingdom and one had a visa for Canada, but had become ill at the last minute and couldn't leave on the boat. Three siblings, the Kropa children, had an invalid father in East Africa, but now there was a consent form in hand, signed by him, and Page hoped that it would be a straightforward matter to arrange their visas — there was just one glitch: the oldest Kropa's x-rays were not satisfactory. Another girl, Eugenia, thirteen years old, had been with the group all along, but had a father in France. Her mother was dead and her father had now remarried. He was also ill and had given his written consent for her to settle elsewhere. Of the twenty outstanding cases, nine (including Helena Kropa, the oldest in the family group) had unsatisfactory chest x-rays. They had all had tuberculosis, but none were infectious anymore. Also, one of these children had a deformed back and pigeon chest from an injury sustained in India. However, she had an uncle in Billings Bridge, Ontario, who was willing to sponsor her and her brother. Page figured that if they could get the two to her uncle, the Ontario Society for Crippled Children would be able to help the girl. Really, Page pleaded, it was amazing that they were as well as they were, given what they had been through.

Then there was the girl who was said to be pregnant. Her three brothers had sailed on the *Heintzelman*. The irony of it was that she had had a visa to Canada some time ago, secured by her aunt, but she had refused to leave her brothers. Page hoped that something could be done for the girl. After all, accidents like this could happen even in "the best regulated families." There were another three girls who had been "furthered for 1 months' (*sic*) because of problematic blood tests, probably a result of suffering from malaria while in Africa." She asked Martin if he would check on this and see if there was some way around this problem. There were also the three Kacpura children, the younger two refusing to leave their older brother. The fourth was a twenty-year-old girl who was partially paralyzed in the right leg and foot, but otherwise fine medically, who had a brother in Alberta. Page praised the Canadian Mission in Bremen area for all they had done for the children, acknowledging that they had done all they could, but that it would take special authorization from Ottawa to settle the remaining twenty cases. She appealed to Paul Martin's conscience and pleaded with him to help these children.

> Two days ago, I had one of the most beautiful experiences in my life. I watched my 123 Polish children walk up the gangplank of the *General Stuart Heintzelman* just before it sailed for Canada.
>
> Someday I may hang for my part in it but I feel now that even I do hang the children are well worth my neck — It has been a strange struggle — beginning (for me) when they landed in Bari on the 19th of June and not ended yet of course — as there are still 25 of the group left here and it is likely there will be devil to pay in more ways than one before the whole matter dies down.
>
> Will you be seeing the children, do you think? Father Krolokowski is a nice little priest who speaks French so you should get along well with him. He will be with the children as far as Montreal, I imagine, and then will go to live in one of the Franciscan monasteries there. He can tell you some tales and show you some pictures taken just after Siberia. Needless to say both tales and pictures are grim.
>
> If you can, meet Czeslawa and Bronislawa Morawska, the two girls that the Warsaw papers have been after. She is slim and fair with beautiful braids round her head. Bronislawa is thirteen and looks younger. She speaks only Polish. They are the two that decided for repatriation to Poland but after being kidnapped from one of our camps near Rome and held for close questioning by members of the Polish Embassy in Rome were too frightened to return to Poland. That evening after the IRO Legal Advisor had placed them both in my care Czeslawa said to me, "I wasn't frightened before, Miss Page, but I am now. I have been in Siberia once. I do not want to go back." After that I just took them both with

me — without so much as 'by your leave' from anybody — on the next 'Rapido' from Rome to the Children's Center in Salerno. Then the fireworks began and we have been running the gauntlet ever since.[5]

Acrimony within the IRO worked against their settlement anywhere. Brigadier Lush and Curtis, of IRO East Africa, were two who had not forgotten these children. However, there was little they could do. As Lush reported to Curtis in early September, he had stopped in the Mass Resettlement Office of the Commonwealth Division of IRO London to see if anything could be done for the remainder.

They represented to me that all your charming orphan children were absolutely grand and fulfilled practically all adjectival conditions except that (a) practically none was an orphan, (b) the majority were of adult age. The fact that several were already or about to be mothers (and probably fathers too) themselves of course made it much easier, and that your request by cable and letter of the KROPA children just tickled them to death.

This was one of the family groups initially held back because they had a father alive, although seriously ill, in Africa. He had given written consent for their resettlement in Canada, as well as medical assurances that he was not fit to care for them. Only after that did Canada grant the children visas. Now, apparently, his health had suddenly recovered enough for him both to move to Australia and to care for his children, as he was requesting that the children be returned to Africa, so they could accompany him. As Lush explained,

They [the staff of the Mass Resettlement Office] said it was just lovely to think of all the stones they had turned and avenues they had explored and lies they had told in order to get the dear children (probably aged 32, 36 and 38 with 5 babies) to Canada, and now all they had to do was extract them from that Dominion and send them, via East Africa, to accompany their <u>father</u> (loud and slightly hysterical laughter) to Australia. At that point, having already aroused somewhat strained relations in that Office by suggesting that some undeserved case should go to the U.K., I thought it better to leave, but my last sight was to see Clabon engraving KROPA on his heart![6]

Whether it was due to Page's efforts or not, slowly resolution was found. On September 18, 22, and 26, twelve more children arrived in Canada. Among them were the three Kacpura siblings (the eldest was the deaf and dumb tailor), the two younger Kropa siblings (Helena, who had tuberculosis, had been left in a sanitorium in Europe), Franciszka Wozyniak (the child with paralysis on the right side), and six more, at least three of whom had been "furthered," or delayed, for more medical tests, two of them ostensibly for venereal disease.[7] Kazimiera Mazur arrived on October 3, a little over a month after her sister and brother. Just before the ship had left on August 29, Kazimiera had had another bout of malaria, which meant she couldn't leave with her siblings.[8]

The remaining children trickled into Canada over the ensuing months. Their initial reactions to the country were mixed — excitement, relief, anticipation, and worry. Stan Paluch wasn't certain that this was a place he wanted to stay, when he got his first glimpse of Canada in the harbour of Halifax. As he explained,

> When I saw the people working on the docks, I was surprised. I said, "Oh, this is not a very good country for me!" [He laughs at himself.] Because everywhere [in] India, Africa, it was black people were working. You don't see white people [working], just brown. "Oh, this is the wrong country!" I said to myself. "Maybe I'm going to stay three, four months, at the most and then I'm going to have to run from here!" But then I started looking around and it was nice. Very nice.[9]

For those who arrived in October, one of the first shocks was the weather. Winter had come early that year and Marian Kacpura remembers being amazed to see that everything was white — he had left Poland and Russia too young to remember snow. He was extremely grateful that the priest who met the ship in Quebec City had blankets in his car, because he was dressed in the Tengeru uniform — short khakis, short sleeves, no shoes, no socks, bare feet.[10] Others were as unprepared for winter. Both Sophia Wakulczyk and Janina Kusa remember the nuns buying winter boots for them after the first snow fell. Janina was working for the nuns and still wearing the shoes she had brought from Africa. They were the only footwear she had. One of the nuns looked at her asked her where her boots were. Janina replied, "What boots? I never had boots!" So the nun said, "Come on, I will buy you a pair of boots and you can pay me back when you have the money."[11] She had no idea if they were stylish or not, but they did keep her feet warm. Canada was going to take some adjusting.

Meanwhile, Poland had not given up. The Polish press had never let up its diatribe against everyone involved in the children's removal to Canada. By late August, the vitriol had become thick and the Polish press flooded with inflammatory articles.[12] An article in the Polish Ministry of Foreign Affairs' *Press and Information Bulletin* of August 31, condemned the IRO, Italy, Britain, Canada, and the United States for the children's abduction. It charged that the IRO had revealed "in a glaring manner the real aim of its activities consisting of supplying cheap manpower to foreign countries."[13] On September 6, a damning letter to the editor appeared in the *Rzeczpospolita*, a Polish pro-government daily. In it, the letter's author expressed his deep indignation and disappointment that the children had not been returned from Canada. Instead,

... [W]armongers and the IRO gangster organization took care of the children, holding them in their clutches, so that the Polish Government was not able to liberate them. The Pope, protector of unhappy Germans, had an opportunity here for intervention in the name of Christian principle. Unfortunately, as he did not raise his voice in defence of murdered Poles, how can he be expected to answer the voice of despairing parents, from whom their children were torn and sentenced to ill-treatment? This unprecedented abduction of children should be made known to the entire world as an illustration of methods used by gangster Governments toward nations which do not want to become cannon food to increase their profits and wealth.[14]

There was another incendiary editorial in the *Zycie Warszawy* on September 10. "This shameful affair, organized by international kidnappers supplying 'merchandise' to modern slave traders, is characterized by monstrous capitalistic hypocrisy!" The editorial decreed that the Polish Government and the Polish people would never forget their children, "kidnapped with the approval of Washington and the IRO."[15]

Then, as if to fan the flames, the *Ensign* published an inflammatory article about the Poles' pursuit of the children across eastern Canada and into the woods of Quebec, a month earlier. The *Ensign*'s article caused some consternation on the part of the Polish Legation in Ottawa, who sent its Presse Attaché, Mr. Mysak, to the Information Division of External Affairs to lodge an informal protest. He complained that the article had painted an unflattering picture of the Polish representatives who had approached the children, having ended the article with:

While no fear is expressed for the safety of the children it has been a most revealing episode. Firstly, the fact that a Communist legation in Ottawa is able to call upon and dispose of Canadian Communists to do their work and continue the work of intimidation in Canada is considered significant. Secondly, the promptness with which in Africa, in Italy, in Western Germany and now even in Canada the Soviet organization works and is able to follow and discover those whom they seek is another and sinister factor.[16]

While nothing much could be done about the article at that point, the Polish displeasure was clear.[17] The Canadian Chargé d'Affaires in Warsaw sardonically pointed out that one advantage could be drawn from the situation: the Polish women working for Dionne appeared to have lost the interest of the Polish people and been replaced by the Tengeru children.[18]

Meanwhile, the diplomatic situation continued to deteriorate and it was becoming increasingly apparent that the matter would eventually be raised in the United Nations General Assembly.[19] At the end of September, the Polish authorities ordered that the IRO office in Warsaw be shut down, and gave the IRO staff a mere two weeks to get out of Poland. The Poles had apparently told J.S. Widdicombe that it was nothing against him personally, "but because [of] the IRO's attitude with respect [to] these children"[20] the IRO had to go. It was no empty threat. IRO Warsaw closed its offices on October 18, and Widdicombe left for Geneva two days later.[21]

All of this was rumbling behind the scenes. The first formal and public condemnation was broached in the Executive Committee of the League of National Red Cross Societies, where the Polish Red Cross condemned the IRO for kidnapping the children. There, the IRO was accused of violating its own constitution by preventing the children's repatriation while their families in Poland waited in vain for their return. The Polish Red Cross claimed that, of the children, ninety-two were under the age of seventeen and that "a great many" had families in Poland. The organization called on the Executive Committee to condemn the transfer of Polish children to Canada by the IRO "as contrary to international law and to humanitarian principles and recommends that the Canadian Red Cross do all that it can to return these children to their country".[22] On October 27, it did so. The Secretary General of the League of Red Cross Societies wrote to W.S. Stanbury, the National Commissioner of the Canadian Red Cross Society, about the children, requesting an explanation and appropriate action. Stanbury quickly referred the letter to Holmes, in External Affairs. Holmes reiterated what was now the Canadians' explanation: they had acted in good faith and in the firm belief all of the children were orphans and properly within the mandate of the IRO. Any concerns that the Polish Government might have would be best directed to the IRO, not the Canadian Government.[23]

Then, on November 4, 1949, in the Third Committee of the General Assembly of the United Nations, Mr. Altman, Representative of Poland, formally denounced the IRO's transfer of the children from Tengeru to Canada. His statement was forceful, condemning, and inflammatory. It was also rife with misrepresentations about the course of events. He began with a lengthy, and rather distorted, account of what he described as a "story of collective kidnapping", expressing the deep umbrage and anger of his administration with the way in which its rights, and the rights of the children, had been trampled. Altman then launched into a round condemnation of the IRO, and a call for the repatriation of all displaced persons who were still in camps.

The story of these children is the crowning achievement of IRO's activities and constitutes the total confirmation of the just appreciation of the work of this organization which we have more than once revealed before the organs of the United Nations. It constitutes also a proof of violation by the IRO of all its international pledges that I mentioned above. And if today we are handed a resolution which attempts to prolong IRO's activities until 1 April 1951, and further to organize a permanent apparatus which would be concerned with a similar protection of refugees, it is clear that my delegation is opposed to it.

With regard to my government's position regarding the protection of its citizens abroad, it was always clear and we do not intend to renounce it. We are always of the opinion that each Polish citizen abroad in need of protection can profit by Polish consular protection. We are obliged to recall our resolution brought before the previous session and unfortunately rejected by the majority, that is, that the repatriation of all refugees and of all displaced persons who are still in camps be completed before 1 July 1950, and that these unfortunates be finally given absolute freedom in taking a decision regarding their future. Then only will this wound vanish from the face of the earth. Then only will there be a stop to the martyrdom of hundreds of millions of men with the sole purpose of poisoning international relations.[24]

In response to the Polish diatribe, Senator Catherine Wilson of the Canadian Delegation took the floor. She went straight to the heart of the matter.

> As the Polish delegate is well aware no one is compelled to remain in Canada. Likewise no one in Canada is prevented from communicating with anyone anywhere in the world. If any of these children should not have been sent to Canada, and arrangements are made for their removal, the Canadian Government will, of course, place no hindrance in the way of their departure; if parents and children have indeed been separated and desire to be reunited the Canadian Government will not stand in the way of their being reunited.[25]

The children could return to Poland if they wanted, but the implication was that none wished to do so.

Canada was not the only entity facing considerable embarrassment from the Polish accusations, the IRO had egg on its face too. The insult could not be ignored and J.D. Kingsley himself, Director General of the IRO, addressed the Committee on Refugees and Stateless Persons (Committee III of the Economic and Social Council) on November 10, when he spoke at length about the Tengeru children. He reviewed the facts of the situation in close detail, explaining that, in fact, of the 148 children who had been moved from East Africa to Germany, eighty-one were over sixteen years of age and thus not children in the sense of the IRO Constitution. Only twenty-four were under thirteen. Of those twenty-four, seven were accompanied by older brothers and sisters. As best as the IRO could determine, only twenty-three in the entire group had a living parent, and sixteen of those twenty-three were in the older age group or accompanied by an adult. Thus, of the 148 children, only seven could be truly classified as minors with a living parent.

Nor, he maintained, was Poland unaware of these children's existence. At least twice the Polish Government had been invited to send a repatriation team to Tanganyika to interview the children. In neither instance was the invitation accepted. As a result, in July the IRO moved the children to Europe, where repatriation officers could interview them. Meanwhile, the Catholic Hierarchy of Canada had offered to take the children and "the Government of Canada had unselfishly offered to permit their entry." Nonetheless, the IRO had decided that the first priority should be given to repatriation, particularly for those twenty-three children who appeared to have at least one parent. A qualified repatriation officer of Polish nationality had interviewed all of the children, and eventually two sisters had opted for repatriation, with approximately a dozen more considering it. However, after the sisters were questioned by officials of the Polish Legation in Rome, as he diplomatically put it, all of them changed their minds. At the invitation of the IRO, three Polish officials later visited the camp, but were unable to budge the children. The IRO then decided to accept the Canadian invitation and moved the group to Bremerhaven, in preparation for shipment. The Polish Red Cross, meanwhile, had made a series of requests to see the children and to get a nominal roll of the children's names, as well as access to the children's files. The IRO offered to allow the Polish Red Cross to interview the children but, as Kingsley explained, it could not give them either the nominal roll or access to the files. The Polish Red Cross then chose not to interview the children.

Kingsley offered to cooperate with the Polish and Canadian Governments in the repatriation of those seven children not accompanied by an older sibling and with a parent living in Poland, if that was what the two governments wanted. But, he concluded, most of the displaced persons under discussion were not, in fact, children but young adults who did not wish to be repatriated. Canada had acted scrupulously and in good faith throughout.[26] The Canadians were quite pleased and heartened with Kingsley's hard-hitting defence of the IRO and the Canadian Government, and that he had placed responsibility for the failure to repatriate the children squarely on the Polish Government.[27]

This did not end the story though, as the Poles refused to let it drop.

In spite of the ever-so-correct dressing down by Kingsley in November, the Polish press continued to rage about the children's kidnapping and the Demokratischer Frauenbund Deutschlands mobilized again. This time, the Frauenbund used its affiliation with the Congress of Canadian Women, through the Women's International Democratic Federation, to reach the Canadian Government and the IRO. On the DFD's behalf, the Congress of Canadian Women wrote IRO Canada, Senator Catherine Wilson (who had responded to the Polish allegations in the Economic and Social Council), and the U.N. Division of External Affairs, demanding an explanation as to why these children were secretly spirited from East Africa to Canada, "despite the protest of the families ... and the Polish Government...." The IRO's response was to explain that the Congress of Canadian Women was misinformed and to send the Congress a copy of Kingsley's statement made to Committee III on November 10, 1949. External Affairs took the same approach — acknowledging the letter and forwarding Kingsley's statement.[28]

The Poles apparently made one last attempt to connect with children directly, via the Czech Consulate in Montreal. Bronislawa Kusa and Helena Koscielniak had become friends and were both attending the same girls' boarding school in Montreal. An older student had befriended them, and one day that student invited Bronislawa and Helena to join her family for dinner one weekend at her home. Thinking nothing of it, but pleased to be invited, the two went to her home for dinner, after getting permission from the school. They didn't realize that her father was the Czech Consul, nor would they have understood the implications at their age. They had a very pleasant dinner and afterwards, the student's mother invited them to sit down with her "for a nice chat." The conversation soon turned into a discussion of how good things were in Poland and how Poland really wanted the two girls to return. As Helena says, "She just went on and on!" Both Helena and Bronislawa became increasingly scared. By the time they returned to the school, they were petrified that they were going to be kidnapped and taken back to Poland. The next day they told Father Krolikowski what had happened. He was furious and he told the school to never let that woman take the girls again. The next year, they were moved to a different school.[29]

The Polish Government continued to pursue the children through diplomatic channels. In December, Canada was chastised in the U.N. General
Assembly and her chief diplomatic representative was summoned to the
Polish Foreign Ministry, where he was presented with a formal note verbale protesting, once again, the children's kidnapping and informing him
that "it was up to the Canadian Government to remedy the situation."[30]
With the children now in Canada and the Polish Government having done
its worst in the U.N., the Canadians no longer felt any rush to respond.
Canada's objective was to strike a balance between wishing to appear co-
operative, and wishing to register displeasure with the high-handed tone of
the Polish note. Finally, in April 1950, the Canadian Legation in Warsaw
responded. The response protested the provocative tone of the note, the
language of which "scarcely seem[ed] calculated to facilitate agreement."
Nonetheless, the Canadians offered to arrange for representatives of the
Polish Legation in Ottawa to interview any of the children at convenient
times and places, in the presence of any other persons who had an interest
in the welfare of the child, including foster parents and representatives of
the Canadian Government, or any provincial government or agency. The
Canadian Legation speculated that these interviews would be a wonderful
opportunity to seek out information on whether the child had a parent in
Poland. If it were determined the child had a parent living in Poland, the
Canadian Government expressed its willingness to help put parent and
child in touch, with a view to possible repatriation.[31]

The Polish Government took a dim view of the Canadian response. In
late July, the Canadian Legation in Warsaw received a letter in which the
Poles declared that they were "forced emphatically to reject these stipulations and to state that, in its note, it has restrained from expressing a justified
indignation, limiting it to a pointed representation of facts and suggesting
well-grounded postulates." They argued that, "in accordance with generally recognized principles of international relations, parents, nearest relatives and in lack of these, homeland authorities or guardians appointed by
them, are exclusively called upon to decide the fate of children." The Polish
Government was "grieved to state that it is … the Canadian Government
by its procedure alone, in the matter of the children as well as in certain
other matters, who evidently does not strive to reach an agreement," rather

than it being Polish intransigence getting in the way of a settlement. The letter ended with the bald statement that the only way in which this matter could be settled properly would be the "speedy return of the children to their country."[32] There were no new requests or proposals. Rather, it was just an acrimonious reiteration of the earlier demands.

The situation was a dead end and the Canadians realized it. It was clear that the Polish Government was not genuinely interested in the welfare of the children, nor was it willing to cooperate in determining the true facts of the matter or reuniting parents and children. This echoed the conclusion drawn by the Canadian Delegation to the U.N. earlier in the year: that Warsaw was more interested in the propaganda value of their anger than in the actual return of wayward Poles. They had certainly got great mileage out of the Tengeru incident in the Polish press. Thus, in late August, a consensus was reached in the Department of External Affairs that there was nothing further to be gained from continuing the conversation with Warsaw and the decision was made to not reply to the Polish Note of July 24. With that, the Polish Government let the matter lie.

The children, meanwhile, were oblivious to all of the political machinations occurring on high. Instead, they were trying to adjust to their new lives in Canada. It was not easy. Once again they were starting from scratch, in yet another foreign country and foreign culture. Those who had finished high school in Africa were found work. The economy in Canada was not terribly strong in 1949, so jobs were scarce. Many of the young women ended up in domestic service. Many of the young men ended up in construction, an industry that was doing well. Stan Paluch, for instance, received his initial training working for the priests. The Catholic Church in Montreal was engaged in some major construction and Stan worked for the priests for one-and-a-half years, training as a painter and plasterer. From there he moved into the construction industry, working whatever jobs he could find. Eventually he built up his own residential painting and decorating company.[33] Michal Bortkiewicz, ever restless, didn't last long in school. He proved very talented on a lathe, and at drilling and milling metal, and his instructor in the technical class wanted to hire him to work in his shop, where he made prosthetic devices. Before that could become a reality, Michal was hired onto a ship as a third-class engineer. The ship supplied the DEW line in northern Canada, and Michal headed north. After a short while, he returned to Montreal, where he held a number of jobs, including one as a mobile repair person for Canadair.[34]

Those who were young enough to be put into schools found themselves quickly distributed across approximately forty day and boarding schools in Montreal and vicinity. Archbishop Charbonneau's office had arranged for a number of schools to take the children in tuition-free, but it meant that they would have to be broken up, as no school was willing to take more than a few of the children. No child was sent to a school alone. They were always in pairs at least, but seldom more. Still, it was very difficult for them, accustomed as they were to living as a kind of tribe. Interestingly, because they had been raised in institutions, the children were used to being segregated according to gender and age. Siblings hadn't lived under the same roof for years. But that did not mean that they were not close; the older siblings were fiercely protective of their younger brothers and sisters. Yet they were accustomed to living apart, and resigned to being separated, at least for the moment. Another bond had been formed over the course of their time in Tengeru, and during the dramatic journey to Canada, one that bound the group together as a whole. This bond was as strong, in some ways, as the family ties. The Catholic Church's decision to break up the tribe and to ignore the family ties may have been done out of practical necessity, but it reflected a profound insensitivity to the group's dynamics and to the children's deep emotional and psychological needs.

For many of the boys this was a particularly difficult period in their lives. Removed from each other — the only support network they knew — and plunged into a rigorous and harsh schooling system that enforced learning through the use of corporal punishment, taught in a language that none of them spoke, and thrown into a new and very different cultural milieu, the children struggled to adapt. The language barrier meant that they spent the first year learning French, which set them back even further. They often found themselves in classes with Canadian children who were considerably younger and smaller than they were, a situation they found embarrassing. And although many Canadian pupils were very open and accepting, there was a degree of latent discrimination apparent among some of the Canadians. There was always someone telling them that "the stupid Polaks" should just go back to where they came from. More than a few of the boys also harboured a deep anger against anyone with authority, and fought back when and where they could — by running away, acting out, and dropping out of school as soon as possible. School was something to be endured.[35]

The children made every effort to get together whenever possible. For those living in Montreal, it was easier. For one group, a Montreal restaurant became a weekly gathering place. For those sent to schools outside of the city, the isolation must have been unbearable.

For those who finished high school some kind of post-secondary training was sometimes possible, though not always. There was little money available to pay for tuition. Many continued on in night school or part-time studies by working at the same time in order to support themselves. This is what Marian Kacpura did; he worked a number of jobs in radio and television servicing, then with an awning manufacturer, and then in construction, while attending Montreal Technical School, where he was studying to be a draftsman. Upon graduation, he ended up working in mechanical design, first in Montreal and ultimately in British Columbia.[36] Al Kunicki ended up doing almost two years of chemical engineering at the University of Ottawa before quitting school and getting a job in construction. He became involved in several big hydroelectric and railway construction projects in Quebec and eastern Ontario, where he was eventually doing quantity estimation. Then he moved to Montreal, where he worked with a private construction company.[37]

Many of the older girls, such as Katie and Stella Koscielniak, Krzysztofa Michniak, Stanislawa Kunicki, and Sophie Matusiewicz, either went to business school or schools of domestic management. It was believed that this would provide them with skills useful in the workplace and help them learn French. Kazimiera Mazur was given the opportunity to go to nursing school, after getting frustrated at the University of Montreal where she and some friends were relegated to a special Polish section. They were being taught in Polish and didn't see the point — they needed to learn English and French. So one of the priests, Father Laramee, who was keeping an eye on the Tengeru children, suggested nursing.[38] Sophie Matusiewicz ultimately ended up in nursing as well.[39] At least two of the girls, Stanislawa Kunicki and Stanislawa Kacpura, discovered their vocation soon after arriving in Canada and became nuns.

In an attempt to compensate for the breakup of the tribe, the Catholic Church of Montreal mustered a panoply of resources. In addition to the numerous boarding schools and day schools that took in the children tuition-free, and to Contrecoeur, that provided their initial housing, the Sisters of the Congregation of Providence took in a number of girls and the Congregation of the Holy Names of Jesus and Mary offered trade school training. However, while these arrangements meant that the children were taken care of during the school terms, because they didn't have families they were left at loose ends for the holidays and summer months. Several Canadian and American Polish organizations donated funds to ensure that the children had proper Christmas and Easter celebrations. The McCombers of Montreal, a prominent family that made its fortune in the fur trade, offered the boys the use of their summer cottage in Châteauguay, outside Montreal. Gerard Tardiff, a notary public from Pointe-Claire, a Montreal suburb, gave the girls use of his summer retreat on Dowker Island. In response to a call from Archbishop Charbonneau, a number of families in Montreal informally adopted individual children, taking them in for the holidays.

All of these were rather "institutional" responses. In addition, and probably most importantly for the children, three priests were assigned to their care and management — Father Caron and Father Dostaler, joined later by Father Laramee. Father Krolikowski was soon sent to the United States by the Catholic Church, although he remained in close contact with the "children" for the rest of their lives. He remains an important figure for many of the "children," who are still deeply grateful for all he did in bringing them to Canada. For many, he still acts as spiritual advisor. However the physical distance meant that he gradually became a more distant figure in their lives. Fathers Caron and Dostaler were the closest the children came to surrogate parents. Father Krolikowski describes Father Caron as "the embodiment of goodness of heart," a kind and tender man, who won the hearts of the children.[40] For many of the boys, he became like a father. Father Dostaler, on the other hand, was a strict disciplinarian with little patience for any who were unruly, ill-disciplined, ill-mannered, or lazy. He was, however, also physically strong and mechanically inclined, two traits the boys admired greatly.[41] He was a man who was respected, if not loved in the same way that Father Caron was.

In spite of the priests' best efforts it was still a very institutional life, and that shaped the children. They clung to each other as much as circumstances would allow. Whenever possible, often once they had finished high school, the siblings got back together. Stan Studzinski moved to Toronto in the early 1950s to attend Ryerson Polytechnical Institute and, more importantly, to join his brother, who had immigrated to Canada from England by that time. He had been sponsored by Stan's sister and her husband, who was a good friend. The two men had rented a house in Toronto, and there was room for Stan and his other sister. This is where Stan met his wife, Halina, who was the sister of the brother-in-law.[42] Katie Koscielniak married her husband, Charlie, in 1951, and moved to Kitchener, Ontario. Within two years, her two sisters, Stella and Helena, had moved to Kitchener as well, to live with them.[43] Whenever possible or practical, it seems, the eldest siblings tried to resume their role of *loco parentis* as soon as they could. And the tribe reconvened when it could, in the summers at Dowker Island and the McComber summer place, at the restaurant in downtown Montreal that became a regular haunt, at weddings and showers. For these people, the other Tengeru children were very much their brothers and sisters. The tribe was, in a very real sense, their family. The ties created in Tengeru and on the voyage to Canada were ties that would never be severed. Sixty years later, in 1999, they held a massive reunion in Montreal, with Father Krolikowski, Father Caron, and Father Laramee at the head table. It was not their first reunion, but it was the most significant, as it became clear that it might be the last.

The communal nature of their upbringing had other consequences as well. As they matured into young adults, there were numerous moments in their lives when they sorely missed their parents. As the young women began to mature physically, the changes to their bodies caught them by surprise and they felt uncomfortable asking anyone for an explanation of what was happening to them. The nuns seemed unapproachable about such intimate things, the language barrier made it impossible to ask other girls at school, and their sisters, if they had any, were at other schools.[44] The young adults, men and women, also felt very much at sea in personal relationships, having never watched their parents negotiate the reefs and shoals, the highs and lows of married life. The Catholic priests and nuns who had raised them were of little help with these kinds of questions. This made it difficult when they began to establish their own relationships, as they had no model of a mature, loving relationship to follow, and no one to turn to for advice. When they had children, they also felt at a loss in raising them, not having been raised in a family environment themselves. They did, however, have a strong sense of what they had missed, if just by observing those with families. All recognized and deeply felt the absence of what one called "a close family life."[45]

It took a long time for many of the children, now mostly young adults, to finally feel like Canada was their home. Some, like Marian Kacpura and Sophie Matusiewicz, had decided the moment they walked down the gangplank in Halifax that Canada was the country where they would stay.[46] Others took much longer. As Kazimiera Mazur so insightfully put it, after spending ten years "sitting on that little valise" that contained all her worldly possessions, waiting to be moved yet again to some unknown destination without being asked or even told where, it was difficult to imagine that the moving had ended.[47] Many, especially the boys, remained very restless, moving from job to job, city to city. Some did that for their entire lives, others eventually put down roots. For many, the turning point came when they married. For others, it was when they purchased their first home, as there is nothing like a mortgage and a family to kill wanderlust.

It was not an easy time they had, building lives for themselves in Canada. But they did it, for the most part very successfully. In spite of the odds, these people established themselves in Canada and have done quite well, with homes and families of their own. Although Canada did not make it easy for them (no support services like those available to immigrants today were in place then, as they are quick to point out), and they had to struggle in the beginning, they still express gratitude to Canada and to God for giving them this opportunity, best summed up in the words of Stan Paluch, who said, "You know, life has been good to me here in Canada. Thanks be to God."[48]

# Notes

## Chapter 1: Deportation to the East

1.  Jan T. Gross, *Revolution from Abroad: The Soviet Conquest of Poland's Western Ukraine and Western Belorussia* (Princeton NJ: Princeton University Press, 1988), 207–11.
2.  Jozef Garlinski, *Poland in the Second World War* (Basingstoke, U.K.: Palgrave Macmillan, 1985), 22.
3.  *Ibid.*, 22.
4.  Andrzej Paczkowski, *The Spring Will Be Ours: Poland and the Poles from Occupation to Freedom* (University Park, PA: Pennsylvania State University Press, 1995), 42.
5.  *Ibid.*, 45.
6.  Katherine R. Jolluck, *Exile and Identity: Polish Women in the Soviet Union During World War II* (Pittsburg: University of Pittsburgh Press, 2002), 9.
7.  Keith Sword, *Deportation and Exile: Poles in the Soviet Union, 1939–48* (London and Basingstoke, U.K.: Macmillan Limited and St. Martin's Press, 1994), 2–4.
8.  Paczkowski, *The Spring Will Be Ours*, 46–47.
9.  Sword, *Deportation and Exile*, 5–7.
10. The number is very inexact because of the nature of the sources available, making it a source of considerable debate among historians. At this point, because of the limited access to Soviet documents (not all archives have been opened to scholars), it is impossible to determine a more precise number. For a revealing discussion of this debate and the range of data available, see Jolluck, *Exile and Identity*, 9–11. See also: General Wladyslaw Anders, *Mémoires (1939–1946)*, translated by J. Rzewuska,

(Paris: La Jeune Parque, 1948); Gross, *Revolution from Abroad* (1st and 2nd editions); N.S. Lebedeva and Alfred J. Rieber, "The Deportation of the Polish Population to the U.S.S.R., 1939–41," *Journal of Communist Studies and Transition Politics*, 16/1-2(2000), 28–45; Paczkowski, *The Spring Will Be Ours*; Sword, *Deportation and Exile*; Z.S. Siemaszko, "The Mass Deportations of the Polish Population to the U.S.S.R., 1940–1941," in *The Soviet Takeover of the Polish Eastern Provinces, 1939–41*, Keith Sword, ed. (New York: St. Martin's Press, 1991).

11. Sword, *Deportation and Exile*, 47; Gross, *Revolution from Abroad*, 19.
12. Jolluck, *Exile and Identity*, 14.
13. Sword, *Deportation and Exile*, 13–14.
14. Jolluck, *Exile and Identity*, 13; Sword, *Deportation and Exile*, 17; Siemaszko, "The Mass Deportations of the Polish Population to the U.S.S.R., 1940–1941," 221.
15. Jolluck, *Exile and Identity*, 13, 15–16; Sword, *Deportation and Exile*, 17–18.
16. Sword, *Deportation and Exile*, 14; N. Lebedeva, "Deportations from Poland and the Baltic States to the U.S.S.R. in 1939–1941: Common Features and Specific Traits," *Lithuanian Historical Studies*, 7 (2002), 98.
17. Interview with Sophia Schreiber.
18. Interview with Helen Atkinson.
19. Interview with Kazimiera Mazur-Pogorzelski.
20. Interview with Janet Przygonski.
21. Interview with Al Kunicki.
22. Interview with Stan Studzinski.
23. Interview with Michal Bortkiewicz.
24. Gross, *Revolution from Abroad*, 207.
25. *Ibid.*, 209; Sword, *Deportation and Exile*, 16.
26. Interview with Christine Babinski.
27. Sword, *Deportation and Exile*, 19; Jolluck, *Exile and Identity*, 18–19.
28. Helen Atkinson.
29. Christine Babinski.
30. Janet Przygonski.
31. Christine Babinski.
32. Michal Bortkiewicz.
33. Sword, *Deportation and Exile*, 21.
34. Helen Atkinson.
35. Sword, *Deportation and Exile*, 17–18; Christine Babinski.
36. Sophia Schreiber.
37. Kazimiera Mazur-Pogorzelski.
38. Janet Przygonski.

39. Michal Bortkiewicz.

40. Jolluck, *Exile and Identity*, 57.

41. *Ibid.*, 60–63.

42. *Ibid.*, 63–65.

43. Interview with Steven Kozlowski.

44. Janet Przygonski.

45. Michal Bortkiewicz.

46. Janet Przygonski.

47. Jolluck, *Exile and Identity*, 60.

48. Sophia Schreiber.

49. Interview with Stanley Paluch.

50. Christine Babinski.

51. Michal Bortkiewicz.

52. Janet Przygonski.

53. Interview with Marian Kacpura.

54. Interview with Sophie Smagala.

55. Kazimiera Mazur-Pogorzelski.

56. Sophia Schreiber.

57. Helen Atkinson.

58. Christine Babinski.

59. John Coutouvidis and Jaime Reynolds, *Poland, 1939–1947* (Teaneck, NJ: Holmes & Meier Publishers, Inc., 1986), 25–26, 41, 46.

60. Paczkowski, *The Spring Will Be Ours*, 77.

61. Coutouvidis, *Poland, 1939–1947*, 52.

62. Paczkowski, *The Spring Will Be Ours*, 79; Garlinski, *Poland in the Second World War*, 88–92.

63. Sword, *Deportation and Exile*, 29–30; Coutouvidis, *Poland, 1939–1947*, 58–60; Garlinski, *Poland in the Second World War*, 104–6.

64. Garlinski, *Poland in the Second World War*, 109–10.

65. Tomasz Piesakowski, *The Fate of Poles in the U.S.S.R. 1939–1989* (London: Gryf Publications, 1990), 73; Sword, *Deportation and Exile*, 31.

66. Paczkowski, *The Spring Will Be Ours*, 81.

67. Sword, *Deportation and Exile*, 34.

68. S.M. Terry, *Poland's Place in Europe: General Sikorski and the Origin of the Oder-Neisse Line, 1939–1943* (Princeton, NJ: Princeton University Press, 1983), 200–02; Paczkowski, *The Spring Will Be Ours*, 106; Anders, *Mémoires*, 88.

69. Anders, *Mémoires*, 87–88.

70. H. Sarner, *General Anders and the Soldiers of the Second Polish Corps* (Cathedral City, CA: Brunswick Press, 1997), 37.

71. Anders, *Mémoires*, 97.
72. Richard Overy, *Russia's War: A History of the Soviet War Effort: 1941–1945* (New York: Penguin, 1999), 87, 170–71.
73. Sword, *Deportation and Exile*, 57; Terry, *Poland's Place in Europe*, 208.
74. Sword, *Deportation and Exile*, 50.
75. Terry, *Poland's Place in Europe*, 208.
76. Paczkowski, *The Spring Will Be Ours*, 108.
77. *Ibid.*, 107; Sword, *Deportation and Exile*, 57.
78. Garlinski, *Poland in the Second World War*, 149–50; Sword, *Deportation and Exile*, 58.
79. Sword, *Deportation and Exile*, 41.
80. Interview with L.P.
81. Stan Studzinski.
82. Stanley Paluch.
83. Michal Bortkiewicz.
84. Sophia Schreiber.
85. Sophia Schreiber; Janet Przygonski; Sophie Smagala.
86. Michal Bortkiewicz.
87. Janet Przygonski.
88. Michal Bortkiewicz; Stanley Paluch.
89. Stanley Paluch.
90. Michal Bortkiewicz.
91. Sophia Schreiber.
92. Sophie Smagala.
93. Christine Babinski.
94. Anders, *Mémoires*, 148–49.
95. Sword, *Deportation and Exile*, 65–67.
96. *Ibid.*, 80–81.
97. Anders, *Mémoires*, 164.
98. Sword, *Deportation and Exile*, 80–81.
99. Christine Babinski.
100. Kazimiera Mazur-Pogorzelski; Marian Kacpura.
101. Stanley Paluch.
102. Janet Przygonski.
103. Kazimiera Mazur-Pogorzelski.
104. Steven Kozlowski.
105. Janet Przygonski.
106. Sophia Schreiber.
107. Marian Kacpura.
108. Sophie Smagala.

109. Steven Kozlowski.
110. Janet Przygonski.
111. Sword, *Deportation and Exile*, 73; Piotrowski, *The Polish Deportees of World War II*, 10.
112. Piotrowski, *The Polish Deportees of World War II*, 10.
113. Stanley Paluch.

**Chapter 2: The Road to Tengeru**

1. Lucjan Krolikowski, *Stolen Childhood: A Saga of Polish War Children* (New York: Author's Choice Press, 1983/2001), 146–47 (see map "Polish Refugee Camps in Africa 1942–1950").
2. Keith Sword with Norman Davies and Jan Ciechanowski, *The Formation of the Polish Community in Great Britain 1939–1950* (London: School of Slavonic and East European Studies, 1989), 246, 248.
3. *Ibid.*, 334–38.
4. Krolikowski, *Stolen Childhood*, 95.
5. Stan Studzinski.
6. Janet Przygonski.
7. Sophie Smagala.
8. Fundacja Archiwum Fotograficzne Tulaczy, *Tulacze Dzieci; Exiled Children* (Warsaw: Muza SA, 1995), 93.
9. Al Kunicki.
10. Christine Babinski.
11. Kazimiera Mazur-Pogorzelski.
12. Fundacja Archiwum Fotograficzne Tulaczy. *Tulacze Dzieci; Exiled Children*, 82.
13. *Ibid.*, 131.
14. Interview with Sister Mary Alfonsa.
15. Helen Atkinson.
16. Christine Babinski.
17. Fundacja Archiwum Fotograficzne Tulaczy. *Tulacze Dzieci; Exiled Children*, 290–92.
18. Stanley Paluch.
19. Christine Babinski; Sister Mary Alfonsa.
20. Sophia Schreiber.
21. Al Kunicki; Kazimiera Mazur-Pogorzelski.
22. Christine Babinski.
23. Kazimiera Mazur-Pogorzelski.
24. Christine Babinski.

25. Al Kunicki.
26. Christine Babinski.
27. Janet Przygonski; Bernice Kusa.
28. Steven Kozlowski.
29. Sophia Schreiber.
30. Steven Kozlowski.
31. Al Kunicki.
32. Kazimiera Mazur-Pogorzelski.
33. Al Kunicki.
34. Marian Kacpura.
35. Marian Kacpura.
36. Krolikowski, *Stolen Childhood*, 88–89.
37. Helen Atkinson.
38. Stan Studzinski.
39. Sophia Schreiber.
40. Janet Przygonski.
41. Janet Przygonski; Sophia Schreiber.
42. Janet Przygonski; Sophia Schreiber.
43. Michal Bortkiewicz.
44. Al Kunicki.
45. Marian Kacpura.
46. Michal Bortkiewicz.
47. Krolikowski, *Stolen Childhood*, 105, 114.
48. Michal Bortkiewicz.
49. Krolikowski, *Stolen Childhood*, 105.
50. Michal Bortkiewicz.
51. Michal Bortkiewicz.
52. Krolikowski, *Stolen Childhood*, 115.
53. Michal Bortkiewicz.
54. Al Kunicki.
55. Marian Kacpura.
56. Al Kunicki.
57. Marian Kacpura.
58. Marian Kacpura.
59. Al Kunicki.
60. Al Kunicki.
61. Krolikowski, *Stolen Childhood*, 112.
62. *Ibid.*, 118.
63. Helen Atkinson.
64. Sophie Smagala.

65. Krolikowski, *Stolen Childhood*, 115.
66. *Ibid.*, 114; Al Kunicki.
67. Krolikowski, *Stolen Childhood*, 109.
68. *Ibid.*, 108, 115.
69. Al Kunicki.
70. Marian Kacpura.
71. Krolikowski, *Stolen Childhood*, 110.
72. UNRRA, PAG 4/1.3.1.3.1.:3 MERRA — History, Organ., and Polish 1942–43, report entitled "Middle East Relief and Rehabilitation Administration Polish Refugee Camps — Iran," December 30, 1943.
73. UNRRA PAG 4/3.0.17.1.3.:5, Displaced Persons. Repatriation, memo, H.H. Lehman to Sir H. Gale, November 6, 1945 (incl. Appendices).
74. NA (U.K.) CO 822/111/19, Accommodation for Refugees in South Africa; Secret East Africa 1942–43, minutes of a conference of Director of Refugees in East Africa, November 17–18, 1943.
75. *Ibid.*, letter, Mr. Gurney, Office of the Conference of East African Governors, Nairobi, Kenya, to G.F. Seel, Colonial Office, London, December 8, 1943.
76. *Ibid.*, "Memorandum regarding the Respective Responsibilities of the East African Governments and the Polish Authorities in East Africa for the General Welfare of Polish Refugees in East Africa and describing the manner in which these responsibilities are to be discharged by the said governments and Polish Authorities in Collaboration," H.L.G. Gurney, Chief Secretary, July 29, 1943.
77. UNRRA PAG 4/1.3.1.1.1.:38, 454.1 MEO EARA Camps; Background, memo, George L. Warren, UNRRA to Mr. Xanthaky, UNRRA, February 3, 1944.
78. UNRRA PAG 4/1.3.1.1.1.:37, 412.2 MEO Reparation of Poles in ME Area, memo, C.M. Pierce to F.K. Hoehler, June 11, 1945.
79. NA (U.K.) CO 822/111/19, Accommodation for Refugees in South Africa: Secret East Africa 1942–1943, minutes of a conference of Directors of Refugees in East Africa, November 17–18, 1943.
80. NA (U.K.) FO 371/42865, 1944 File No. 97 (WR), telegram no. 823, Deputy Governor, Tanganyika Territory to Secretary of State, Colonies, London, July 26, 1944.

**Chapter 3: The Postwar Settlement**

1. NA (U.K.) FO 371/42865, 1944 File No. 97 (WR), telegram no. 823, Deputy Governor, Tanganyika Territory to Secretary of State, Colonies, London, July 26, 1944.

2.  Sword, Davies, and Ciechanowski, *The Formation of the Polish Community in Great Britain 1939–1950*, 185.

3.  George Woodbridge, ed., *UNRRA: the History of the United Nations Relief and Rehabilitation Administration* (New York: Columbia University Press, 1950), 4.

4.  NA (U.K.) FO 371/42865, 1944 File No. 97 (WR), telegram no.38, Relief, British Delegation Montreal to Foreign Office, September 23, 1944.

5.  *Ibid.*, letter, P. Mason, Foreign Office, Refugee Department, London to G.S. Dunnett, Treasury, November 2, 1944.

6.  *Ibid.*, draft of note verbale, Foreign Office, London to Polish Ambassador, London, November 1944.

7.  Sword, Davies, and Ciechanowski, *The Formation of the Polish Community in Great Britain*, 176–77.

8.  "The Yalta Conference," The Avalon Project at Yale Law School, *http://avalon.law.yale.edu.*

9.  Sword, Davies, and Ciechanowski, *The Formation of the Polish Community in Great Britain*, 179, 184–85.

10.  *Ibid.*, 231.

11.  *Ibid.*, 231.

12.  *Ibid.*, 233–34.

13.  *Ibid.*, 182.

14.  *Ibid.*, 185.

15.  *Ibid.*, 222–23.

16.  *Ibid.*, 224.

17.  NARA RG 260, Office of the Adjutant General, General Correspondence and Other Records, 1945–49, 390/40/21/2 box 91 file AG 383.7 Displaced Persons (Refugees, Expellees, Internees) 1 of 2, letter, HQ USFET to Commanding Generals: 3rd U.S. Army Area, 7th U.S. Army Area, Berlin District, subject: Repatriation of Soviet Citizens Subject to Repatriation under the Yalta Agreement, January 4, 1946.

18.  UNRRA PAG 4/3.0.17.1.3.:5 Displaced Persons. Repatriation, C.M. Drury, Chief, UNRRA Mission to Poland to Displaced Persons Division, ERO London, November 19, 1945; memo, C. Van Hyning, Director, Displaced Persons Division, ERO to C.M. Drury, Chief, UNRRA Mission to Poland, December 14, 1945.

19.  *Ibid.*, memo to file by C.M. Drury, January 15, 1946.

20.  NA (U.K.) FO 371/57780, WR 382, minutes of meeting held at UNRRA ERO, London, January 8, 1946; FO 371/57780, WR 39, minutes of meeting held at Foreign Office, January 4, 1946.

21. *Ibid.*, minutes of meeting held at UNRRA ERO, London, January 8, 1946; NA (U.K.) FO 371/57780, WR 39, minutes of meeting held at Foreign Office, January 4, 1946; UNRRA, *The Central Committee of the Council: Documents of the Special Subcommittee on Resolution 71 1946.*

22. UNRRA PAG 4/3.0.17.1.3.:5 Displaced Persons. Repatriation, memo to file, C.M. Drury, January 15, 1946.

23. NA (U.K.) FO 371/57780, WR 382, minutes of meeting held at UNRRA ERO, London, January 8, 1946.

24. *Ibid.*, WR 266, letter, Brigadier G.M.O. Day, War Office Liaison Staff (Poles) to War Office, CA(DP), January 17, 1946.

25. *Ibid.*, WR 345, memo, Lt. Col. V.M. Hammer, War Office CA(DP), London to D.S. MacKillop, Refugee Department, Foreign Office, London, January 30, 1946.

26. *Ibid.*, WR 266, minute sheet, February 8–18, 1946; letter, D. MacKillop, Foreign Office to Lt. Col. V.M. Hammer, War Office CA(DP), February 14, 1946.

27. *Ibid.*, WR 398, minute sheet (February 12–22, 1946) in response to telegram 243, Warsaw to Foreign Office, February 8, 1946.

28. *Ibid.*, WR 768, memo, C. Van Hyning, Director, Division of Welfare and Repatriation, ERO, UNRRA to D. MacKillop, Foreign Office, London, March 13, 1946.

29. UNRRA PAG 4/1.3.1.3.1.:3 Middle East Mission Budget 2nd Quarter 1945, memo, Deputy Chief of Mission for Finance and Administration to M.A. Menshikov, Deputy Director General, Bureau of Areas, UNRRA Washington, att: Mr. Dayton, February 23, 1945.

30. In a memo from J. Marynowski, Delegate of the Ministry of Finance to the Commissioner, East African Refugee Administration, Nairobi, dated November 25, 1944, it was reported that the total expenses for the Polish refugees in East Africa, Northern Rhodesia, and Southern Rhodesia was £417,839. (UNRRA PAG 4/1.3.1.1.1.:38, 454.3 MEO EARA Camps; Reports)

31. UNRRA PAG 4/3.0.2.0.5.:3, Historical Records HR XVI Polish Refugees, memo, C.M. Pierce, Division on Displaced Persons, UNRRA to N. Miller, Senior Deputy Chief of Balkan Mission, UNRRA, November 23, 1944.

32. UNRRA PAG 4/1.3.1.1.1.:38 "454.2 MEO EARA Camps; UNRRA-EARA Relations," letter, S.K. Jacobs, Displaced Persons Specialist, UNRRA, Nairobi, January 15, 1945.

33. NA(U.K.) FO 371/51150, Refugees, 1945, File No. 93, pp No. 1624, censor intercept of letter, Friends Relief Service, London to American Friends Service Committee, Philadelphia, March 2, 1945.

34. UNRRA PAG 4/1.3.1.1.1.:38 "454.2 MEO EARA Camps; UNRRA-EARA Relations," letter, S.K. Jacobs, Displaced Persons Specialist, UNRRA, Nairobi, January 15, 1945.

35. NA (U.K.) FO 371/51150, Refugees, 1945, File No. 93, pp No. 1624, censor intercept of letter, Friends Relief Service, London to American Friends Service Committee, Philadelphia, March 2, 1945.

36. NA (U.K.) FO 371/51150, Refugees, 1945; File No. 93; to pp. No. 1624, letter, E.M. Rose, Refugee Department, Foreign Office to C.W. Footman, Colonial Office, April 19, 1945.

37. UNRRA PAG 4/1.3.1.1.1.:38 "454.2 MEO EARA Camps; UNRRA-EARA Relations," letter, Commissioner, East Africa Refugee Administration (EARA), Nairobi to S.K. Jacobs, Displaced Persons Specialist, UNRRA, January 16, 1945.

38. *Ibid.*, letter, C.L. Bruton, EARA, Nairobi to C.M. Pierce, Office of the Commissioner, Nairobi, with letter, S.K. Jabobs, Displaced Persons Specialist, UNRRA, February 13, 1945.

39. "Stateless" meant exactly what it said: to be without a state, without citizenship, or national identity. Tens of thousands of DPs found themselves in this condition, due to changing borders, changing political complexions in their homelands resulting in their governments denying their citizenship, and several other reasons. It meant that the individual did not fall under the protective umbrella of any state, being the citizen of none. They literally had no homeland to which they could return, or to protect them.

40. UNRRA PAG 4/1.3.1.1.1.:37, 412.2 MEO Repatriation of Poles in ME Area, cable 851, Cairo to London, 757 repeated Washington DC, September 7, 1945.

41. *Ibid.*

42. UNRRA PAG 4/3.0.17.1.3.:5, Displaced Persons. Repatriation, memo, H.H. Lehman to Sir H. Gale, November 6, 1945.

43. UNRRA PAG 4/1.3.1.1.2.0.:7, M.E.-Misc, Report on Middle East Displaced Persons Problems as Noted During the Mission to the Middle East, October 26 – November 8, 1945 (Part II), by W. Langrod, November 20, 1945.

44. UNRRA PAG 4/3.0.17.1.3.:5, Displaced Persons. Repatriation, memo, H.H. Lehman to Sir H. Gale, November 6, 1945.

45. NA (U.K.) FO 371/57780, WR 761, memo, Count Raczynski to His Majesty's Government, March 15, 1946.

46. *Ibid.*, minute sheet (May 10, 1946, March 19–20, 1946), March 15, 1946.

47. UNRRA PAG 4/1.3.1.1.1.:37, 412.2 MEO Repatriation of Poles in

ME Area, cable 11255 to London, repeated Belgrade 3133 (for Director General), July 25, 1946.

48. NA (U.K.) AST 18/96, Admission of Refugee Poles from East Africa and the Lebanon, February–July 1950, Appendix F, letter, Sir H. Gale, Personal Representative of the Director General, UNRRA, Geneva to Under-Secretary of State, Foreign Office, London, August 7, 1946, attached to a memo-to-file, "Polish Refugees in East Africa," Colonial Office, March 8, 1950.

49. British currency at this time was pounds, shilling, and pence. There were twenty shillings to a pound, and one hundred pence to a pound.

50. NA (U.K.) AST 18/96, Admission of Refugee Poles from East Africa and Lebanon, February–July 1950, Appendix F, letter, Sir H. Gale, Personal Representative of the Director General, UNRRA, Geneva to Under-Secretary of State, Foreign Office, London, August 7, 1946, attached to a memo-to-file, "Polish Refugees in East Africa," Colonial Office, March 8, 1950.

51. NA (U.K.) FO 371/57781, Refugees, 1946, File No. 39, pages 1242 to end, minute sheet, "UNRRA Acceptance of Financial Responsibility for Polish Refugees in the Middle East, E. Africa & India," August 22–24, 1946.

52. NA (U.K.) T 236/1437, Poland: Polish refugees in East Africa, transfer of financial responsibility from the ITC to UNRAA (*sic.*), H.H. Eggers to J.D. Bates, Colonial Office, London, November 14, 1946.

53. *Ibid.*, extract from report.

54. *Ibid.*, C.I. Bruton, Office of the Commissioner, Nairobi, East African Refugee Administration to H.H. Eggers, January 29, 1947; C.I. Bruton, Office of the Commissioner, Nairobi, East African Refugee Administration to Director, Aliens and Internees, Kenya; Director, Refugees, Dar es Salaam and Kampala; Director, War Evacuees and Camps, Lusaka; Director, Internment Camps and Refugee Settlements, Salisbury, January 29, 1947.

55. NA (U.K.) FO 371/66163, Poland File No. 148, 1947, H. Eggers, Treasury to R.M.A. Hankey, January 30, 1947; NA (U.K.) T 236/1438, Poland: Polish refugees in East Africa, transfer of financial responsibility from the ITC to UNRRA, letter, H.H. Eggers to C.B. Burgess, Colonial Office, May 16, 1947.

56. *Ibid.*, H. Eggers, Treasury to R.M.A. Hankey, January 30, 1947.

57. *Ibid.*, H. McNeil to R.H.S. Crossman, MP, February 12, 1947.

58. Sword, Davies, and Ciechanowski, *The Formation of the Polish Community in Great Britain*, 189–90.

59. NA (U.K.) T 236/1438, Poland: Polish refugees in East Africa, transfer of financial responsibility from the ITC to UNRRA, Prince E. Sapieha,

Chairman, Polish Civic Committee, Nairobi to the Secretary of State for the Colonies, London, April 18, 1947; Zygmunt Rusinek, Chairman, Association of Polish War Émigrés, Brussels to C. Jones, Secretary of State for the Colonies, London, April 23, 1947.

### Chapter 4: Doors Closing

1. IRO 43/AJ/787, 34/5, memo, H.A. Curtis, Chief of Mission IRO, East Africa to W.P. Black, June 24, 1949.
2. Sophia Schreiber.
3. NA (U.K.) FO 371/71588, Poland 1948, letter, Nairobi Office, PCIRO to Leslie Dow, Chief of PCIRO London Office, London, June 18, 1948.
4. *Ibid.*, letter, Sir A. Rucker, Office of the Executive Secretary, PCIRO to C.J. Edmonds, Foreign Office, Refugee Department, London, June 28, 1948.
5. *Ibid.*, carrier sheet, note by P.J. Hancock, 8 July 1948; note by P.J. Hancock, July 14, 1948.
6. *Ibid.*, carrier sheet, P.J. Hancock to Major Pett-Ridge, War Office, July 14, 1948; draft of letter, Mr. Rundall to Sir A. Rucker, PCIRO Geneva, July 15, 1948.
7. *Ibid.*, memo, Anthony Meyer, for P.J. Hancock, Foreign Office, London to S.A. Goulborn, Commonwealth Relations Office, March 20, 1948.
8. LAC, RG 76, vol. 660, reel C-10596, file B-74072, letter, District Superintendent, Ottawa to Immigration Inspector-in-Charge, Halifax, Nova Scotia, September 27, 1948.
9. *Ibid.*, letter, G.G. Congdon, Superintendent, Immigration Service, Department of Mines and Resources, London to Officer in Charge, Canadian Government Immigration Mission, Karlsruhe, U.S. Zone, Germany, September 30, 1948.
10. *Ibid.*, letter, G.G. Congdon, Superintendent, Immigration Service, Department of Mines and Resources, London to Officer-in-Charge, Canadian Government Mission, Karlsruhe, U.S. Zone, Germany, September 30, 1948.
11. IRO, 43/AJ/1073, letter, M.D. Lane, Chief, Welfare Division, Health, Care and Maintenance Department, IRO Geneva to J. Widdicombe, IRO Warsaw, October 29, 1948.
12. Krolikowski, *Stolen Childhood*, 176.
13. Christine Babinski; Sophia Schreiber; Sophie Smagala.
14. Krolikowski, *Stolen Childhood*, 175.

15. *Ibid.*, 175.
16. IRO 43/AJ/604, 39/3 Legal Status, letter, H.A. Curtis, Senior IRO Representative, East Africa and Rhodesia to Director General, IRO Geneva, att: Chief of Welfare Division, November 29, 1948.
17. *Ibid.*, letter, H.A. Curtis, Senior IRO Representative, East Africa and Rhodesia to Director General, IRO Geneva, attention: Chief of Welfare Division, November 29, 1948.
18. IRO, 43/AJ/604, 39/3, Legal Status, memo, Yvonne de Jong to M.D. Lane, December 15, 1948.
19. LAC, RG 76, vol. 660, reel C-10596, file B-74072, letter, Irene Dalgiewicz, Supervisor Polish Projects, War Relief Services, National Catholic Welfare Conference, Washington DC to Rt. Reverend Monsignor Basil Markle, Permanent Secretariat of the Canadian Episcopate, Ottawa, December 7, 1948.
20. *Ibid.*, letter, Joseph Charbonneau, Archbishop of Montreal to A.C. Joliffe, Immigration Branch, Ottawa, December 9, 1948.
21. *Ibid.*, letter, A.L. Jolliffe, Director, Immigration Service, Department of Mines and Resources, Ottawa to Mrs. D.B. Sinclair, Executive Assistant to the Deputy Minister of National Health and Welfare, Ottawa, December 11, 1948.
22. *Ibid.*, memo, A.L. Jolliffe, Office of the Director, December 14, 1948.
23. *Ibid.*, letter, A.L. Jolliffe, Director, Immigration Branch, Department of Mines and Resources, Ottawa to Msgr. J-Lucien Beaudoin, Secretary of the Canadian Episcopate, Ottawa, December 28, 1948; letter, J-Lucien Beaudoin, Secretary to the Canadian Episcopate, Ottawa to A.L. Jolliffe, Director of Immigration, Department of Mines and Resources, Ottawa, January 4, 1949.
24. *Ibid.*, letter, A.L. Jolliffe, Director, Immigration Branch, Ottawa to J. Colley, PCIRO Canada, Ottawa, January 10, 1949.
25. *Ibid.*, letter, J. Colley, Chief of Operations, IRO Canada, Ottawa to A.L. Jolliffe, Director, Immigration Branch, Department of Mines and Resources, Ottawa, January 13, 1949
26. *Ibid.*, letter, O'Brien, Acting Under-Secretary of State for External Affairs, Ottawa to Chief Secretary to the Government of Tanganyika, Dar es Salaam, Tanganyika, January 14, 1949.
27. NA (U.K.) HO 213/1241, Polish Orphans in Tanganyika, memo, Under Secretary of State, Home Office, Aliens Department, London, N. Warrington, Repatriates Poles and E.V.W.'s Welfare Department, Women's Voluntary Services, London, att: Mr. Storr, January 28, 1949.
28. IRO, 43/AJ/604, 39/3 Legal Status, letter, H.A. Curtis, Chief of Mission,

IRO East Africa to Director General, IRO HQ Geneva, att: A.F. Schnitzer, Legal Adviser, February 4, 1949.

29. NA (U.K.) FO 371/78185, Refugees 1949, file no. 6, pages 571–1382, letter, Myer Cohen, Assistant Director-General, Health, Care and Maintenance Department, IRO to H.A. Curtis, IRO East Africa, Nairobi, cc'd to Brigadier Lush, February 23, 1949.

30. IRO 43/AJ/1040, Description of Salerno.

31. NA (U.K.) FO 371/78185, Refugees 1949, file no. 6, pages 571–1382, letter, Myer Cohen, Assistant Director-General, Health, Care and Maintenance Department, IRO to H.A. Curtis, IRO East Africa, Nairobi, cc'd to Brigadier Lush, February 23, 1949.

32. IRO 43/AJ/787 39/1, cable, H.A. Curtis, Chief of Mission, IRO East Africa to IRO Representative for Tanganyika, March 7, 1949.

33. Krolikowski, *Stolen Childhood*, 176.

34. NA (U.K.) HO 213/1241, Polish Orphans in Tanganyika, letter, A.L. Pennington, Director of Refugees, Dar es Salaam, Tanganyika Territory to Mrs. Warrington, Women's Voluntary Services, London, March 15, 1949; LAC, RG 76, vol. 660, reel C-10596, file B-74072, letter, A.L. Pennington, for Acting Chief Secretary, Tanganyika Territory, Dar es Salaam to Acting Under-Secretary of State for External Affairs, Ottawa, March 26, 1949.

35. *Ibid.*, letter, A.L. Pennington, Director of Refugees, Dar es Salaam, Tanganyika Territory to Mrs. Warrington, Women's Voluntary Services, London, March 15, 1949.

36. LAC, RG 76, vol. 660, reel C-10596, file B-74072, letter, A.L. Pennington, for Acting Chief Secretary, Tanganyika Territory, Dar es Salaam to Acting Under-Secretary of State for External Affairs, Ottawa, March 26, 1949.

37. NA (U.K.) HO 213/1241, Polish Orphans in Tanganyika, memo to file, W. Storr, Home Office, March 11, 1949.

38. LAC, RG 76, vol. 660, reel C-10596, file B-74072, telegram, Mr. Cormier, Karlsruhe to Ottawa, March 21, 1949.

39. *Ibid.*, letter, A.L. Jolliffe, Director, Immigration Branch, Ottawa to Deputy Minister, March 23, 1949.

40. *Ibid.*, memo, H.L. Keenleyside, Deputy Minister, Department of Mines and Resources, Ottawa, to A.L. Jolliffe, Director, Immigration Branch, March 26, 1949.

41. *Ibid.*, cable, Immigration to Mapleleaf Karlsruhe, March 31, 1949.

42. LAC, RG 25, file 5475-DS-40 vol.1, letter, Canadian Delegation to the United Nations to the Secretary of State for External Affairs, Ottawa, March 2, 1949.

43. *Ibid.*, letter, Canadian Delegation to the United Nations to the Secretary of State for External Affairs, Ottawa, March 29, 1949.

44. *Ibid.*, letter, Office of the Secretary of State for External Affairs, Canada to Canadian Delegation to the United Nations, Geneva, March 29, 1949.

45. *Ibid.*, letter, Canadian Delegation to the United Nations to the Secretary of State for External Affairs, Ottawa, March 29, 1949.

46. NARA, RG 84, Foreign Service Posts of the Department of State, Poland, Warsaw Embassy, General Records 1945–49, 1949: 511.2–570.3, box 100, file 570.1 People. Memo, Cecil B. Lyon, Counselor of Embassy, American Embassy, Warsaw, Poland, to Secretary of State, Washington DC, no.368, June 7, 1949.

47. LAC, RG 25, file 5475-DS-40, vol. 1, letter, L. Dionne, Member of Parliament to M.H.M. Pearson, Secretary of State, Ottawa, April 20, 1949.

48. IRO 43/AJ/600, 39/1 Unaccompanied Children — General Policies and General Reports 1949 (Jan–June), letter, Orphans Board of Guardians, Polish Refugee Camp, Tengeru, PO Arusha Tanganyika to Governor of Tanganyika, March 16, 1949.

49. *Ibid.*, letter, H.A. Curtis, Chief of Mission, IRO East Africa to Myer Cohen, Director General, IRO Geneva, March 22, 1949.

50. IRO 43/AJ/787, 39/1, letter, S. Raregiewicz, Vice Chairman, Board of Guardians, Tengeru, Tanganyika to IRO Representative, Tengeru, March 23, 1949.

51. *Ibid.*, letter, H. Curtis, Chief of Mission, IRO East Africa to the Commissioner, East African Refugee Administration, Nairobi, March 24, 1949.

52. *Ibid.*, letter, H.A. Curtis, Chief of Mission, IRO East Africa to IRO Representative, Nyali, Mombasa, March 24, 1949.

53. *Ibid.*, unnumbered cable, Nairobi to Geneva, March 26, 1949; letter, A.L. Pennington, Director of Refugees, Dar es Salaam, Tanganyika Territory to Chief of Mission, IRO East Africa, March 25, 1949.

54. IRO 43/AJ/787, 39/1, letter, K. Papee, Ambassador for Poland to the Vatican, March 17, 1949.

55. NA (U.K.) HO 213/1241, Polish Orphans in Tanganyika, memo, N.W. to Mr. Strutt, March 28, 1949.

56. *Ibid.*, minute sheet, March 25, 1949; April 5, 1949; both initialled J.B.H.

57. *Ibid.*, May 2, 1949, initialled J.B.H.

58. *Ibid.*, letter, F.A. Newsam to Lady Reading, May 5, 1949.

59. *Ibid.*, letter, Lady Reading, Women's Voluntary Services, London to Sir Frank Newsam, Home Office, London, May 18, 1949.

60.  *Ibid.*, letter, F.A. Newsam, Home Office, London to Lady Reading, Chairman, Women's Voluntary Services, London, May 20, 1949.

## Chapter 5: Confrontation

1.  IRO 43/AJ/600, Unaccompanied Children 39/1 General Policies and General Reports 1949, letter, M.D. Lane, Chief, Welfare Division, Health, Care and Maintenance Department to Admiral G. Mentz, IRO Rome, April 1, 1949.

2.  IRO 43/AJ/787, 39/1, letter, H.A. Curtis, Chief of Mission, IRO East Africa to IRO Representative for Tanganyika, Arusha, April 1, 1949; IRO 43/AJ/600, Unaccompanied Children 39/1 General Policies and General Reports 1949, summary of telephone conversation between A. Curtis, Chief of Mission IRO Nairobi (initiator of call) and Brigadier M.S. Lush, IRO Geneva, April 4, 1949.

3.  NA (U.K.) FO 371/78185, Refugees 1949, file no. 6, pages 571–1382, cable Misc 580, Marie D. Lane for Myer Cohen, Welfare, Health, Care and Maintenance Department, IRO Geneva (authorized by Sir A. Rucker, Director General, IRO) to Secretariat, Dar es Salaam, Tanganyika, March 29, 1949).

4.  IRO 43/AJ/926, Recovery Program, 1949. Administrative Order No. 109, issued by IRO, U.S. Zone HQ, October 7, 1948.

5.  NA (U.K.) FO 371/78185, Refugees 1949, file no. 6, pages 571–1382, cable Misc 580, Marie D. Lane for Myer Cohen, Welfare, Health, Care and Maintenance Department, IRO Geneva (authorized by Sir A. Rucker, Director General, IRO) to Secretariat, Dar es Salaam, Tanganyika, March 29, 1949.

6.  *Ibid.*, cable Geneva 296, Governors' Deputy, Dar es Salaam to Brigadier Lush, IRO Geneva, April 4, 1949 (cc'd to Mrs. Lane, IRO Geneva).

7.  *Ibid.*, cable (no number), Brigadier Lush, IRO to Surridge, Secretariat, Tanganyika, April 5, 1949.

8.  *Ibid.*, WR 726, letter, Sir Arthur Rucker, Director General, IRO Geneva to C.J. Edmonds, U.K. Delegate to the IRO, Geneva, April 5, 1949.

9.  IRO 43/AJ/600, Unaccompanied Children 39/1 General Policies and General Reports 1949, letter, M.D. Lane, Chief, Welfare Division, Health Care and Maintenance Department, IRO Geneva to M. Thudichum, International Tracing Services, IRO Arolsen, April 6, 1949.

10. Robert A. Ventresca, *From Fascism to Democracy: Culture and Politics in the Italian Election of 1948* (Toronto: University of Toronto Press, 2004), 4–5, 236–37.

11. IRO 43/AJ/600, 39/1 Unaccompanied Children — General Policies and General Reports 1949 (Jan–June), letter, Captain Williams, Camp Commandant, Polish Refugee Camp Tengeru to H.A. Curtis, Chief of Mission, IRO East Africa, April 12, 1949.

12. *Ibid.*, H.A. Curtis, Chief of Mission, IRO East Africa to Director of Refugees for Territory of Tanganyika, Dar es Salaam, Tanganyika, April 12, 1949.

13. *Ibid.*

14. LAC, RG 76, vol. 660, reel C-10596, file B-74072, letter, E.H. Gilmour, Under-Secretary of State for External Affairs, Ottawa to Director, Immigration Branch, Department of Mines and Resources, Ottawa, April 4, 1949; letter, L. Fortier, Associate Commissioner, Overseas Service, Ottawa to Msgr J-L. Beaudoin, Secrétaire Français de l'Episcopate, Ottawa, April 6, 1949; letter, A.L. Jolliffe, Director, Immigration Branch, Ottawa to Under-Secretary of State for External Affairs, Ottawa, April 6, 1949; letter, J-L. Beaudoin, Secretary for the Episcopate of Canada, Ottawa to L. Fortier, Associate Commissioner, Overseas Service, Immigration Branch, Ottawa, April 7, 1949; letter, L. Fortier, Associate Commissioner, Overseas Service, Immigration Branch, Ottawa to Msgr J-L. Beaudoin, Secretary to the Secretariat, Episcopate of Canada, April 9, 1949; letter, J-L. Beaudoin, Secretary to the Episcopate of Canada, Ottawa to L. Fortier, Associate Commissioner, Department of Mines and Resources, April 11, 1949.

15. *Ibid.*, letter, A.L. Jolliffe, Director, Immigration Branch, Ottawa to Under-Secretary of State for External Affairs, Ottawa, April 13, 1949.

16. *Ibid.*, letter, R. Innes, Acting Chief of Operations, IRO Canada to L. Fortier, Commissioner, Overseas Service, Immigration Branch, Ottawa, May 25, 1949.

17. *Ibid.*, cable 44-ACAP-40, Secretary of State for External Affairs to the Secretariat, Dar es Salaam, Tanganyika Territory, East Africa, April 15, 1949.

18. IRO 43/AJ/787, 39/1, cable 93, Geneva to Nairobi, April 21, 1949.

19. *Ibid.*, letter, H.A. Curtis, Chief of Mission, IRO East Africa to Brigadier M.S. Lush, Special Adviser on Middle East Affairs, IRO HQ, Geneva, April 13, 1949.

20. *Ibid.*, letter, K. Burke, Polish American Congress Inc., Washington DC to Reverend P. Roginski, Shobdon Camp Nr. Kingsland, Hereford, England, April 16, 1949.

21. Krolikowski, *Stolen Childhood*, 178.

22. IRO 43/AJ/787, 39/1, letter, Camp Commandant, Polish Refugees

Camp, Tengeru to Director of Refugees, Dar es Salaam, and attachments, April 21, 1949.

23. *Ibid.*, letter, F.J. Lorriman, IRO Representative, Tanganyika to H.A. Curtis, IRO Representative, Nairobi, Kenya, April 22, 1949, with attachments (two cables from Director of Refugees, Dar es Salaam to Tengeru Camp, Arusha, AL/275/311 and AL/275/315).

24. *Ibid.*, letter, F.J. Lorriman, IRO Representative, Tanganyika to H.A. Curtis, IRO Representative, Nairobi, Kenya, April 22, 1949, with attachments (two cables from Director of Refugees, Dar es Salaam to Tengeru Camp, Arusha, AL/275/311 and AL/275/315).

25. *Ibid.*, cable TC/36/73, from campcom, Arusha, April 22, 1949.

26. *Ibid.*, cable 1346/2204, from Ebb, East African Refugee Administration, April 22, 1949.

27. IRO 43/AJ/787, 39/1, cable TC/3681, to Camp Commandant, Polish Refugee Camp, Tengeru, April 23, 1949.

28. *Ibid.*, note, Fred (Lorriman) to Arnold (Curtis), no date, plus two attachments, both dated April 24, 1949.

29. NA (U.K.) FO 371/78185, Refugees 1949, file no. 6, pages 571–1382, minute sheet, note by A.W. Williamson, April 25, 1949; letter, E.B. Boothby, Foreign Office, London to Sir Arthur Rucker, IRO Geneva, April 29, 1949.

30. IRO 43/AJ/787, 39/1, cable 96, IRO Nairobi to IRO Geneva 96, sent April 24, 1949, received April 25, 1949.

31. IRO 43/AJ/600, Unaccompanied Children 39/1 General Policies and General Reports 1949, resolution, five illegible signatures, inmates of Polish Camp at Tengeru, Tanganyika, April 26, 1949.

32. IRO 43/AJ/600, 39/1 Unaccompanied Children — General Policies and General Reports 1949 (Jan–June), memo, M.D. Lane to Admiral G. Mentz, IRO Rome, April 29, 1949, attachment: "Report on Unaccompanied Children and Youth in East Africa — April 1949."

33. IRO 43/AJ/787, 39/1, letter, Camp Commandant, Polish Refugee Camp, Tengeru to Director of Refugees, Dar es Salaam, May 7, 1949.

34. Stan Studzinski; Sophie Smagala.

35. Christine Babinski.

36. IRO 43/AJ/787, 39/1, letter, H.A. Curtis, Chief of Mission, IRO East Africa to Director of Refugees, Dar es Salaam, Tanganyika, cc'd to Board of Guardians, April 29, 1949; 43/AJ/600, Unaccompanied Children 39/1 General Policies and General Reports 1949, unnumbered cable, Arusha to Geneva, April 30, 1949.

37. IRO 43/AJ/600, Unaccompanied Children 39/1 General Policies and

General Reports 1949, memo, Brigadier M.S. Lush to Assistant Director General, Department of Health, Care and Maintenance, IRO, May 2, 1949.

38. IRO 43/AJ/600, 39/1 Unaccompanied Children — General Policies and General Reports 1949 (Jan–June), letter, A.L. Pennington, Director of Refugees, Tanganyika to Camp Commandant, Tengeru, May 2, 1949.

39. IRO 43/AJ/600, Unaccompanied Children 39/1 General Policies and General Reports 1949, letter, H.A. Curtis, Chief of Mission, IRO East Africa to Chief of Mission, IRO Italy, May 2, 1949.

40. IRO 43/AJ/787 39/1, cable 10204, Geneva to Nairobi, May 4, 1949.

41. *Ibid.*, cable 04004 (no. 41), Nairobi to Director of Refugees D. Salaam, May 4, 1949.

42. *Ibid.*, letter, H.A. Curtis, Chief of Mission, IRO East Africa to IRO Representative for Tanganyika, Arusha, May 4, 1949.

43. *Ibid.*, letter, Camp Commandant, Polish Refugee Camp, Tengeru to Director of Refugees, Dar es Salaam, May 7, 1949.

44. *Ibid.*, letter, S. Rarogiewicz, Vice Chairman, Orphans Board of Guardians, Arusha Tanganyika to Chief of IRO Mission, East Africa, Nairobi, May 4, 1949.

45. *Ibid.*, letter, A.L. Pennington, Director of Refugees, Dar es Salaam to Camp Commandant, Tengeru, May 6, 1949.

46. *Ibid.*, letter, H.A. Curtis, Chief of Mission, IRO East Africa to IRO Representative for Tanganyika, Arusha, May 17, 1949.

47. LAC, RG 76, vol. 660, reel C-10596, file B-74072, letter, A.D.P. Heeney, Under-Secretary of External Affairs to Director of Immigration, Department of Mines and Resources, Ottawa, May 13, 1949.

48. *Ibid.*, cable 44-ACAP-40, External Affairs to Orphans Board Guardians, Arusha, Tanganyika, May 13, 1949.

49. *Ibid.*, letter, L. Fortier, Commissioner, Overseas Service, Immigration Branch, Ottawa to Wing Commander R. Innes, IRO Canada, Ottawa, May 16, 1949.

50. IRO 43/AJ/600, Unaccompanied Children 39/1 General Policies and General Reports 1949, letter, A.L. Pennington, Director of Refugees, Dar es Salaam, Tanganyika to Sir. A. Rucker, IRO Geneva, May 19, 1949.

51. Krolikowski, *Stolen Childhood*, 182.

52. Michal Bortkiewicz.

53. Marian Kacpura.

54. Al Kunicki; Christine Babinski.

55. Michal Bortkiewicz; Marian Kacpura; Al Kunicki; Steven Kozlowski.

56. Krolikowski, *Stolen Childhood*, 188.

57. IRO 43/AJ/600, 39/1 Unaccompanied Children — General Policies

and General Reports 1949 (Jan–June), letter, J. Powell to M.D. Lane, June 24, 1949.

58. NA (U.K.) FO 371/78185, Refugees 1949, file no. 6, pages 571–1382, saving telegram no. 474, Governor, Dar es Salaam to the Secretary of State for the Colonies, London, June 1, 1949.

59. *Ibid.*, letter, Brigadier M.S. Lush, IRO Geneva (for Sir Arthur Rucker) to E.B. Boothby, Foreign Office, London, July 20, 1949.

## Chapter 6: Warsaw Strikes

1. Michal Bortkiewicz; Christine Babinski.
2. Christine Babinski; Kazimiera Mazur-Pogorzelski.
3. Marian Kacpura.
4. Steven Kozlowski.
5. Kazimiera Mazur-Pogorzelski; Sophia Schreiber; Sophie Smagala.
6. LAC, RG 76, vol. 660, reel C-10596, file B-74072, letter, R. Innes, Chief of Operations, IRO Canada to L. Fortier, Commissioner, Immigration Overseas Service, Department of Mines and Resources, Ottawa, May 2, 1949; letter, Polish Ambassador to the Holy See, Rome to Canadian Ambassador, Rome, May 9, 1949; letter, A.D.P. Heeney, Under-Secretary of External Affairs to Director of Immigration, Department of Mines and Resources, Ottawa, May 13, 1949.
7. *Ibid.*, letter, G.G. Congdon, Superintendent, Immigration Service, Department of Mines and Resources, London to Commissioner, Overseas Service, Immigration Branch, Ottawa, May 25, 1949.
8. *Ibid.*, letter, L. Fortier, Commissioner, Overseas Service, Immigration Branch, Ottawa to Superintendent of European Immigration, London, United Kingdom, June 1, 1949.
9. *Ibid.*, letter, G.G. Congdon, Superintendent, Immigration Service, Department of Mines and Resources, London to Commissioner, Overseas Service, Immigration Branch, Ottawa, May 25, 1949; letter, R. Innes, Acting Chief of Operations, IRO Canada to L. Fortier, Commissioner, Overseas Service, Immigration Branch, Ottawa, June 1, 1949; letter, L. Fortier, Commissioner, Overseas Service, Immigration Branch, Ottawa to R. Innes, Acting Chief of Operations, IRO Canada, June 3, 1949; telegram BMW28/G84, Innes Geneva to Immigration Ottawa, June 13, 1949.
10. *Ibid.*, letter, Msgr. J. Charbonneau, Archbishop of Montreal to A.L. Jolliffe, Director of Immigration, Department of Mines and Resources, Ottawa, June 14, 1949.
11. *Ibid.*, letter, L. Fortier, Commissioner, Overseas Service, Immigration

Branch, Ottawa to A. MacNamara, Deputy Minister of Labour, Ottawa, June 16, 1949.

12. *Ibid.*, letter, F.B. Cotsworth, for Superintendent of European Immigration, London, England to Officer-in-Charge, Visa Office, Canadian Embassy, Rome, June 28, 1949; IRO 43/AJ/604, 39/2, letter, A.W. Clabon, Chief, British Commonwealth Branch for Director, Division of Mass Resettlement to O. Cormier, Officer-in-Charge, Canadian Government Immigration Bureau, Karlsruhe, July 1, 1949.

13. LAC, RG 76, vol. 660, reel C-10596, file B-74072, letter, L. Fortier, Commissioner, Overseas Service, Immigration Bureau, Ottawa to G.G. Congdon, Superintendent of European Immigration (Canada), London, England, June 22, 1949.

14. *Ibid.*, letter, L. Fortier, Commissioner, Overseas Service, Immigration Bureau, Ottawa to Acting Chief of Operations, IRO Canada, Ottawa, June 22, 1949.

15. *Ibid.*, letter, L. Fortier, Commissioner, Overseas Service, Immigration Bureau to Msgr Joseph Charbonneau, Archbishop of Montreal, Canadian Catholic Conference, Ottawa, June 22, 1949.

16. *Ibid.*, letter, C.K. Wicks, Resettlement Branch, for Acting Chief of Operations, IRO Canada to L. Fortier, Commissioner, Overseas Service, Immigration Branch, Ottawa, June 24, 1949.

17. IRO 43/AJ/604, 39/2, letter, A.W. Clabon, Chief, British Commonwealth Branch for Director, Division of Mass Resettlement to O. Cormier, Officer-in-Charge, Canadian Government Immigration Bureau, Karlsruhe, July 1, 1949.

18. LAC, RG 76, vol. 660, reel C-10596, file B-74072, letter, A.D.P. Heeney, Under-Secretary of State for External Affairs, Ottawa to Director of Immigration Branch, Ottawa, July 5, 1949.

19. In fact, the visas were restricted to children over the age of five and under the age of sixteen at the time of presentation for the visa; *Ibid.*, telegram RAA50 39/38 Coml ORdy BGovt, Torosus London to Immigration Ottawa, September 27, 1948; cable B74072, Immigration Ottawa to Torosus London, September 28, 1948.

20. *Ibid.*, letter, IRO Canada to J.D. McFarlane, Immigration Branch, Department of Mines and Resources, Ottawa July 18, 1949; letter, J. Charbonneau, Archbishop of Montreal to A.L. Jolliffe, Director of Immigration Branch, Department of Mines and Resources, Ottawa, July 29, 1949; letter, A.L. Jolliffe, Director of Immigration Branch, Department of Mines and Resources, Ottawa to J. Charbonneau, Archbishop of Montreal, August 10, 1949.

21. *Ibid.*, cable 274, Inorefug Geneva to IRO Ottawa, July 16, 1949.

22. Provisional Order No. 75 provided that unaccompanied children whose nationality was determined were to be repatriated or resettled in accordance with the rights and wishes of the government of their established country, or nationality. However, this would not be done if it was contrary to the wishes of the child. Such wishes were to be assessed in light of the child's age and circumstances. The child's wishes were to be taken into account only if they were expressed freely and, when the child was over seventeen years of age, if they could be considered valid objections. In practice, that meant that the IRO could arrange a child's resettlement without their country's permission and in spite of its objections. The most fundamental principle to which the IRO ascribed in the matter of repatriation was that it did not participate in forcible repatriation. IRO 43/AJ/600, Unaccompanied Children 39/1 General Policies and General Reports 1949, inter-office memo, L.C. Stephens, Deputy General Counsel, to Dr. A. Cohen, Chief, Division of Protection, IRO, March 31, 1949; IRO 43/AJ/927, 1947/Constitution of IRO/IRO-CINCEUR Agreement; IRO 43/AJ/926, Recovery Program 1949, Provisional Order No. 75, issued by PCIRO, July 26, 1948.

23. IRO 43/AJ/600, Unaccompanied Children 39/1 General Policies and General Reports 1949, letter, M.D. Lane, Chief, Welfare Division, Health, Care and Maintenance to H. Meyer, ITS, U.S. Zone, May 27, 1949.

24. *Ibid.*, letter, R.J. Youdin, Director of Repatriation to M.J. Wiazemski, Chief, Department of Repatriation and Resettlement, IRO Rome, June 17, 1949; letter, R.J. Youdin, Director of Repatriation to J.E. Folger, Personnel Officer, June 17, 1949.

25. IRO 43/AJ/600, 39/1 Unaccompanied Children: General Policies and General Reports 1949 (Jan–June), letter, J. Powell to M.D. Lane, June 24, 1949.

26. IRO 43/AJ/598, 39/1 Unaccompanied Children: General Policies and Reports 1948 (Jan–June), PCIRO Provisional Order No. 33, "Unaccompanied Children," November 18, 1947.

27. IRO 43/AJ/601, Unaccompanied Children 39/1 General Policies and General Reports 1949, "Field Trip to Italy, 4th – 11th July, 1949," by Y. de Jong, Child Welfare consultation, Geneva, August 1, 1949.

28. *Ibid.*

29. Christine Babinski.

30. Michal Bortkiewicz.

31. Al Kunicki.

32. Stanley Paluch.
33. IRO 43/AJ/604, 39/2, Narrative Report on Special Registration Assignment at the IRO Children's Centre, Salerno, Italy, C.M. Babinski, Deputy Chief, Tracing Section to H.H. Meyer, Chief, Child Search Branch, August 4, 1949.
34. Kazimiera Mazur-Pogorzelski.
35. Steven Kozlowski; Stan Studzinski.
36. IRO 43/AJ/604, 39/2, Narrative Report on Special Registration Assignment at the IRO Children's Centre, Salerno, Italy, C.M. Babinski, Deputy Chief, Tracing Section to H.H. Meyer, Chief, Child Search Branch, August 4, 1949.
37. *Ibid.*
38. IRO 43/AJ/787, file 39/1, extract from letter, Mrs. Grosicka to Mrs. Czolowska, written from Salerno, Italy, dated July 10, 1949.
39. Al Kunicki.
40. IRO, 43/AJ/601, file 39/1 Unaccompanied Children: General Policies and General Reports 1949 (July–Dec), letter, Krycz to Wiaszembski, Chief of Reestablishment Department, IRO Rome, July 25; girls' statement witnessed by Charlotte Babinski, July 25, 1949; letter, I. Page, Child Welfare Officer to Chief, Department of Health, Care and Maintenance, Rome, July 25, 1949.
41. *Ibid.*, letter, Krycz to Wiaszembski, Chief of Reestablishment Department, IRO Rome, July 26, 1949; 43/AJ/604, 39/2; memo, I.P. Krycz, Repatriation Officer to Irene Page, Welfare Officer, August 13, 1949.
42. IRO 43/AJ/604, 39/2, cable, Inorefug Nairobi to Inorefug Geneva 179, repeated Rome 119, August 5, 1949 (received August 6, 1949); 43/AJ/787, 39/1, letter, M. Rule, Acting IRO Representative, Tanganyika to Chief of Mission, IRO East Africa, Nairobi, August 13, 1949.
43. IRO 43/AJ/787, 39/1, memo to file, telephone conversation between H.A. Curtis and Brigadier Lush, August 5, 1949.
44. IRO 43/AJ/604, 39/2, unnumbered cable, A.W. Clabon, Resettlement, IRO Geneva to W.G. Fuller, Acting Chief of Mass Resettlement, IRO Geneva, August 6, 1949.
45. IRO 43/AJ/601, Unaccompanied Children 39/1 General Policies and General Reports 1949, inter-office memo, P. Jacobsen to M. Cohen, July 27, 1949.
46. IRO 43/AJ/457, No. 51 Group of Polish Children from Nairobi to Mr. Hacking's Office, letter, A. Ostrowski, Ambassador for Poland, Rome to General Metz, Chief of Mission, IRO Italy, July 20, 1949.

47.   Krolikowski. *Stolen Childhood*, 201–3; IRO 43/AJ/604, 39/2, cables and telex exchange, folio 240B, August 18, 1949.
48.   IRO 43/AJ/457, No. 51 Group of Polish Children from Nairobi to Mr. Hacking's Office, letter, T.D. Daly, for the Chief of Mission, IRO Italy to A. Ostrowski, Ambassador for Poland, Rome, August 2, 1949.
49.   IRO 43/AJ/604, 39/2, letter, Comte E.H. Czapski, Ministre Pléniptentiare, Rome to P. Jacobsen, Vice-Directeur de l'OIR, Geneva, August 8, 1949.
50.   IRO 43/AJ/1073, Poland Volume 2, letter, J.S. Widdicombe, Chief, PCIRO Office in Poland to K. Lapter, Chief, Department of Foreign Organizations, Ministry of Foreign Affairs, Warsaw, Poland, August 3, 1949.
51.   *Ibid.*, letter, J.S. Widdicombe, Chief, PCIRO Office in Poland to K. Lapter, Chief, Department of Foreign Organizations, Minister of Foreign Affairs, Warsaw, Poland, August 4, 1949.

**Chapter 7: The Scramble for Canada**

1.   IRO 43/AJ/927, 1949/General, cable SC-14207, CINCEUR, at IRO HQ, Bad Kissingen to Assistant Secretary of the Army; OMGUS Berlin from CAD, OMGUS Frankfurt for Poland and Bremen Military Post, sent August 16, 1949.
2.   IRO 43/AJ/787, 39/1, memo, H.A. Curtis to Father Wierzbinski (parish priest, Tengeru), August 6, 1949; IRO 43/AJ/787, 39/1, letter, Brigadier M.S. Lush, Special Adviser to the Middle East, Geneva to H.A. Curtis, Chief of Mission, IRO East Africa, August 27, 1949.
3.   Krolikowski, *Stolen Childhood*, 207–9.
4.   Sophia Schreiber; Marian Kacpura; Stan Studzinski; Al Kunicki; Christine Babinski.
5.   IRO 43/AJ/604, 39/2, cover memo, I.P. Krycz, Repatriation Officer to I. Page, Welfare Officer, August 10, 1949, with nominal rolls attached and results of interviews with the twenty-seven questionable cases; memo, I.P. Krycz, Repatriation Officer to I. Page, Welfare Officer, August 13, 1949.
6.   Krolikowski, *Stolen Childhood*, 209.
7.   IRO 43/AJ/604, 39/2, letter, Comte E.H. Czapski, Ministre Plénipotentiare, Rome to P. Jacobsen, Vice-Directeur de l'OIR, Geneva, August 8, 1949: cable, Monsignor Meysztowicz, Bremen to IRO Geneva, for Jacobsen and Sir Arthur Rucker, August 6, 1949.
8.   LAC, RG 76, vol. 660, reel C-10596, file B-74072, letter, L. Fortier, Commissioner, Overseas Service, Immigration Branch, Ottawa to

Officer-in-Charge, Canadian Government Immigration Mission, Karlsruhe, Germany, August 10, 1949; telegram London 11, Congdon, London to Immigration Branch, Ottawa, August 11, 1949.

9. *Ibid.*, telegram London 11, Congdon, London to Immigration Branch, Ottawa, August 11, 1949; letter, P.W. Bird, Officer-in-Charge, Canadian Government Immigration Mission to Superintendent of European Migration, London, August 12, 1949.

10. LAC, RG 25, vol. 3689, file 5745-T-7-40, vol.1, memo, W.W. Schott, Office of United States Political Adviser, Frankfurt to Miss Wellington, Office of Political Affairs, Berlin, August 11, 1949; letter, Major Kjanowski, Konsul Republic of Poland to W.W. Schott, U.S. POLAD, Chief Foreign Governmental Representation, August 10, 1949.

11. LAC, RG 76, vol. 660, reel C-10596, file B-74072, letter, P.W. Bird, Officer-in-Charge, Canadian Government Immigration Mission to Superintendent of European Migration, London, August 12, 1949.

12. LAC, RG 25, vol. 3689, file 5745-T-7-40, vol.1, memo, W.W. Schott, Office of United States Political Adviser, Frankfurt to Miss Wellington, Office of Political Affairs, Berlin, August 11, 1949; letter, Major Kjanowski, Konsul Republic of Poland to W.W. Schott, U.S. POLAD, Chief Foreign Governmental Representation, August 10, 1949.

13. NARA, RG 48 Office of the U.S. Political Adviser to Germany, Berlin, Classified General Correspondence, 1945–1949, box 277: 1949 (560.2-570.5), "570.1 Displaced Persons, Refugees, General 1949," note verbale, Polish Military Mission to Control Council for Germany, Nr. 532/37/49 to Office of Political Adviser, OMGUS, Berlin, August 11, 1949.

14. *Ibid.*, letter, R.W. Benton, Berlin, Germany to Polish Military Mission, August 11, 1949.

15. LAC, RG 25, vol. 3689, file 5745-T-7-40, vol. 1, telegram 115, Canadian Military Mission, Berlin to Secretary of State for External Affairs, Ottawa, August 11, 1949.

16. *Ibid.*, letter, P.T. Molson, Acting Head of Mission, Canadian Military Mission, Berlin to Secretary of State for External Affairs, Ottawa, August 12, 1949.

17. IRO 43/AJ/604, 39/2, memo, DBH Vickers, Repatriation Division, recipient unidentified, August 13, 1949.

18. *Ibid.*, letter, J. Bikart, Polish Red Cross, Senior Representative for Germany to P.E. Ryan, Chief of Operations, IRO U.S. Zone, August 12, 1949.

19. IRO 43/AJ/1073, no file name, letter, Z. Radomski, Senior Representative of the Polish Red Cross, British Zone, Germany to Zone Welfare Officer, 400 IRO HQ BAOR 15, August 13, 1949.

20. IRO 43/AJ/604, 39/2, P.E. Ryan, Chief of Operations, IRO U.S. Zone to J Bikart, Polish Red Cross, Delegation for U.S. Zone, August 18, 1949; IRO 43/AJ/1073, no file name, cover letter, T. Jamieson, Assistant Director, Chief, Care and Maintenance for Zone Director, IRO HQ Geneva, att: Chief, Welfare Division, Health, Care and Maintenance Department, August 17, 1949; letter, E. W. Francel, Zone Welfare Officer, for Assistant Director, Chief, Care and Maintenance to Polish Red Cross, British Zone, Spenge, Germany, August 17, 1949.

21. *Ibid.*, memo, D.B.H. Vickers, Repatriation Division, recipient unidentified, August 13, 1949.

22. *Ibid.*,

23. LAC, RG 25, vol. 3689, file 5745-T-7-40, vol. 1, cable 117, Canadian Military Mission, Berlin to Secretary of State for External Affairs, Ottawa, August 16, 1949.

24. *Ibid.*, cable 64, Secretary of State for External Affairs, Ottawa to Canadian Military Mission, Berlin, August 16, 1949; LAC RG 76, vol. 660, reel C-10596, file B-74072, cable 346, IRO Geneva to IRO Canada, August 15, 1949; cable (no number), J.D. MacFarlane, Immigration to Karlsruhe, August 17, 1949.

25. IRO 43/AJ/604, 39/2, memo, I.P. Krycz, Repatriation Officer to I. Page, Welfare Officer, August 13, 1949.

26. LAC, RG 76, Vol. 660, reel C-10596, file B-74072, cable 346, IRO Geneva to IRO Ottawa, August 15, 1949; unnumbered cable, J.D. MacFarlane Immigration to Karlsruhe, August 17, 1949.

27. *Ibid.*, cable COMO47/11 Bremen 207/206 1/51/50 11, Msgr Meysztowicz and Dorothy Sullivan to Archbishop Charbonneau, August 17, 1949.

28. Sophia Schreiber.

29. LAC RG 25, vol. 3689, file 5745-T-7-40, vol. 1, dispatch 736, P.T. Molson, Acting Head of Canadian Military Mission, Berlin to Secretary of State for External Affairs, Ottawa, August 19, 1949; note verbale, Polish Military Mission, Berlin to P.T. Molson, Acting Chief, Canadian Military Mission, August 11, 1949; telegram, Canadian Military Mission, Berlin to Polish Military Mission, Berlin, August 19, 1949.

30. NARA RG 84, Poland, Warsaw Embassy, General Records, 1945–49, 1949:511.2-570.3, box 101, "571 Calamities, Relief Measures. 1949, June," telegram 1105, C.B. Lyon, American Embassy, Warsaw, Poland to Secretary of State, Washington DC, August 16, 1949.

31. NARA RG 48, Office of the Political Adviser to Germany, Berlin; Classified General Correspondence, 1945–1949, box 277: 1949(560.2-570.5), "570.1 Displaced Persons, Refugees, General 1949," letter,

C.B. Lyon, American Embassy, Warsaw, Poland to Secretary of State, Washington DC, August 24, 1949.

32. IRO 43/AJ/604, 39/2, digest of article in *Il Paese*, Rome, August 17, 1949.

33. LAC, RG 25, vol.3689, file 5745-T-7-40, vol. 1, dispatch 664, K.P. Kirkwood, Charge d'Affaires, Canadian Legation, Warsaw to Secretary of State for External Affairs, Ottawa, August 18, 1949.

34. IRO 43/AJ/604, 39/2, cables and telex exchange, folio 240B, August 18, 1949.

35. NARA RG 84, Poland, Warsaw Embassy, General Records, 1945–49, 1949: 511.2-570.3, box 101, "571 Calamities, Relief Measures. 1949, June," telegram 493, Acheson, Secretary of State, Washington to Geneva, repeated to Berlin 901, Heidelberg 58, Warsaw 493, Rome 1874, August 19, 1949.

36. IRO 43/AJ/927, 1949/General, cable SC-14207, CINCEUR, sent August 16, 1949, received August 17, 1949, at IRO HQ, Bad Kissingen, also to Assistant Secretary of the Army; OMGUS Berlin from CAD, OMGUS Frankfurt for Poland and Bremen Military Post.

37. IRO 43/AJ/604, 39/2, cable 40, R.J. Youdin, Repatriation, Inorefug Geneva to Inorefug Warsaw, August 17, 1949.

38. *Ibid.*, cables and telex exchange, folio 240B, August 18, 1949.

39. *Ibid.*, cable, Jacobsen, Acting Director-General, IRO Geneva to Grohn, August 19, 1949.

40. *Ibid.*, letter, P. Jacobsen, Assistant Director General for Repatriation and Resettlement, IRO to H. Allard, Chief of Mission, IRO Canada, September 12, 1949.

41. *Ibid.*, cable, Kalmanowicz, Polish Red Cross, Munich to General Director, Geneva, August 25, 1949.

42. IRO 43/AJ/927, 1949/General, letter, the Demokratischer Frauenbund Deutschlands, Berlin to IRO Bad Kissingen, August 19, 1949, plus a copy of the resolution.

43. Alvin Roseman, a Foreign Service Reserve Officer for the U.S. Government, was appointed to this post in June 1949. He was to work with the IRO informally, advancing the views and policies of the United States Government, reporting to the U.S. Government on IRO activities and responses to American views and policies, and assisting any formal American delegations to the IRO, as necessary. He was the proverbial "fly on the wall" for the U.S. State Department.

44. NARA RG 84, Poland, Warsaw Embassy, General Records, 1945–49, 1949: 511.2-570.3, box 101, "571 Calamities, Relief Measures. 1949,

June," telegram 493, Acheson, Secretary of State, Washington DC to Geneva, August 19, 1949.

45. LAC RG 76, vol. 660, reel C-10596, file B-74072, memo, author unknown, Tirpitz Camp, Bremen, August 18, 1949.

46. *Ibid.*, letter, G.G. Congdon, Superintendent of European Immigration, London to A.L. Jolliffe, Director of Immigration, Ottawa, August 19, 1949.

47. *Ibid.*, letter, P.W. Bird, Officer-in-Charge, Canadian Government Immigration Mission, Karlsruhe to Superintendent for European Immigration, London, England, August 20, 1949.

48. *Ibid.*, letter, Dorothy Sullivan, Catholic Immigration Aid Society to Mr. Gertson, Canadian Visa Officer, Tirpitz Camp, Bremen, 18 August 1949; memo, F.C. Gertson, Visa Officer, Tirpitz, Bremen to Officer-in-Charge, Canadian Government Immigration Mission, Karlsruhe, August 18, 1949.

49. *Ibid.*, cable, Immigration Branch, Ottawa to Superintendent of European Immigration, London, August 23, 1949.

50. NARA RG 84, Poland, Warsaw Embassy, General Records, 1945–49, 1949: 511.2-570.3, box 101, "571 Calamities, Relief Measures. 1949, June," letter, Ministry of Foreign Affairs, Poland to American Embassy, Warsaw, August 23, 1949.

51. *Ibid.*, telegram 1125, C.B. Lyon, American Embassy, Warsaw to Secretary of State, Washington DC, August 24, 1949.

52. LAC RG 25, vol. 3689, file 5745-T-7-40, vol.1, dispatch 290, Secretary of State for External Affairs, Ottawa to Chargé d'Affaires, Canadian Legation, Warsaw, August 31, 1949.

53. *Ibid.*, dispatch 691, K.P. Kirkwood, Charge d'Affaires, Canadian Legation, Warsaw to Secretary of State for External Affairs, Ottawa, August 31, 1949.

54. LAC RG 25, vol.3689, file 5745-T-7-40, vol. 1, collection of articles.

55. NARA RG 48, Office of the U.S. Political Adviser to Germany, Berlin; Classified General Correspondence, 1945–1949, box 277: 1949 (560.2-570.5), 570.1 Displaced Persons, Refugees, General 1949, letter, Lyon, American Embassy, Warsaw, Poland to Secretary of State, Washington DC, August 24, 1949.

56. NARA RG 84, Poland, Warsaw Embassy, General Records, 1945–49, 1949: 511.2-570.3, box 101, "571 Calamities, Relief Measures. 1949, June," airgram A-1060, C.B. Lyon, American Embassy, Warsaw to Secretary of State, Washington DC, August 26, 1949; IRO 43/AJ/604, 39/2, memo, I.P. Krycz, Repatriation Officer to I. Page, Welfare Officer, August 10, 1949, plus nominal rolls, prepared August 10 and 11, 1949.

57. NARA RG 84, Poland, Warsaw Embassy, General Records, 1945–49, 1949: 511.2-570.3, box 101, "571 Calamities, Relief Measures. 1949, June," telegram 1129, C.B. Lyon, American Embassy, Warsaw to Secretary of State, Washington DC, August 23, 1949.

58. *Ibid.*, report, "The 'Kidnapping' of Polish Children," Alvin Roseman, Representative for Specialized Agency Affairs, the Foreign Service of the U.S.A., Geneva to Col. B. Ferris, HQ EUCOM, Heidelberg, Germany, August 29, 1949 (Same report submitted to State Department on August 26, 1949).

59. IRO 43/AJ/604, 39/2, cable, A.W. Clabon, Resettlement No. 352, Inorefug, Geneva, August 22, 1949.

60. *Ibid.*, press release, the Office of Public Information, IRO Rome, August 23, 1949.

61. NARA RG 59, Records Relating to the International Refugee Organization (IRO) and the Displaced Persons Commission (DPC), DP Subject File, 1944–1952, box 12, DP Poland, telegram 1131, C.B. Lyon, American Embassy, Warsaw to Secretary of State, Washington DC, August 25, 1949.

62. NARA RG 59, Records Relating to the International Refugee Organization (IRO) and the Displaced Persons Commission (DPC), DP Subject File, 1944–1952, box 12, DP Poland, telegram 1102, Acheson, Department of State, Washington DC to Amconsul, Geneva, August 25, 1949; RG 84, Poland, Warsaw Embassy, General Records, 1945–1949, 1949:511.2-570.3, box 101, "571 Calamities, Relief Measures. 1949, June," telegram 499, Acheson, Secretary of State, Washington DC to Berlin, August 25, 1949.

63. NARA RG 84, Poland, Warsaw Embassy, General Records, 1945–1949, 1949: 511.2-570.3, box 101, "571 Calamities, Relief Measures. 1949, June," telegram 1141, C.B. Lyon, American Embassy, Warsaw to Secretary of State, Washington DC, August 26, 1949.

64. *Ibid.*, telegram 8, Riddleberger, Heidelberg to Secretary of State, Washington DC, August 27, 1949; telegram 24, Troutman, Geneva to Secretary of State, August 27, 1949; NARA RG 59, General Records of the Department of State, Records Relating to the International Refugee Organization (IRO) and the Displaced Persons Commission (DPC), DP Subject File, 1944–1952, box 12, DP Poland, telegram 1005, Troutman, Geneva to Secretary of State, Washington DC, August 27, 1949.

Chapter 8: Canada — A Home at Last

1.  Krolikowski, *Stolen Childhood*, 223.
2.  LAC, RG 25, vol. 3689, file 5745-T-7-40, vol. 1, "Refugee Orphans in Canada Met By Terror Agents Here: Polish Legation and Agents Use Same Soviet Tactics as in Africa, Italy, Germany," *The Ensign*, October 8, 1949, p. 3 and elsewhere (clipping).
3.  Sophia Schreiber.
4.  Bernice Kusa.
5.  LAC, RG 25, vol. 3689, file 5745-T-7-40, vol. 1, letter, I. Page, Camp Tirpitz, Bremen to Paul Martin, Minister of National Health and Welfare, Ottawa, August 31, 1949.
6.  IRO, 43/AJ/787, file 39/1, letter, Brigadier M.S. Lush, Special Adviser on the Middle East, IRO Geneva to H.A. Curtis, Chief of Mission, IRO East Africa, September 19, 1949.
7.  LAC, RG 25, vol. 3689, file 5745-T-7-40, vol. 1, list, "The Following Polish Orphans arrived at Quebec on Sept. 18th, 1949, Ex SS *Samaria*"; "Sailed SS *Scythia* Sept. 22nd, 1949"; "Expected to Sail Sept 26th, 1949," undated.
8.  Kazimiera Mazur-Pogorzelski.
9.  Stanley Paluch.
10. Marian Kacpura.
11. Janet Przygonski.
12. LAC, RG 25, vol 3689, file 5745-T-7-40, vol. 1, collection of articles.
13. NARA RG 84, Poland, Warsaw Embassy, General Records, 1945–49, 1949: 511.2-570.3, box 101, "571 Calamities, Relief Measures. June," airgram A-1118, C.B. Lyon, American Embassy, Warsaw to Secretary of State, Washington DC, September 7, 1949.
14. NARA RG 84, Foreign Service Posts of the Department of State, Poland, Warsaw Embassy, General Records, 1945–49, 1949: 511.2-570.3, box 101, "571 Calamities, Relief Measures. 1949, June," airgram A-1127, Lyon, American Embassy, Warsaw to Secretary of State, Washington DC, September 9, 1949.
15. NARA RG 84, Poland, Warsaw Embassy, General Records, 1945–49, 1949: 5601.-570.5, box 251, 570.1-570.1, airgram A-1175, C.B. Lyon, American Embassy, Warsaw, Poland to Secretary of State, Washington DC, September 16, 1949.
16. LAC, RG 25, vol. 3689, file 5745-T-7-40, vol. 1, "Refugee Orphans in Canada Met by Terror Agents Here: Polish Legation and Agents Use Same Soviet Tactics as in Africa, Italy, Germany," *The Ensign*, October 8, 1949, p. 3 and elsewhere (clipping).

17. *Ibid.*, memo, A. Anderson, Information Division, External Affairs, Canada to T.W.L. MacDermot, European Division, External Affairs, Canada, October 14, 1949.

18. *Ibid.*, dispatch 784, K.P. Kirkwood, Chargé d'Affaires, Canadian Legation, Warsaw to Secretary of State for External Affairs, October 21, 1949.

19. NARA RG 84, Poland, Warsaw Embassy, General Records, 1945–49, 1949: 511.2-570.3, box 101, "571 Calamities, Relief Measures. 1949, June," note, C.B. Lyon, American Embassy, Warsaw to R.F. Corrigan, Office of U.S. Political Adviser on German Affairs, Heidelberg, September 26, 1949.

20. *Ibid.*, telegram 1271, C.B. Lyon, American Embassy, Warsaw to Secretary of State, Washington DC, September 28, 1949.

21. *Ibid.*, airgram A-1302, Gallman, for C.B. Lyon, American Embassy, Warsaw to Secretary of State, Washington DC, October 18, 1949.

22. LAC, RG 25, vol. 3689, file 5745-T-7-40, vol. 1, letter, B. de Rougé, Secretary General of League of Red Cross Societies to W.S. Stanbury, National Commissioner, The Canadian Red Cross Society, October 27, 1949.

23. *Ibid.*, letter, J.W. Holmes, for Secretary of State for External Affairs, Ottawa to W.S. Stanbury, National Commissioner, Canadian Red Cross Society, Toronto, November 17, 1949.

24. *Ibid.*, Mr. Altman, Representative of Poland, statement in the Third Committee re: Polish Refugee Children, November 4, 1949 (translation).

25. *Ibid.*, memo, A.D.P. Heeney to the Minister of External Affairs, December 30, 1949.

26. *Ibid.*, cable 306, Chairman, Canadian Delegation to the U.N., New York to the Secretary of State for External Affairs, Ottawa, November 11, 1949.

27. *Ibid.*, dispatch 371, J.W. Holmes, for Secretary of State for External Affairs, Ottawa to Chargé d'Affaires, Canadian Embassy, Warsaw, November 17, 1949.

28. *Ibid.*, letter, H. Allard, Chief of Mission IRO Canada to E. Neilson, Congress of Canadian Women, Toronto, November 21, 1949; letter, E. Neilson, Congress of Canadian Women, affiliate of Women's International Democratic Federation, Toronto to IRO Ottawa, November 16, 1949; letter, J.W. Holmes, U.N. Division, External Affairs, Ottawa to Senator Cairine R. Wilson, Ottawa, November 28, 1949.

29. Bernice Kusa; Helen Atkinson.

30. NARA, RG 84 Foreign Service Posts of the Department of State, Poland, Warsaw Embassy, General Records, 1945–49, 1949: 511.2-570.3, box

101, "571 Calamities, Relief Measures. 1949, June," airgram 853, C.B. Lyon, Counselor of Embassy, December 8, 1949; LAC, RG 25, vol 3689, file 5745-T-7-40, vol. 1, letter, K.P. Kirkwood, Chargé d'Affaires, Canadian Legation, Warsaw to Secretary of State for External Affairs, Ottawa, December 14, 1949.

31. LAC, RG 25, vol. 3689, file 5745-T-7-40, vol. 1, letter, Canadian Legation, Warsaw to Polish Ministry of Foreign Affairs, Warsaw, April 11, 1950.

32. *Ibid.*, letter, Polish Ministry of Foreign Affairs, Warsaw to Canadian Legation, Warsaw, July 24, 1950.

33. Stanley Paluch.

34. Michal Bortkiewicz.

35. Krolikowksi, *Stolen Childhood*, 226–27; Al Kunicki; Steven Kozlowski; Stanley Paluch; Sophia Schreiber.

36. Marian Kacpura.

37. Al Kunicki.

38. Kazimiera Mazur-Pogorzelski.

39. Sophie Smagala.

40. Krolikowski, *Stolen Childhood*, 256.

41. *Ibid.*, 257.

42. Stan Studzinski.

43. Helen Atkinson.

44. Helen Atkinson.

45. Helen Atkinson; Janet Przygonski; Stanley Paluch.

46. Marian Kacpura; Sophie Smagala.

47. Kazimiera Mazur-Pogorzelski.

48. Stanley Paluch.

# Bibliography

## Archives Consulted

IRO — International Refugee Organization, National Archives of France.
LAC — Library and Archives of Canada, Ottawa, Canada.
NA (U.K.) — National Archives of the United Kingdom.
NARA — National Archives and Records Administration, College Park, MD, United States.
UNRRA — United Nations Relief and Rehabilitation Administration, United Nations Archives, New York City, United States.

## Interviews

Atkinson, Helen (née Helena Koscielniak), November 26, 2006.
Babinski, Christine (née Krysztofa Michniak), November 23, 2006.
Bortkiewicz, Michal, November 18, 2006.
Kacpura, Marian, November 21, 2006.
Kozlowski, Steven (Stefan), November 17, 2006.
Kunicki, Al, November 17, 2006.
Kunicki, Sister Mary Alfonsa, November 3, 2006.
Kusa, Bernice (née Bronislawa Kusa), November 24, 2006.
L.P., March 7, 2007.
Mazur-Pogorzelski, Kazimiera (née Mazur), November 17, 2006.
Paluch, Stan, November 17, 2006.
Przygonski, Janet (née Janina Kusa), November 24, 2006; March 6, 2007.
Schreiber, Sophia (née Wakulczyk), November 9, 2006.
Smagala, Sophie (née Matusiewicz), December 11, 2006.
Studzinski, Stan, November 6, 2006.

## Secondary Sources

Anders, General Wladyslaw. *Mémoires (1939–1946)*, trans. J. Rzewuska. Paris: La Jeune Parque, 1948.

Bingle, Jean C. "Labour for Bread: The Exploitation of Polish Labor in the Soviet Union During World War II." Ph.D. dissertation, West Virginia University, 1999.

Brudorowycz, Bohan B. *Polish-Soviet Relations 1932–1939*. New York: Columbia University Press, 1963.

Coutouvidis, John and Jaime Reynolds. *Poland 1939–1947*. Teaneck, NJ: Holmes & Meier Publishers, Inc., 1986.

Davies, Norman. *Heart of Europe: A Short History of Poland*. Oxford: Oxford University Press, 1984.

Fundacja Archiwum Fotograficzne Tulaczy. *Tulacze Dzieci; Exiled Children*. Warsaw: Muza SA, 1995.

Garlinski, Jozef. *Poland in the Second World War*. Basingstoke, U.K.: Macmillan, 1985.

Gross, Jan T. *Revolution from Abroad: The Soviet Conquest of Poland's Western Ukraine and Western Belorussia*. Princeton, NJ: Princeton University Press, 1988.

Grudzinski-Gross, Irena and Jan Tomasz Gross, eds. *War Through Children's Eyes*. Stanford: Hoover Institution Press, 1981.

Holborn, Louise W. *The International Refugee Organization: A Specialized Agency of the United Nations: Its History and Work 1946–1952*. London: Oxford University Press, 1956.

Jolluck, Katherine R. *Exile and Identity: Polish Women in the Soviet Union During World War II*. Pittsburgh: University of Pittsburgh Press, 2002.

Jolluck, Katherine R. "'You Can't Even Call Them Women': Poles and 'Others' in Soviet Exile During the Second World War." *Contemporary European History*, 10/3 (2001), 463–80.

Kacewicz, George. *Great Britain, the Soviet Union and the Polish Government-in-Exile.* The Hague: Martinus Nijhoff Publishers, 1979.

Krolikowski, Lucjan. *Stolen Childhood: A Saga of Polish War Children.* New York: Author's Choice Press, 1983/2001.

Lebedeva, Nataliia. "Deportations from Poland and the Baltic States to the U.S.S.R. in 1939–1941: Common Features and Specific Traits." *Lithuanian Historical Studies,* 7 (2002), 95–110.

Lebedeva, N.S., and Alfred J. Rieber. "The Deportation of the Polish Population to the U.S.S.R., 1939–41." *The Journal of Communist Studies and Transition Politics,* 16/1-2(2000), 28–45.

Lipper, Elinor. *Eleven Years in Soviet Prison Camps.* Washington DC: Regnery Publishing, Inc., 1951.

Marrus, Michael R. *The Unwanted: European Refugees in the Twentieth Century.* New York: Oxford University Press, 1985.

Paczkowski, Andrzej. "Poland, the 'Enemy Nation,'" in Stéphane Courtois, ed., *The Black Book of Communism: Crimes, Terror, Repression.* Boston: Harvard University Press, 1999.

Paczkowski, Andrzej. *The Spring Will Be Ours: Poland and the Poles from Occupation to Freedom.* University Park, PA: Pennsylvania State University Press, 1995.

Piesakowski, Tomasz. *The Fate of Poles in the U.S.S.R. 1939–1989.* London: Gryf Publications, 1990.

Piotrowski, Tadeusz. *The Polish Deportees of World War II: Recollections of Removal to the Soviet Union and Dispersal Throughout the World.* Jefferson, NC: McFarland & Company, Inc., 2004.

Proudfoot, Malcolm J. *European Refugees: 1939–52, A Study in Forced Population Movement.* London: Faber and Faber Ltd, 1957.

Raczynski, Count Edward. *In Allied London.* London: Weidenfeld and Nicolson, 1962.

Rystad, G., ed. *The Uprooted: Forced Migration as an International Problem in the Post-War Era*. Lund, Sweden: Lund University Press, 1990.

Siemaszko, Z.S. "The Mass Deportations of the Polish Population to the U.S.S.R., 1940–1941," in Keith Sword, ed. *The Soviet Takeover of the Polish Eastern Provinces, 1939–41*. New York: St. Martin's Press, 1991.

Statiev, Alex. "Motivations and Goals of Soviet Deportations in the Western Borderlands." *Journal of Strategic Studies*, 28/6 (December 2005), 977–1003.

Sukiennicki, Wiktor. "The Establishment of the Soviet Regime in Eastern Poland in 1939," *Journal of Central European Affairs*, 23/2 (July 1963), 191–218.

Sword, Keith. *Deportation and Exile: Poles in the Soviet Union, 1939–48*. London and Basingstoke, U.K.: Macmillan Limited and St. Martin's Press, 1994

Terry, Sarah Meiklejohn. *Poland's Place in Europe: General Sikorski and the Origin of the Oder-Neisse Line, 1939–1943*. Princeton, NJ: Princeton University Press, 1983.

Ventresca, Robert A. *From Fascism to Democracy: Culture and Politics in the Italian Election of 1948*. Toronto: University of Toronto Press, 2004.

Viatteau, Alexandra. *Staline Assassine La Pologne 1939–1947*. Paris: Éditions du Seuil, 1999.

Woodbridge, George, ed. *UNRRA: The History of the United Nations Relief and Rehabilitation Administration*, 3 vols. New York: Columbia University Press, 1950.

Zajdlerowa, Zoe. *The Dark Side of the Moon*. New edition, edited by J. Coutouvidis and T. Lane. New York: Harvester Wheatsheaf, 1989.

# OF RELATED INTEREST

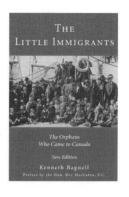
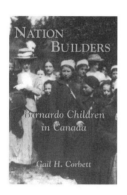

Marquis Book Printing Inc.

Québec, Canada
2009